Khalil Maleki

RADICAL HISTORIES OF THE MIDDLE EAST

SERIES EDITORS

Dr Mezna Qato, University of Cambridge

Dr Siavush Randjbar-Daemi, University of Manchester

Dr Eskandar Sadeghi-Boroujerdi, University of Oxford

Dr Omar AlShehabi, Gulf University of Science and Technology

Dr Abdel Razzaq Takriti, University of Houston

For current information and details of other books in the series, please visit oneworld-publications.com/radical-histories

Khalil Maleki

The Human Face of Iranian
Socialism

Homa Katouzian

ONEWORLD
ACADEMIC

Oneworld Academic

An imprint of Oneworld Publications

Published by Oneworld Academic, 2018

Copyright © Homa Katouzian 2018

The moral right of Homa Katouzian to be identified as the Author of
this work has been asserted by him in accordance with the Copyright,
Designs, and Patents Act 1988

ISBN 978-1-78607-293-1
eISBN 978-1-78607-294-8

Typeset by Siliconchips Services Ltd, UK
Printed and bound in Great Britain by Clays Ltd, St Ives plc

Oneworld Publications
10 Bloomsbury Street, London WC1B 3SR, England

Stay up to date with the latest books,
special offers, and exclusive content from
Oneworld with our newsletter

Sign up on our website
oneworld-publications.com

FSC
www.fsc.org
MIX
Paper from
responsible sources
FSC® C018072

To Mohamad Tavakoli-Targhi
In honour of his many qualities

CONTENTS

ACKNOWLEDGEMENTS

I am indebted to Manouchehr Rassa, Kamal Ghaemi, Amir Pichdad, Siavush Randjbar-Daemi, Eskandar Sadeghi-Boroujerdi, Houshang Sayyahpour, Hamid Ahmadi, Hormoz Homayounpour, Houshang Tale Yazdi, Mohammad Sadeqi, Reza Goudarzi and MariaLuisa Langella, the most efficient Librarian of the Middle East Centre of St Antony's College, University of Oxford, for helping out with sources which were difficult to access. I also benefited from the views and comments of the three able and competent (though anonymous) scholars who read a draft of the manuscript for Oneworld. All the faults and shortcomings are mine, of course.

HK

A Note on Transliteration

In transliterating Persian words I have applied the transliteration scheme of the journal *Iranian Studies* which also allows for anglicised spellings such as Hossein.

INTRODUCTION

The Age of Khalil Maleki

Khalil Maleki was born in 1901, a few years before the Constitutional Revolution of 1906, and died in 1969, six years after the shah's White Revolution of 1963; he would have been seventy-six in 1977 when the protest movement which led to the revolution of February 1979 began. Thus, in much of this long and eventful period, Maleki played a significant role in politics and society, as an intellectual, a political thinker, activist and organiser, and a communist-turned-socialist, believing in freedom, democracy and social justice, and pursuing these goals through peaceful means. And since he split with the Tudeh party in 1948 he almost constantly faced a barrage of abuse, libel and invective from that party, and later from other revolutionaries as well. He was thus a unique figure caught in a generally intolerant age, now jailed by rulers and now castigated by much of the opposition. It is only in recent times that his ideas and approaches are making inroads in the political attitude and praxis of some, especially younger, Iranians – both men and women. He was not generally known even in Iran from the late 1960s until the twenty-first century, the great age of revolutionary idealism and revolution.

The Constitutional Revolution of 1906 was first and foremost fought for the establishment of government by law as opposed to arbitrary rule, although various secondary programmes, notably modernisation, were also floated through the movement. And it was supported by virtually all the urban social classes (the peasantry being still apolitical): merchants, small traders, artisans, intellectuals, clerics, Qajar princes and notables, tribal leaders, etc. And although in many ways it was very different from the revolution of February 1979, the resemblance to the consensus of all social classes to remove the shah (and thus overthrow arbitrary rule) is uncanny.

Once Mohammad Ali Shah was deposed and exiled, however, conflict, chaos and anarchy began to replace his rule, quite like the aftermath of the fall of every arbitrary government throughout the centuries. The intervention in Iran of warring parties in the First World War simply exacerbated the situation, since before it chaotic trends had already begun both in the centre and the provinces. Come the end of the war, Iran was on its knees, even in danger of being fragmented as had happened before. Most erstwhile revolutionaries were regretting this to the extent that in 1920 a radical leader of the revolution, Seyyed Mohammad Reza Mosavat, wrote to another, Seyyed Hasan Taqizadeh, repenting what they had done to the country. A few, like the poets Mirzadeh Eshqi and Abolqasem Lahuti, were yearning for another revolution, but many if not most intellectual, nationalist and modernist elites hoped for a strong government which would stamp out the chaos and modernise the country virtually overnight. As we shall see, the young Khalil Maleki was one of them wishing for the establishment of a modern republic (Chapter 1).

Various factors led to the emergence of Reza Khan, but once he appeared on the scene he proved to be the 'saviour' many

educated Iranians had longed for. Even his establishment of a
dictatorship went down well at first, to the extent that when
he bid to become shah in 1925, he also had the support of the
ulama in Najaf. He quickly brought general security and stabil-
ity to the country and began a process of modernisation, in fact
pseudo-modernism, since it was a case of straight copying from
the West.

However, it did not take long for dictatorship to turn into the
traditional arbitrary rule (*estebdad*), a modern form of a 'one-
person regime' as the shah himself described it, which increasingly began to alienate various social classes, so that when, in
1941, he had to abdicate in the wake of the Allied occupation
of Iran, he had very few friends left in the country. An example
of his reforms was sending state students to study at European
(mainly German, French and Belgian) universities, from which
at first Maleki benefited, only to be returned to Iran before he
had completed his studies on the false charge of being a communist. And an example of the shah's arbitrary rule was the arrest
and incarceration of a group of young men (later known as the
Fifty-Three) in 1937, who included Khalil Maleki, on charges
of belonging to a communist organisation, which they did not
(Chapter 1).

Shortly after Reza Shah's abdication, the Tudeh party was
formed by some members of the Fifty-Three and other democratic and anti-fascist (mainly young) people, which resembled
the resistance movements in occupied Europe's popular fronts.
Its membership ranged from Marxists through to social democrats, democrats and liberals. It took Maleki a couple of years to
join the party mainly because he did not trust certain members
of the Fifty-Three, and, when he did, he began to lead the young
party dissidents who were critical of many of the attitudes and
policies of its leadership (Chapter 2).

Once again, the country was almost on its knees in many ways, except that the occupying forces stopped it from falling apart or getting entangled in revanchist and factional struggles of the kind that was experienced after the revolution of February 1979. The Tudeh party was, to say the least, the best organised and, sometime later, the most popular party in Iran in spite of its internal disagreements. It organised (though not exclusively) the trade union movement, and its press and publications spread new political values and encouraged modern cultural and literary activities. After the 1943 Soviet victory at Stalingrad, it became the strongest centre of social and intellectual activity, and Maleki was one of its most famous and most popular writers, journalists and teachers, at the same time as he was the elder member of the internal party critics (Chapter 2).

The party's support for the 1944 Soviet demand for the concession of north Iranian oil, which Maleki endorsed, put it in a difficult situation, but the party made the biggest stir when its members demonstrated in support of the Soviet demand under the protection of the occupying Soviet troops. However, the internal party disagreements came to a head in 1946 when the party leadership supported the Azerbaijan Democrats' forceful declaration of autonomy which smacked of separatism, and forced their own local party organisation to join them as a result of Soviet pressure. Maleki led the opposition to that policy which failed abjectly, and this provided the turning point that ended in the party split of January 1948. This was under Ahmad Qavam's premiership with whom – against Maleki's advice – the Tudeh leaders had formed a short coalition government which they later regretted (Chapter 2).

The winds of the Cold War had begun to blow in 1946 and the Tudeh party split could have been an indirect result of that, although the splinter group still had faith in the Soviet Union (though not the Soviet embassy in Tehran). But it did not take Maleki long to see through Soviet communism. By this time the Tudeh, having been banned in 1949, had become a fully-fledged Stalinist party. Meanwhile, the conflict with the Anglo-Iranian Oil Company (AIOC) had begun to flare up, which had as its background the great oil workers' strikes of the mid-1940s, the rejection of the Soviet demand for the north Iranian oil concession and the general dissatisfaction with AIOC's interference in the political affairs of Iran. That is how the National Front(NF) led by Mohammad Mosaddeq and the newspapers *Bakhtar-e Emruz* and *Shahed,* which supported it, came into existence. Maleki began to write in Mozaffar Baqa'i's *Shahed,* criticising British policy in Iran as well as the Tudeh party and the very current and popular conspiracy theory of politics (Chapter 3).

Maleki had become a socialist who firmly believed in parliamentary democracy, while during that period and for a long time to come the Tudeh and other Marxist-Leninists regarded democracy as a bourgeois conspiracy, and contemptuously described Western liberties as bourgeois freedoms. Meanwhile, the country was in a fever over election rigging which was largely tied up with the struggle over oil. In 1950 General Razamara, the able and intelligent chief of the general staff, became prime minister and met Mosaddeq head-on as the leader of the sixteenth Majlis (parliament) opposition. In March 1951 a member of the *Fad'iyan-e Islam* (Devotees of Islam) assassinated Razmara, which was followed by the nationalisation of Iranian oil by the Majlis and Mosaddeq's premiership in April 1951. He had the support of the leading political Mojtahed, Ayatollah Kashani (Chapters 3 and 4).

Shortly after Mosaddeq became prime minister, Maleki, Baqa'i and their supporters formed the Toilers party and soon became the strongest and most organised party supporting the nationalisation of Iranian oil and Mosaddeq's government. However, the oil dispute with Britain dragged on during which, in February 1952, Mosaddeq eventually turned down the offer of the International Bank for mediation between Iran and Britain which led to the international boycott of Iranian oil. Meanwhile, Britain was trying to arrange Mosaddeq's removal by parliamentary means, and when the shah and Mosaddeq clashed over which of them should appoint the war minister, the latter resigned and Qavam replaced him. There was a public revolt called by Kashani and the strong Majlis minority which supported Mosaddeq, in which the Toilers party played a significant role and which resulted in Mosaddeq's return to power within a few days (Chapter 4).

This was the peak of the Popular Movement (*Nehzat-e Melli*), as it was known then, but later developments led to its gradual decline, when Kashani, Baqa'i and some other leading figures in the Popular Movement went over to the opposition and began to attack Mosaddeq. This was anticipated by a split in the Toilers party, most of whom, led by Maleki, formed the Toilers Third Force party, which gave crucial support to Mosaddeq. Maleki had already put forward the theory of the Third Force which was his elaborate formulation of independence from both Eastern and Western blocs (Chapter 5).

The oil dispute continued and Mosaddeq's government rejected Britain and America's final proposal for settlement in February 1953, which Maleki thought ought to have been accepted. Meanwhile, the Anglo-American powers were busy organising a coup against Mosaddeq which was unwittingly helped by Mosaddeq's decision to close the Majlis via a referendum, against which Maleki and some other leading figures had advised him. The first attempted coup of 16 August 1953 failed but the subsequent one, on 19 August, succeeded. The Tudeh party, which had castigated Mosaddeq as an American agent but had later somewhat toned down its vehement opposition to him, did not resist the coup despite their repeated slogan that they would 'turn *coup d'état* into a counter *coup d'état*' (Chapter 6).

Mosaddeq and some Popular Front leaders were arrested, tried and imprisoned, Hossein Fatemi, the foreign minister, was executed, and Maleki was thrown in jail without trial, together with many prominent Tudeh members and activists, for a year. Within a couple of years the regime of the shah and General Zahedi had suppressed the Popular Movement and virtually destroyed the Tudeh party. They settled the oil dispute at least against the spirit of the oil nationalisation, resulting in the Consortium Oil Agreement which was opposed in the Majlis by Mohammad Derakhshesh, the teachers' union leader, whose long speech had been written by Maleki (Chapter 6).

The period 1953–60 was one of dictatorship, first led jointly by the shah and Zahedi, then by the shah alone after he dismissed Zahedi in 1955. It was not a regime of absolute and arbitrary rule which commenced from 1963 onwards, and so a certain amount of semi-legal activity was possible. Maleki tried hard both in person and in writing to rally the erstwhile leaders of the Popular Movement to organise themselves quietly and prepare for the opportunity which he believed would come, but they had been largely demoralised and would not be motivated. Maleki himself kept in contact with the core of Third Force activists and edited *Nabard-e Zendegi* (Battle of Life), a theoretical-cum-intellectual journal in which several university professors and intellectuals wrote articles which were not politically highly charged (Chapters 6 and 7).

By 1960 the regime was in acute crisis. Inflation, a large balance of payments' deficit, the Soviet Union's vehement propaganda campaigns against the shah, the election of John F. Kennedy to the US presidency, a man who had been openly critical of corrupt third world regimes, including Iran's, not to mention the domestic discontent, impelled the shah to allow a certain amount of opening up when he declared that the forthcoming (twentieth) Majlis elections were free. Quickly, some former leaders of the Popular Movement, in addition to some others they had invited, declared the formation of the second NF, but they did not invite Maleki who, together with the core of Third Force activists plus some newcomers, formed the Socialist League of the Popular Movement of Iran (Chapter 7).

The new NF, which at first had a considerable following mainly on account of past associations with Mosaddeq, did not issue a manifesto; they simply demanded free elections, and set about dissolving the NF parties into simple members of the Front, which, by definition, excluded the Socialist League. They soon boycotted the elections which were largely rigged in any case, and the twentieth Majlis, which had been thus elected, was dissolved by the shah a couple of months later, in early 1961, a condition which Ali Amini had made for his accepting the premiership (Chapter 7).

The shah both disliked and feared Amini who was an able and independent-minded former minister and former ambassador to Washington, but he made him prime minister nonetheless, both because the situation was desperate and because he thought that that was what the Americans desired. Amini's main policy was a comprehensive reform of the land tenure, and he therefore asked for the dissolution of parliament as it was packed with landlords and their supporters. He also wished to trim some of the shah's powers. Maleki believed that the second NF should not get into a life- and-death struggle against Amini but turn themselves into a shadow government: he argued that the fall of Amini without his being replaced by the Front would result in 'black dictatorship'. The Front did not heed his advice, and, after the fall of Amini, a now confident shah launched his White Revolution in January 1963, which included land reform and women's franchise, followed by absolute and arbitrary rule that would last for almost fifteen years (Chapter 7).

Thus, for the second time the Popular Movement was defeated. Mosaddeq tried to intervene through correspondence to reform the second NF but they were ready to quit the scene and his intervention gave them the pretext for doing so. But the Socialist League continued its opposition until August 1965 when Maleki and three of his colleagues were arrested and convicted in a military court. Maleki was sentenced to three years' imprisonment but was released after eighteen months largely as a result of pressure put on the shah by European socialists. He continued to read and translate books, none of which were allowed to be published under his name. He died in July 1969 at the age of sixty-eight (Chapter 8).

1

KHALIL MALEKI AND
THE FIFTY-THREE

Khalil Maleki was born in Tabriz, Iran, into an old Turkic-speaking Azerbaijani family. His father, Fath'ali Maleki, was a well-to-do merchant descended from one of the generals of Nader Shah (ruled 1736–47) whose descendants in turn became major merchants in Tabriz. They were probably distant relatives of Hajj Hossein Aqa Malek, the renowned collector of books, including rare manuscripts and other antique items, in whose name there is now a museum in Tehran. Maleki's mother, Fatemeh, later known as Hajj Khanom, was his father's relative and lived with Khalil all her life, dying a few years before him.[1]

Maleki was the oldest son of five children; the other sons were Shafi' and Reza, the daughters La'ya and Zahra. He grew up in Tabriz amid the turmoil of the Constitutional Revolution. This began in 1905 in Tehran and the provinces and led to the abolition of the traditional arbitrary rule (*estebdad*) and establishment of constitutional monarchy. There followed a protracted power struggle between Mohammad Ali Shah – who acceded to the throne after his father died almost as soon as he had signed the constitution – and the Majlis ending with the shah ordering the bombardment of the Majlis and his subsequent abolition of constitutional government in 1908. This was followed by revolt and resistance, especially in Tabriz where a heroic fight was put up against the forces of arbitrary government, until the tide turned in July 1909, and the second constitutional monarchy was declared after the shah was forced to abdicate and leave Iran.[2]

Maleki grew up in this environment, witnessing the siege of Tabriz by government forces, followed by the triumph of 1909 which was in turn quickly followed by the chaos that increasingly engulfed the country. In 1911, the conflict with Russia over decisions made by Iran's young American financial adviser, Morgan Shuster, obliged the government either to dissolve the Majlis or face the Russian military occupation of Tehran, since Russian forces were already occupying the north of the country.[3] Maleki was ten at the time and these events left their mark on him.

A few years later his father died during a cholera epidemic at a young age. His uncle Mohsen, who was then a carpet merchant in Istanbul, came back to Tabriz, and, according to the traditions of the time, married his brother's widow, the fruit of their union being Hossein Malek, Maleki's half-brother. Not long afterwards the family moved from Tabriz to Arak – which at the time was called Soltanabad – because the central customs office for exporting carpets was in that city. Hossein's father died when he was seven and Shafi' and Reza sustained the family by opening a pharmacy.[4]

According to Taqi Makkinezhad – an Araki intellectual who knew the Malekis well and was destined to be Khalil's cell mate and later comrade in the Tudeh party, and still later accompany him in the party split of 1948 – the Maleki brothers ran a pharmacy in Arak when Khalil was eighteen. Makkinezhad further attests that the family were highly respected and deeply religious.[5]

2

'THE TRAGEDY OF OUR CENTURY'

Maleki finished his schooling in a traditional *madrasa*, a college for Islamic instruction, in Arak and a few years later went to Tehran in pursuit of his political ideals. Two memories of this period stood out in his mind in a few semi-autobiographical essays that he wrote in 1960–1. He recorded them in the weekly *Elm o Zendegi* (Science and Life), in a column entitled 'The Tragedy of Our Century' and signed them, as usual, a 'student of the social sciences'. He wrote in the first essay:

> The tragedy of our century, i.e. the greatest tragedy of all the historical epochs, arose from the expectations that the intellectuals and freemen of the world had of the wonderful values which would result from the great [Bolshevik] revolution of the century, and which instead led to the disgusting ugliness brought about by that promised revolution. A European person who has experienced this tragedy has likened the wish for that bright future which had turned into this terrible darkness to the group who were looking for the great forest which they thought would burn for ever and keep them warm, and yet discovered that it had burnt down and turned into ashes ... But some bigots had gone blind and deaf while their eyes and ears were open, and did not want to believe that there were no more than ashes left.[6]

The first lasting memory was his meeting with Soleyman Mirza Eskandari, the socialist leader, who was a descendant of Abbas Mirza Qajar, the modernising Crown Prince under Fath'ali Shah. Maleki had come across the representative whom Soleyman had sent to Arak to set up a branch in that city. He writes that he did not need much persuasion because at the time Soleyman was the idol of the young people who had lofty ideals about progress and modernisation and who, like Soleyman Mirza, supported Reza Khan against 'the corrupt Qajar court'. This was certainly the case in Arak, Maleki writes, where the younger generation were eager to make Reza Khan the first president of Iran and were singing in demonstrations the following verse from the romantic revolutionary poet Aref Qazvini:

I am happy that the hand of nature has put
The lantern of the shah's kingship in the window of the wind.

Instead of leading to a democratic government, the Constitutional Revolution of 1906–11 had resulted in increasing chaos both at the centre and in the provinces. That is why the modern elite and middle classes were more and more eager for order and modernisation and they began to put their hopes in Reza Khan's success. The republican movement was a movement from above to put Reza Khan at the helm. It failed, but not long afterwards the Qajars were toppled and Reza Khan was made shah. All the newspapers that came to Arak, Maleki writes, were full of support for the change of regime and Reza Khan's rule.[7] After the failure of the republican movement which clearly depressed him, he decided to go to Tehran, meet 'the greatest political leader and public idol' – Soleyman Mirza – and ask him why the movement that was sacred to both of them had failed. This was in the month of Ramadan and, in his response to Maleki's questions, the socialist leader explained that he could not name the culprits since he was fasting, and backbiting would make his fast null and void. Maleki was not put off at all by Soleyman's religious commitment (which was well known) as he himself had been devoutly religious until his youth. But he believed that what

Soleyman had said was just an excuse, the result of duplicity and demagogy. However, this does not necessarily follow. It is hardly surprising that a leading political figure would refuse to name those people to 'a simple and provincial young man' whom he was meeting for the first time. On the other hand, it does show that two of Maleki's outstanding characteristics, honesty and openness, were already evident.[8]

And that is how the idol of his youth fell, so much so that he says for a while he was living in a state of limbo. In the end, he decided to turn to higher studies and registered at the Iran-German Technical College to study chemistry. This is where the second incident occurred which reveals another side to Maleki that was to remain with him all his life. He used to describe it as 'the refrain of my life'.

BERLIN

The German principal of the college, a Dr Strung, initially treated the students in a democratic manner but as a result of their indiscipline his attitude hardened and the German teachers followed suit. On one occasion a German teacher said something about Iranians in the class which the students took as an insult. They declared a strike unless the teacher apologised. He did not. The students wrote a letter of complaint to Strung, parts of which Maleki advised were too strong, but the others thought the letter was not strong enough.

However, they did not heed his advice and sent the letter as it was. The principal gathered them all together, protested about some parts of the letter and made them stay behind one afternoon, supervised by the German teacher. After he left, the students issued emotional slogans about not submitting to the punishment, insisting again on an apology. However, Strung came down with both feet and demanded that they submit or be expelled. They all gave in except Maleki and one other student. Under further pressure, the latter also gave in but Maleki insisted on a one-man strike. Eventually he left the college and Strung used his influence to prevent any other school from admitting him. He decided to escape to Russia and continue his education there, but when he explained what had happened to a leading educationalist, he let him enrol in his school. Shortly afterwards, arrangements were made for Maleki and Strung to bury their differences, and he returned to the college.[9]

Maleki refers to this as the refrain of his life because in such situations he would first advise caution in the face of romantic and revolutionary slogans, then he would commit himself to collective action, then his comrades – those who shouted the loudest – would give in and he would be left stranded.

In 1927 the Iranian government decided to send a hundred students to European universities for a few years. The successful students were selected in a stiff competition. Maleki took the examination and passed with flying colours. One candidate with good connections had finished 109th but rather than fail him, it was decided to send 110 so that he could be included.

Maleki was one of the top seven students who were sent to Germany in 1928, under a supervisor whose pay was ten times more than the combined scholarships of the seven students, and yet he decided to live in Switzerland. One day this supervisor went to Berlin, summoned the seven to a room in the Iranian embassy, offered a few words of appreciation for their academic efforts and ended by saying that as soon as he had reached Berlin he had contacted all the universities there, and they told him how disciplined and hard-working the Iranian students were. He did not know that at the time there was only one university in Berlin.[10]

Shortly after arriving in Berlin, the group of seven state students decided to join the Iranian students' union. Taqi Arani, later to become an icon in the annals of the Iranian left, ran the union together with Morteza Alavi, older brother of the famous novelist Bozorg Alavi, of whom more later. At first the union did not want to admit them, thinking that because they were state students they must inevitably be the government's stool pigeons. But the unions' constitution would not allow their exclusion. This led to the emergence of two factions in the union, but the old members soon realised their mistake, especially as the newcomers stood firm with the union in their disagreements with the students' office of the embassy. There was a central student department in Paris which oversaw all the offices in other European capitals, and its head, Isma'il Mer'at, was the strong lawgiver for both state and private students everywhere in Europe. Many of the students' union members had leftist tendencies and a few were communists. Arani and Mohammad Bahrami (who were later to become Maleki's cell mates in Iran) as well as Morteza Alavi (later to disappear in Stalin's purges in Russia) were already communists.[11] Iraj Eskandari, who was then in France and was in contact with Arani and Alavi, recalls that they were publishing 'a highly radical' newspaper and a magazine.[12]

This was a highly critical period in German history when the Nazis and communists had the better of the democratic parties, and were struggling for total power, which culminated in Hitler's rise in 1933. Thus they were caught between extremes and they felt they had to choose between one or the other, like the German people themselves who had been disappointed in the Weimar Republic. Maleki quotes a German girl as having told him at the time that, one way or another, she wanted to see a major change.

Maleki had vaguely leftist tendencies: he was not a communist but was a devoted member of the students' union. However, one particular incident overturned Maleki's fortunes as an Iranian student in Europe. A fellow student had a major grievance against the officials of the students' office in the Iranian embassy in Berlin. And when his protests were dismissed with contempt, one day he turned up in the students' office of the embassy and shot himself. Something like the episode at the college in Tehran was repeated, though this time with disastrous consequences for Maleki. The union members swore to fight to the last drop of their blood. The situation became so critical that Mer'at himself travelled from Paris to Berlin and ordered the students to leave the union. Once again epic slogans were issued for resistance, but when Mer'at threatened to send them back home all but Maleki and Ahmad Hami relented.

The authorities in Europe reported to Tehran that Maleki and Hami were involved in communist activities, and that was enough for their counterparts in Tehran to terminate their state scholarships. Hami went to Tehran and used high-level contacts to overturn the decision in his own case and subsequently returned to Berlin. Maleki was left alone with his principles.

Maleki, who had been very successful in his studies, decided to hold out and try to manage by taking a job, in addition to the little help that he received from his brothers in Iran. His main work was part-time translating German brochures into Persian for German firms exporting to Iran. The earnings were far from sufficient, but although some of the students offered to lend him money, he turned them down. Once, a student whom he did not know sent him a cheque via his post office box. He wrote back saying that since he did not know the benefactor he could not accept his help and was returning the cheque. He accepted financial assistance only from one of his fellow students in the old Tehran College, Reza Ganjeh'i, who was a student in Switzerland and, by chance, would become his brother-in-law.[13]

RETURN TO IRAN

Inevitably, however, this could not last for long and Maleki had to return to Iran in 1933 without finishing his studies. But he did not sulk or remain idle. He went to the Tehran Teacher Training College and qualified as a school teacher of chemistry after finishing his three-year course of study. A couple of years later, in 1935, he met Sabiheh Ganjeh'i, later a biology teacher, and they married shortly afterwards.[14] (Sabiheh was a daughter of Hajj Alinaqi Ganjeh'i, a well-to-do merchant, a leading Tabriz figure in the Constitutional Revolution of 1906–11 and several times a parliamentary deputy. Her brother Reza was to become a leading satirist as well as a minister. Another brother, Javad, became a Majlis deputy under Mosaddeq.) Thus, both remained in education, Sabiheh later becoming principal of a girls' school. She was an able and courageous person and remained her husband's devoted wife, indeed his soulmate, until his death. Writing to Mosaddeq on 29 November 1962 Maleki said:

> Throughout our lives when I have not had mental or physical rest even for a few months, she has been courageously at my side and has run our life by tireless efforts. Knowing that I have chosen this mode of living willingly, she has never put me under moral pressure to choose a way other than acting for the Iranian popular movement and my social ideals. On the contrary, she has always been a solid support for me in the rough path that I have trodden.[15]

The country to which Maleki had returned was considerably different from the one he had left five years before. Some modernising changes (mainly copying Europe) had taken place, but the hopes and enthusiasm of the young middle classes who had supported Reza Shah's rise to power had been dashed. In 1928, when Maleki went to Europe, the elections for the seventh Majlis were held, for the first time without a single member of the parliamentary opposition being elected.[16]

Yet, although it was a dictatorship, absolute and arbitrary power – or what the shah himself described as 'a one-person government'[17] – was still to come. This had been established quickly so that at least by 1931 the shah's wishes ruled supreme over all laws and public decisions. In 1933, the year Maleki returned to Iran, Teymurtash, the powerful court minister and second only to the shah, was in jail (later to be murdered in his cell), and the highly controversial 1933 oil agreement had been made with the Anglo-Persian (later Anglo-Iranian) Oil Company. However, by far the greatest grievance of the young educated class against the regime was the total absence of freedom of expression. Nothing could be spoken or written which even remotely smacked of the slightest criticism.

THE ARANI CIRCLE

Meanwhile, Taqi Arani had got his doctorate in chemistry and returned to Iran in 1930. He began to teach at a secondary school, and, being an able and charismatic young teacher, he had begun to attract a few of his students into his circle. According to Bozorg Alavi, Arani was appointed director general of all technical schools, including the same Iran-German College at which Maleki had studied and Alavi was now teaching.[18] Alavi was a young writer as well as teacher and was close to Sadeq Hedayat.[19] He had studied in Germany, had not been involved in politics there but had become radicalised as a result of 'the suffocating dictatorship' in Iran.

Alavi himself says that he witnessed Farrokhi Yazdi, the dissident poet who had been put in the Majlis for appearances' sake, being assaulted, beaten and thrown out of the House because he was criticising the bill for the establishment of an agricultural bank, arguing that it would only benefit the landlords; all parliamentary bills were first approved by the shah:

> I then realised that Farrokhi's speech had aroused the anger and enmity of the Majlis majority all of whom were stooges of the shah and the police. Watching that scene I got so horrified that when I was returning home I came across Dr Arani whom I had met in Germany and knew he was a friend of my brother [Morteza] and told him about it in full detail. ... Arani listened quietly ... and said come and see me sometime so we talk about such issues. By going to Arani's home my political life began, willy-nilly.[20]

Iraj Eskandari, whose uncle Soleyman Mirza was the old socialist leader, had also returned to Iran, having studied law and economics in France, but while he was a doctoral student he had his allowance cut off and had to come back.[21] According to Eskandari his allowance was discontinued because he had published a pamphlet against Teymurtash.[22] Arani and Alavi's relationship had already begun in 1930 when they were reading Marx's *Capital* together. Eskandari had returned to Tehran later and the three of them read Nikolai Bukharin's *The ABC of Communism*.[23]

The old Communist party of Iran, which had held its first congress in June 1920, after holding its third congress in 1928, had been so thoroughly suppressed and its daily organ *Haqiqat* (Pravda!) outlawed that it no longer existed as a party, and many of its leading figures – Ardeshir (Ardashes) Avanesian, Ja'far

Pishevari, Yusef Eftekhari, among others – were in jail.[24] In fact, a law of 1931 formally banned 'collectivist' (i.e. communist) activities on pain of up to ten years' imprisonment.

None of Arani's circle had been members of the old Communist party, but they intended to study and promote Marxism both cautiously and discreetly. They began to contact their students and some friends and acquaintances that they had known in Europe, such as Mohammad Bahrami and Khalil Maleki, and in order to provide a central focus for their activities they decided to publish an intellectual (effectively scientific) journal. They initially thought of calling the journal Materialism, but the licensing authorities would not accept that title because it was a European word![25] So they called it *Donya* (The World). Its first issue was published in February 1934.[26]

The fact that the licensing authorities did not understand the meaning of 'materialism' and its Marxist connotations shows the degree of ignorance of the censors regarding Marxist ideology. This played into the hands of *Donya*'s editors (Arani, Alavi and Eskandari) who could publish articles on materialism, dialectics, determinism and indeterminism, etc., with impunity. However, at the same time they published articles on industry and technology – even the arts and psychology – as a cover. All three editors published their own articles under pseudonyms.[27] Arani and Eskandari tried hard to involve Maleki in the journal but he agreed only to buy the journal and give them additional financial support.[28]

This was a very unusual journal at the time and attracted a small group of young intellectuals, some of whom, such as Eprime Eshagh and Anvar Khameh'i, were only at the last stages of their secondary education. Arani began to invite a select group to his house on Monday afternoons initially to discuss questions arising from the journal's articles but later extending them to other matters such as philosophical and social issues, as long as they did not touch on the current political situation in Iran.[29]

According to Khameh'i, these meetings provided the foundation of the group of Fifty-Three, whose members were later arrested and charged with communist activities. Apart from the triumvirate of Arani, Alavi and Eskandari, they were attended by Khalil Maleki and Mohammad Bahrami among other old hands. The result was a group of twenty activists. Only a few of those who attended the meetings were aware of the underlying ideology of Marxism, the others had no idea. *Donya* ceased publication after a year; according to Arani, it had run into financial difficulties.[30]

It is at about this time that a 'communist party' was formed. A three-man committee was established: Arani, general secretary; Abdossamad Kambakhsh (an old communist), chief executive; and Bahrami, treasurer. The meetings in Arani's home were cancelled and contact between members was made through Kambakhsh who often used various pseudonyms.[31] That is how Maleki and Kambakhsh, known by the pseudonym Sariri, met once a week in 'a two-person meeting'.[32] Still, the so-called party of at most twenty people did nothing other than keep in contact with each other indirectly and continued their Marxist studies. There was no publication, not even the occasional leaflet. They did not even have a typewriter while material they translated from French was handwritten and circulated among the group.[33] According to Eskandari, they had not formally organised a party, but Arani was in contact with a communist nucleus through Kambakhsh who was a communist and in touch with Comintern (the Communist International). He says that he and some of the others had become aware of its existence only after their arrest.[34]

THE FIFTY-THREE

This so-called party was uncovered by the authorities purely by chance. In May 1937 a certain Mohammad Shureshyian was

13

arrested because of an indiscretion, and he told the police that he was a member of the Communist party which had once published *Donya*, and that the party's aim was to establish a socialist republic in Iran.[35] He mentioned the names of five of its members whom he knew, including Arani and Kambakhsh. They were subsequently arrested, and Kambakhsh, an ardent Russophile who had spent a long time in Russia, told the police everything, including, of course, the names of everyone he knew.[36] As Maleki and Eskandari put it, he had submitted what almost amounted to a complete party congress report to the police.[37] Kambakhsh had even confessed that they had received a small sum of money from Comintern.[38]

Next day, forty others were arrested, and the remainder on the following day. Some of the leading figures, notably Arani, Bahrami and Alavi, were heavily tortured, but not Kambaksh who had needed no persuasion to speak. Among Alavi's papers they had found a poison-pen letter signed by 'the secret committee'. This had been written by one of his students who had received a bad mark from him. Now the police were torturing him and others to reveal all that they knew about this 'secret committee'.[39]

Most of those arrested knew nothing about 'the party': some had simply been readers of *Donya*. Others had even been arrested as a result of mistaken identity.[40] One was arrested because, years earlier, he had written to his brother from Isfahan that 'the people of Isfahan are very uncivilised'. Now his brother had been arrested as a student of Arani, and the police believed that, by 'uncivilised', he had meant that the Isfahanis were not communist![41] Altogether they were fifty-two men, and by accident another man was added to their list.

This man was Reza Radmanesh, a European-educated scientist. He had been arrested before with a group in Rasht with no connections to the Arani group, almost all of whom were released within a few months. But in the belief that the fifty-two would soon be released, his family had used influence to include him in the fifty-two's dossier. And that is how the Fifty-Three came into being.[42] He was destined to become secretary general of the Tudeh party for many years. However, Alavi's version is that he had been added to the group simply because he had once met Arani.[43]

The Fifty-Three were first taken to the Tehran police prison and put in solitary confinement, yet somehow they managed to keep in contact, although many of them did not know each other. After a couple of months, the authorities transferred some of the leading figures to a general ward and kept the others in solitary confinement; curiously, they left the doors of their cells open. After a while they moved them all to three rooms. Maleki, Eskandari, Alavi and a couple of others who were financially better off were put in the first room and the others were put in the other two rooms. The first room became known as the 'bourgeois' room, the second the 'petit bourgeois' room and the third the 'proletarian' room.[44]

Maleki had been among the group of forty who were arrested on 11 May 1937, the day after Kambakhsh's confession to the police. Predictably, the inmates talked and argued among themselves. But the one issue that preoccupied all of them was who had been responsible for their arrest; who had named them to the police? Kambakhsh had very cleverly convinced most of his companions that the culprit was Arani rather than himself, as a result of which Arani was regarded by most of the others with disdain. Maleki says that he defended Arani from the start and the others accused him of doing this just because both he and Arani were from Azerbaijan.[45]

It was only later, when they were transferred to Qasr prison and, crucially, were sent to the criminal court where everyone's dossiers were read out, that the role of Kambakhsh became clear.

As a result, Arani vehemently attacked Kambakhsh in court, accusing him of writing a long report in which he had resorted to libel and named anybody and everybody he had ever known, and had named Arani himself as leader of the group. The Tudeh party subsequently cut out this part of Arani's defence in their publication of his speech in court, Arani having died in prison in 1939.[46]

According to Alavi and Eskandari, after their release from prison and the founding of the Tudeh party, Kambakhsh went to the Soviet Union for a few months and convinced the Soviets that it was not he who had given the Fifty-Three away.[47] Alavi further says:

> Some gullible people like me believed that the Tudeh party would realise their ideal of freedom and social justice and so joined the party, little knowing that Kambakhsh after wheeling and dealing with the Russians would be at the helm of the Tudeh ship and take it as far as it would become a news agency for the Russians.[48]

Years later, the issue of Kambakhsh's confession was raised in the fourth plenum of the Tudeh party which met in exile, in Moscow, but no decision was taken on it because the matter had not been raised at the time he had joined the party, and later in the first and second party congresses. Kambakhsh's main defence, however, had been that he had reported everything to Comintern and they had agreed that he was innocent.[49]

Alavi says in his memoirs, 'I got upset when a couple of months after the foundation of the Tudeh party Kambakhsh had gone missing, but it was later discovered that he'd gone to Baku and told them that Arani, not he, had exposed the Fifty-Three. And now he had returned and personally organised a meeting at a school in which he spoke and referred to the Tudeh party as "my party" … Then I heard he was in the central committee as well. I asked Radmanesh, what's this? He said I can't do anything; it's in the hands of those who are running things. I said you mean the Russians. He said yes …' He adds that he wanted to resign but Radmanesh and Eskandari made him change his mind. 'This was the biggest mistake of my life. I wish I had resigned in the very first months.'[50]

MALEKI DEFIES THE JAILERS

While they were still being detained in the police prison something happened that became almost a legend in its own time. There was a disagreement between the inmates of one of the rooms and a policeman. He reported to his superiors that the prisoners had tried to 'disarm' him, i.e. grab his baton and beat him with it.[51] As a result, they transferred four of them, including Khameh'i and Kambakhsh, to solitary confinement for punishment.[52]

When the news reached the 'bourgeois' room, they saw it as an insult to all of them and decided to react strongly to it. Fiery speeches were made to the effect that all of the Fifty-Three were prepared to shed the last drop of their blood to rectify the situation. Maleki says that, although he knew that any advice to the contrary would be put down to his conservatism, he nevertheless argued that a strong reaction was not warranted by the case, and that they should not overreact. But his argument carried no weight and the 'revolutionaries' still persisted in demanding satisfaction.

Maleki then said if they insisted on taking action they should call the officer on duty and protest to him. However,

Maleki told them that he would not do the speaking and that he would stand in the last row; and if he or those who spoke up were taken out for disciplinary punishment, all the others should continue to protest until all of them were punished in the same way. He called a witness from another room and repeated their agreement in front of him. Decades later, he wrote in his memoirs:

> Right from the beginning I felt that the most radical of speech-makers were more hesitant than the rest. The officer on duty arrived and [while the prisoners were standing in a few rows facing him] he challenged anyone who had anything to say to step forward ... Following the agreement we had made, I stood in the last row ... Even after the officer's second warning no one stepped forward. I felt ashamed that a group of the society's first-rank revolutionary intellectuals were cowed by the challenge of such a base individual.
>
> I remember I was pushing forward when the officer issued his third warning. I told him of our grievance and demanded satisfaction ... He said, 'well if I send you somewhere would you not demand to be released from it.' I said 'why should I not make that demand. From the word go I protest at the fact that you have put me in prison. Therefore I always demand to be released from prison and from the prison that you have made inside the prison. I protest against all this.'[53]

According to Alavi, Maleki said, 'why should I not protest. Of course, as long as you have not released me from prison I would protest. And even when I am released I would protest.'[54] Both Alavi and Khameh'i describe Maleki's action as heroic. 'The duty officer went', Maleki continued, 'and a few minutes later two officers showed up … and, without a single person protesting, they took me to Ward Five.'[55]

MALEKI ADDRESSES THE MOST UNFORTUNATE INMATES

Ward Five was a room measuring 15 x 8 metres where, according to Khameh'i, Maleki and Alavi they kept four hundred of the worst, most hardened criminals and the most pitiable people imaginable. It was not just the place of ordinary criminals (that was Ward Six), but for the forgotten, the 'dead souls', to use the title of Gogol's famous novel. Both Khameh'i and Maleki say that there was not enough room for them to sleep on their backs next to each other, and there was one cesspit which several of them used at the same time. Both Alavi and Khameh'i say that when some of them were taken to the yard through the back of their rooms, the smell was intolerable and both agree that the worst possible punishment for a political prisoner was to be thrown into that ward.[56]

When Maleki entered the room the deafening noise decreased. Then, one of the inmates who had thought Maleki was a prison inspector, stepped forward and complained that another inmate had stolen some money from him:

> I said loudly that he has stolen one rial from you while the prison authorities steal 3.5 rials of your daily ration. Slowly, those who had realised I was a political prisoner told everyone to be quiet. A miracle had happened and for some time there was complete silence in the room. I spoke to them of the wretchedness of the petty thieves whom the social maladies had forced to steal; of those who without the slightest guilt had been put there …; of

the big millionaire thieves who, not far from where they were, were in the large hotel-like prison rooms ...; and, finally, of the necessity of unity among them which could result in a better daily ration, and of the help that we the political prisoners could provide in organising them ... I did not have to wait too long for the prison authorities to loudly announce that I should leave the room.[57]

Alavi says that they heard a policeman shouting to the prison governor 'he is making a speech'.[58]

Maleki was taken to the administrative rooms where the prison governor and others told him he had committed a heinous crime and that he would be court-martialled. They took him to a solitary cell and wanted to handcuff him and put his legs in fetters but he ran out of the cell and began to make such a racket that the duty policeman ordered them to leave him alone, fearing a reaction from other prisoners. The prison authorities did not proceed with the threatened court-martial mainly because they were afraid that they themselves would also be blamed for sending Maleki to Ward Five.

Maleki was released from solitary confinement after several weeks but chose not to return to his old room because he had discovered that, despite all the revolutionary speeches that had been made before his arrest, no action at all had been taken by his friends and inmates to protest against the treatment he had received.[59] This he called in his memoirs 'the first bitter test', though it was the third time that he had had this kind of experience, the other two being in the technical college and, following that, in Berlin. Perhaps he meant that this was the first bitter test in the Fifty-Three prison, for there were others to come.

As mentioned, the Fifty-Three were arrested in May 1937; in midsummer they were transferred to Qasr prison. This was a worrying move. At the time, the prisoners who had not yet been charged were kept in the police prison and only sent to Qasr if and when they were convicted by a court. Now, being sent to Qasr without trial implied that the inmates were to be incarcerated indefinitely, as had been the case with its old communist prisoners such as Ardeshir Avanesian, Ja'far Pishevari and Reza Rusta, and many nomadic chiefs and khans. It was seen by many as Tehran's Bastille, although it had once been a Qajar palace.[60]

On the plus side, there was more freedom of movement in Qasr, and, besides, the Fifty-Three were happy to be in the same jail as the old communists whom they looked up to. However, this was not invariably the case; for example, a couple of the old communists, such as Ardeshir and Rusta, and a few of the Fifty-Three, and Eskandari in particular, did not like Pishevari and treated him with contempt.[61] Apart from that, there would soon be conflict among the old communists on the Moscow purges of the Old Bolsheviks. Some, like Yusef Eftekhari and Ali Omid, were critical of those purges whereas others, especially Ardeshir, defended them and described the critics as Trotskyists. The conflict inevitably involved many of the Fifty-Three as well.[62]

However, sometime after being transferred to Qasr prison the Fifty-Three were told that they would soon be put on trial and it was then that they insisted the police dossiers were read out to them, at which point it became clear that Arani had not given their names to the police. Thus Arani became the hero and leader of the group and believed that they should reinforce their resistance to the jailers, chief among whom was Colonel Nirumand, the prison governor.

The old political prisoners suggested that they should go on hunger strike so the jailers would meet some of their demands. Alavi mentions the return of their stoves which had been removed for no reason and which they needed to warm up their meals.[63]

Maleki writes that, once again, he was opposed to strong action, arguing that the balance of power was hugely in favour of the prison authorities, and if they went on strike and then had to break it without their demands being met it would be a catastrophic failure. At first, not even Arani agreed with him but upon further discussion he came round to his view and the strike did not take place.[64]

MALEKI'S SECOND ACT OF DEFIANCE

The irony is that the strike did take place but in protest against Maleki's punishment by the jailers and in his absence! One night at 11p.m. they heard the duty officer shouting at one of the old political prisoners at the top of his voice because he had been walking in the corridor, pointing out that the official time of silence was 10 p.m., and claiming that the prisoner was disturbing the sleep of the others. He went on shouting such that 'his drunken bellowing' woke everyone up.

Maleki, whom Alavi describes as 'one of the bravest of the Fifty-Three',[65] got up, went into the corridor and shouted back at the duty officer. He told him that it was not that prisoner's quiet walk which woke up everyone but his own drunken outburst. He told him silence must be observed by everyone and not just the prisoners, and it was in fact the heavy boots of the wardens that disturbed the prisoners' sleep every night. A crowd gathered to watch the scene. The duty officer issued a couple of threats and left.[66]

Next morning they came, pulled Maleki from his bed in his pyjamas and took him to Nirumand. The officer slapped Maleki, and in a torrent of abuse told him that he had on one occasion broken the silence in the police prison and because he had not been properly punished at the time had now done it again. Maleki did not hit him back but responded vigorously to his insults and abuse. He was taken into the garden and whipped. He was then sent back to the police prison in his pyjamas, put in a solitary cell which had a cesspit in one corner, while he was handcuffed and his feet were put in fetters. He was put on half-rations. Sometime later they took him out and he and Bahrami, who had also been moved to the police prison, were taken back to Qasr. On the way there Bahrami feared that they were going to be executed but when they got there they were relieved to see the whipping board. They were both thrashed and the colonel in charge then told Maleki 'now carry on fasting'![67]

The colonel was referring to the hunger strike that had been declared in Qasr in response to Maleki's punishment, which the inmates regarded as an insult to all of them. As noted, there were already some grounds for such an action but 'what they did to Maleki made it certain'.[68] The hunger strike spread but after a few days was broken. The reason for this was that Colonel Nirumand ordered that ten of the hunger strikers should be brought over, among them Arani and Kambakhsh, to be heavily beaten; he summoned Iraj Eskandari to witness the flogging and told him to go and tell the others what he had seen. At first there was disagreement among the strikers, but in the end they decided to end their hunger strike. Alavi writes that 'in this struggle we were defeated',[69] just as Maleki had predicted. Alavi, Khameh'i and (to a lesser degree) Eskandari have all recalled the hunger strike in detail.[70]

As indicated, the Fifty-Three were put on trial in the criminal court but, contrary to the expectations of many of them, they were condemned to various terms between three and ten years' imprisonment, as had been stipulated in the anti-communist law of 1931, even though most of them knew little or nothing about communism. Arani and Kambakhsh were sentenced to ten years each, some others to five years, and Maleki to four years followed by banishment to a small town. Yet many of them managed to become familiar with the principles of Marxism in jail in the years after their convictions. While in jail they even managed to get hold of a copy of Marx's *Capital* in German, had it 'buried' in the prison courtyard, and every day Maleki and Bahrami would translate ten pages of it into Persian for the others, which was followed by group discussion. 'This way about a hundred persons or more studied *Capital*, though only the first ten of them knew that the book was inside the prison.'[71]

MALEKI'S THIRD ACT OF DEFIANCE

Arani died of typhoid in 1939, all his fellow prisoners believing that this was due to lack of proper food, medicine and care, while the jailers moved him from one cell to another. The jailers did not even accept the food and medicine brought for him by his mother and sister, something they would normally permit. Maleki lost his two-year-old son Hormoz, whom he had only seen in the arms of his wife from behind prison bars, which came as a terrible blow.[72] Now that they had received long jail sentences the Fifty-Three were active in self-education, especially learning languages. Maleki knew German and French so he learned English in jail.

In his political memoirs Maleki praises the friendship and cooperation of many of the Fifty-Three, especially after the conviction and the death of Arani. But at the same time he is critical of many of them regarding collective action as well as narrow-mindedness, petty jealousies, dogmatism and lust for power. The last specific incident which he recalls is when the prison authorities ordered them not to walk in the corridors after 9 p.m. There was anger and the usual slogans about resistance to the last drop of blood, but this time Maleki agreed that they should take action. It was decided that all of them should come out into the corridors and walk around after nine o'clock. This happened, but after a while they began to drift back to their rooms one by one so that only Maleki and one other man were left in a corridor. They were both arrested and taken to disciplinary cells for some time.[73] Maleki wrote:

> Although this event compared to the bitter experiences of the past was not so important, it made me decide more strongly than before not to join an organisation outside prison led by a member of the Fifty-Three.[74]

2

THE TUDEH PARTY

THE ALLIED INVASION

In August 1941 British and Russian forces invaded Iran. There were several reasons for this. The shah, the army and, not least, the people were pro-German, although the country was officially neutral. There was fear of Rommel and his Afrika Korps breaking through the British defence of Egypt, linking up with the Palestinians, who were also pro-German, and pushing through to Iran. Another, perhaps lesser, possibility was that the German Army Group South in Russia would reach the Caucasus Mountains and invade (a probably welcoming) Iran from the north.[1] The most disturbing prospect for the Allies was the possibility that one way or another Iranian oil would fall into the hands of the Germans. There was also the prospect of their using the trans-Iranian railway and roads for supplying arms and other equipment to Russian and British forces.[2]

However, they kept warning the Iranian government about the activities of around 2,400 Germans in the country whom they described as agents and spies of the Nazi regime. No doubt some of them were, but it cannot be the main reason why the invasion came. Reza Shah did not understand the gravity of the situation, the real possibility of an Anglo-Soviet invasion now that the two powers had been united in war against Germany. And if anyone else did, he would never have dared point it out to him in a political situation so insecure and unfree that, as an upper-class correspondent of the politician and diplomat Taqizadeh was to write later, even the upper classes 'were afraid of seeing their own relatives'.[3]

He was therefore caught completely by surprise when Ali Mansur, the prime minister, woke him early on the morning of 25 August to inform him of the invasion. By all accounts he kept his nerve, but to his horror the army on which he prided himself so much and on which he had lavished so much money and privilege behaved in such an undignified manner that many believed that officers had run away from the invaders wearing a chador to cover their uniform.[4] Furious, the shah physically assaulted the minister of war and the chief of staff so violently that he hurt his own hand.[5] By the time he abdicated, the shah had dismissed Mansur and appointed the loyal and respectable Mohammad Ali Forughi as prime minister.

It has now become commonplace to say that the Allies forced Reza Shah to abdicate. In some platitudinous sense this may be true, but it calls for two important qualifications. According to Sir Reader Bullard, the British minister in Tehran, the Allies never formally made such a demand and there is no evidence to contradict this, though he admitted that the news of the movement of the Russian forces from Qazvin towards Tehran had probably frightened the shah.[6] According to Abbasqoli Golshah'iyan, then minister of finance, the Russian ambassador had denied the news. During the 1921 coup, British diplomats and officers had accompanied Iranian officials to Mehrabad ostensibly to dissuade

Reza Khan's Cossacks from marching to Tehran, which became a fruitless exercise. Now, by an irony of history, the military attachés of both Russia and Britain had left for Qazvin ostensibly to prevent such a move, but later the news came that the Russian were approaching Karaj.[7] However, Golshai'iyan states explicitly that it was the cabinet that asked Forughi to tell the shah to abdicate, and that Forughi, having said he personally believed that that was the wish of the Allies, saw the shah and told him so.[8]

Further support for the suggestion that the Allies did not force the shah to abdicate is the fact that the shah had to do so simply because he had nothing to stand on. Virtually the whole of the society was against him. Had he had a reasonable social base, with at least the backing of the upper classes, he would not have had to abdicate and the Allies would not have insisted on it now that he had agreed to cooperate with them.[9] Instead, even before he abdicated, the Majlis deputies who had been in effect appointed by him were implying that he had misappropriated some of the crown jewels,[10] and when he did abdicate they led scathing attacks on his humanitarian record and violation of public and private property, etc.[11] Shortly after the abdication, court cases began to be brought against the shah by those whose relatives had been murdered in jail and those whose properties had been confiscated.[12] Golsha'iyan says in his contemporary diaries that, the shah being so unpopular, those in government posts had been worried about their own fate (as a result of the public backlash) if he died or was assassinated, and almost rejoices in the fact that he had to abdicate while the Allies occupied the country and kept the peace.[13] The British briefly toyed with the idea of returning the Qajars,[14] but soon agreed to let Crown Prince Mohammad Reza succeed to the throne.

An absolute and arbitrary ruler having fallen, there was chaos in the centre and the provinces, as had always been the case in Iranian history. The big difference with the revolution of February 1979 was that it was not in the interest of the Allies for the forces of revenge, killing and looting to be unleashed. At any rate, people were much freer and at least in the first few months anything could be said and published. In January 1942, the young Mohammad Reza Shah signed the Tri-Partite Alliance with Britain and Soviet Russia, and in September 1943 Iran declared war on Germany (and later Japan), and so became a member of the United Nations. The following November, the Tehran Conference was attended by the Allied heads – Joseph Stalin, Franklin D. Roosevelt and Winston Churchill – who reaffirmed their commitment to Iranian independence and territorial integrity. Thus, almost from the outset, the Allies did not treat Iran as an occupied country to be run by themselves, although they did indirectly interfere in Iranian politics to serve their collective as well as individual interests in the country. Furthermore, the British and Americans effectively controlled Iran's transport and communications system, and even beyond that, as the British minister reported to the Foreign Office, 'the compelling need to save shipping also forced us into a considerable degree of interference in local affairs ...'[15]

THE TUDEH PARTY

The release of political prisoners created the opportunity for setting up parties, groups and factions. It took a month from the Allies' invasion for the Tudeh party to be formed. According to Eskandari, it was he who christened the party. Later developments turned it into an authentic communist party, but in the beginning it was similar to the European popular fronts – the anti-fascist movements of the 1930s and 1940s – consisting of various leftist and democratic tendencies with a broadly reformist programme: it declared its loyalty to constitutional monarchy and that it was a legal party using peaceful means.[16]

Eskandari denies that the Soviets were involved in the formation of the party.[17] However, both Kiyanuri and Tabari say that the party was formed under the instructions of Comintern.[18] This is confirmed by Chaqueri's detailed study of Soviet archival documents.[19] They looked for an old, established political leader and they found it in Soleyman Mirza Eskandari, Qajar nobleman, Iraj's uncle and former socialist leader (see Chapter 1). The constituent assembly was made up of various progressive and moderate individuals as well as members of the Fifty-Three.[20] Old communists such as Reza Rusta and Ja'far Pishevari were also active in the formation of the party, as was Abbas Eskandari, Iraj's maternal uncle who did not enjoy a good reputation and was later expelled from the party. Ardeshir (Ardashes) Avanesian at first insisted that the party should be openly communist but later relented and joined it.[21] The party attracted a few hundred people and this was to continue until 1943, especially after the earth-shaking Soviet victory at Stalingrad in February of that year, when thousands joined the party. Kambakhsh claims that in February 1942, thousands of people participated in the memorial meeting that was held at Arani's graveside.[22] This is not true and, in any case, Kambahksh was in the Soviet Union at the time. He may have confused the dates since there was a similar gathering in February 1944, which thousands attended.[23]

The Tudeh party brought more than a breath of fresh air to Iranian politics, culture and society, and was soon to become the most popular and best organised party in the country. It could be claimed that virtually all modern Iranian intellectuals under the age of forty joined it or sympathised with it. Their growing press and publications not only provided forums for modern politics and literature, but became vehicles for the publications of young and enthusiastic intellectuals. They organised the largest and in some ways the most authentic labour movement, much more widespread, better organised and more effective that anything that the old and now defunct communist party of Iran had managed. This was not only true of the period up to 1949, when the party believed in peaceful and gradual change, but also after being banned in that year, going underground and becoming a fully-fledged revolutionary Stalinist party; and as long as it could operate publicly (up to the 1953 coup) through proxy organisations and publications. Maleki was to write nostalgically of the earlier period after he had already split with the party:

> After August [1941, the Allied invasion of Iran], the Iranian society was thirsty for a social movement based on scientific theories which would see to the needs of the deprived classes of the people via plans and appropriate actions. The emergence of the Tudeh party was a response to these needs. Soon enough, a growing number of the best social forces welcomed the Tudeh party. And the party with the help of many intellectuals from different social classes including workers who had joined it made possible to formulate a social school, and in addition to that taught the methods of struggle to the deprived people ...[24]

THE PARTY REFORMISTS

As one of the superheroes of the Fifty-Three – for they were now seen as heroes by young modern intellectuals – Maleki was conspicuously absent in the formation of the Tudeh party, nor did he join it, as he had pledged to himself while still in prison. Eskandari says he told Maleki: 'You cannot shy away from political activity.'[25] According to him, Maleki's objection mainly concerned certain individual members in the party such as Abbas Eskandari and Morteza Yazdi. For that reason he describes him as 'puritanical'. But his further claim, that after some discussion Maleki agreed to join the party, is contrary to the facts, since it took almost two years and much interaction with party members and fellow travellers for Maleki to become a party member.[26]

Maleki's refusal to join the party attracted the attention of some members of the new party, especially the younger generation who had not experienced imprisonment. One of the first to establish contact with Maleki in the hope of persuading him to join the party was Abdolhossein Nushin, the talented theatre director and actor and close friend of Sadeq Hedayat. At first Maleki would not state clearly his reasons for not joining the party based on his experience in prison, but in time Nushin heard some of it from a few of the younger members of the Fifty-Three.

However, what began to change the situation was Nushin's and his friends' experience of the Tudeh leaders' attitude and behaviour. Nushin told Maleki that initially he had had complete faith in the Tudeh leaders and could not understand his refusal to join the party. But now they had come to the same conclusion as Maleki, namely a belief in the unreliability of their leaders. He then informed Maleki that a circle had been formed comprising mainly the younger members of the party committed to reforming the party leadership, and invited Maleki to join their discussions without necessarily becoming a member of the party.[27] They usually met in Sadeq Hedayat's home. He was not particularly political but had sympathy for the new party and was friends with Nushin and his circle.

Thus, the opposition to the party leadership had been formed from the early months. They would even make fun of the party central committee. Khameh'i quotes Nushin as saying that someone enters the committee meeting and Rusta says he is one of our leftist comrades. Now, 'left' in Persian is *chap*, and a cross-eyed person is also called *chap*. A committee member says, 'he is not *chap* at all; his eyes are perfectly all right'.[28] They objected to the presence of some individuals in the party and especially its leadership, and demanded greater commitment in promoting the interests of workers, peasant and women, distribution of the state lands and Reza Shah's agricultural estates, etc. The party's first Tehran provincial conference sat in October 1942 and on paper the opposition won some of these concessions, although Maleki, not being a party member, was not at the conference. But in practice there was very little change. The leadership's argument for not encouraging active dissent was that it would endanger 'the behind-the-front interests of the Soviet Union'.[29]

THE ROLE OF THE ALLIES

Having declared non-interference in Iran's domestic affairs, the Allies nevertheless made important demands on the country that Iranian governments had little choice but to meet as long as Allied troops remained in the country. The rial (Iranian currency) was devalued by more than 100 per cent. This meant that, in terms of gold and foreign exchange, Allied purchases of Iranian goods and services cost them less than half, and Iranian imports of their products cost Iran more than twice as much as before. The supply of Iranian paper money was increased in order to extend credit to the Allies for their expenditure in Iran, to be paid back after the war. Between 1941 and 1944 there was more than a threefold increase in money supply.[30] These policies, added to hoarding and speculation, which they encouraged, led to rampant inflation, scarcity of goods (especially bread) and greater pauperisation in the country at large.[31]

Yet at the same time, Allied diplomats and representatives in Iran kept pressing various Iranian authorities for social reform aimed at a better deal for the majority of the population. Under Reza Shah the landlord power vis-à-vis the peasantry had remained intact, but otherwise they, too, had been subject to arbitrary rule, having no political power as a class, and their property rights being at the mercy of the almighty state. They had now stepped into the power vacuum created by the fall of Reza Shah, enjoying the privileges of wealth and political power, but displaying little sense of responsibility towards the peasantry and society at large. In 1943, the British minister Reader Bullard regarded the Tudeh party's reform programme as being 'mild in comparison with the conditions of the poor classes'.[32]

After Abbas Eskandari's newspaper *Siyast* (Politics), which for a short period was the party newspaper, Iraj Eskandari agreed to cooperate with Mostafa Fateh, the highest ranking Iranian employee of the AIOC, in publishing *Mardom-e Zedd-e Fascist* (Anti-fascist People), its title later changing to *Nameh-ye Mardom* (People's Letter). 'The British paid the money; the Soviets, the paper',[33] an action to which Ardeshir Avanessian was dead opposed.[34] Many Iranians were still pro-German, partly because they were anti-British, so the Allies felt it was necessary to conduct anti-fascist propaganda, some of which was being carried out by the British Victory House in Tehran led by Miss (later Professor) Lambton, and assisted by Bozorg Alavi and Ehsan Tabari.[35] Just before the victory at Stalingrad in February 1943,

KHALIL MALEKI

the new party newspaper *Rahbar* (Leader) was founded under the editorship of Eskandari.

MALEKI JOINS THE PARTY

All members of the Tudeh party, certainly the leftists, were anti-fascist and admired the Soviet Union. But the leadership as a whole was bound by the advice and instructions of the Soviet embassy in Tehran. This was what many in the reformist opposition most resented. Maleki says that even before he joined the party early in 1944, his party interlocutors (reformists he normally talked to) often used to refer to some leaders as 'lackies of the embassy': 'When the party reformists contacted me [they used to say that the party leaders] "are incapable of leadership and, worse, they are not even lackeys, but lackeys of the lackeys of the [Soviet] embassy".'[36]

Maleki, 'because of his brilliant background in jail, his prominent personality ... strong logic, broad knowledge, the effectiveness of his spoken word, and, especially, his boldness and courage was made into a personality who would be very useful and necessary in this struggle'.[37] Yet he had serious reservations even about some members of the reformist movement and Ehsan Tabari in particular on account of his scandalous behaviour in jail.[38] However, they managed to convince him that he had changed so that, after Tabari defected to the party leadership, Maleki used to remind the other reformists of his original objection. Khameh'i admits that that was a big mistake but he goes on to add that the unforgivable mistake they made

> was to trust a dangerous person like Kambakhsh despite his criminal past and let him take control of the party

36

and destroy both groups of the party leaders, i.e. both left and right! Who was more dangerous for the reform of the party and its freedom and independence: the Eskandaris, the Radmaneshes, the Yazdis and the Rustas, or Kambakhsh and his assistants such as the Kiyanuris or the Gholamyahyas?[39]

Meanwhile elections for the fourteenth session of the Majlis began in September 1943 and the Tudeh party put up a number of candidates mainly in Tehran and the northern provinces. Maleki was not yet a party member; had he been, it is very likely that he would have been nominated for Tabriz. Influence was used in many of the constituencies, including that of the Russians in the northern provinces which were under their occupation. For example, Eskandari, who was elected for the Mazandaran capital city, admits that he received indirect help from the Russians.[40]

Eight Tudeh deputies out of the total of 136 were elected, including Eskandari, Kambakhsh, Radmanesh, Avanesian, Ferydun Keshavarz and Taqi Fadakar, the powerful trade union leader of Isfahan. Pishevari was elected for Tabriz, but his credentials were rejected by the full House. This tradition was intended to ensure that every deputy's election had been fair and free from irregularities. And it provided for the most sensational debate on the credentials of Seyyed Zia, the deputy for Yazd. Zia was the Anglophile journalist who, together with Reza Khan, had led the *coup d'état* of February 1921, though he had been exiled by Reza Khan three months later, and ended up farming in mandated Palestine.

Now he had returned to Iran, and many if not most (including the shah) believed that he was the British candidate for the premiership. No longer the nationalist-modernist zealot that he had been at the time of the coup, he was now an advocate of traditional values and posed as the leader of conservative politicians. He was seen as their arch enemy by the Tudeh party as well as Mohammad Mosaddeq, Tehran's first deputy. Mosaddeq led a vehement attack on Zia's credentials for election, having got the agreement of the Tudeh deputies not to initiate it themselves. Zia defended himself and the majority of deputies voted for him.[41]

The first Tudeh party congress met at the end of July 1944 as a result of the reformists' campaign. The reformist delegates, including Maleki, were in the majority and managed to amend the party constitution largely along the lines described, as well as having a number of members whom they regarded as undesirable expelled from the party. Pishevari, whom the party bosses disliked, was a delegate from Tabriz but his credentials were rejected, although Maleki used his influence to stop this being made public.[42] According to Eskandari, that was the root of Pishevari's enmity towards the Tudeh party,[43] although in fact it went back to the period in prison when a number of his fellow prisoners led by Ardeshir had treated him with contempt.

The congress elected an eleven-man central committee, the majority being reformists, but Maleki was not one of them as he came twelfth, Keshavarz being the eleventh member.[44] Maleki put this down to the personal animosity he had created in the congress by being outspoken about individuals and programmes. He was, however, elected to the nine-man investigative committee – the second highest body in the party – whose majority was also made up of the reformists.[45] These majorities, however, were eroded through time as a number of original reformists such as Kambakhsh, Tabari, Ahmad Qasemi and Kiyanuri defected to the other side, although they were replaced by many more later who were not in the leadership positions. It is doubtful that

Kambakash was ever a genuine reformist. Years later he wrote that in the congress Khalil Maleki tried to take full advantage of reasonable critiques of the past party activities for his long-term plan, which was then unknown, and later he continued to sow division until he split the party.[46]

At any rate after the congress, reformist activity experienced a lull for about a year, partly because the reformists had – or so the reformlists thought – the leadership majority, and partly because they could now put forward their ideas in the regular party cells, and partly because some of them were sent on provincial missions.[47] After the party split of 1948, one of the milder charges that the Tudeh brought against Maleki was that he led the split in 1948 because he had not been elected to the central committee in 1944! This charge was repeated in the military prosecutor's indictment against Maleki in the mid-1960s, no doubt on the advice of former Tudeh members who were then in SAVAK, the Iranian secret service (see Chapter 8).

THE SOVIET DEMAND FOR AN OIL CONCESSION

Maleki and Nushin kept in touch with young members of the party and thus spread their views and concerns among them. An important and successful initiative of Maleki's was to launch regular 'critique and discussion' (*bahs o enteqad*) meetings which soon made him one of the most famous members of the party. The meetings were open to the public. A small panel led by Maleki would receive any and all political questions and would answer them. It attracted large members of both the party and the public and became an efficient channel for recruitment. Indeed, it became so popular that one or two members of the central committee also joined the panel.[48]

Late in September 1944, Sergei Kaftaradze visited Iran in public pursuit of the granting of a concession for north Iranian oil to the Soviet Union. Earlier, demands for further oil concessions had been made privately by AIOC and American companies, but this had been leaked and so prepared the ground for the Soviet demand. Mohammad Sa'ed and the conservatives were opposed to the idea but their pro-British stance did not afford them much moral authority for it. Mosaddeq stepped in and passed a bill in the Majlis that would forbid the granting of any concessions without approval of parliament. That put paid to the Soviet demand for the time being. The official position of the party, as expressed in a *Rahbar* leader, was that in the weak economic circumstances of Iran 'it is not possible to generally oppose the principle of concessions but the question is the conditions by which they are bound'.[49] The Tudeh faction in parliament hesitated at first but in the end voted against Mosaddeq's bill.[50]

This did not go down well with the Iranian public but what was by far the worst incident occurred when Soviet forces protected a demonstration organised by the Tudeh party and its affiliated United Workers Central Council (led by Rusta) in support of the Soviet demand. Almost everyone was disgusted with this, and that included many Tudeh members. Jalal Al-e Ahmad, who was then a young Tudeh reformist, says that as soon as he saw the Soviet forces he felt deeply ashamed and ran off from the crowd.[51] According to Khameh'i, Eskandari and Radmanesh did not join the demonstration but Rusta, Kambakhsh and Keshavarz did.[52] Eskandari says he had been in Isfahan at the time of the demonstration but describes the Russian intervention as wrong.[53] According to Rahim Abedi, a prominent reformist, Maleki shouted at Eskandari, 'Tell the blasted red-boots to stop destroying our reputation.'[54]

On the other hand, virtually all the leaders and writers of the party, including Maleki, were in favour of the Soviet demand. Tabari went as far as suggesting that the government should open negotiations for oil concession with Russia, Britain and the US, and said that 'refusal to grant [oil] concessions is an incorrect and one-sided policy'. He went even further and all but described southern Iran as the British sphere of influence and northern Iran as the Soviet, reminiscent of the hated 1907 Anglo-Russian convention.[55] It is now clear that the idea came straight out of Kaftaradze's own mouth, when he told Sa'ed: 'We want a security zone. By northern Iran we don't just mean [north] Iranian oil, but that this area should be under our influence, and be our security zone.'[56]

Meanwhile, Sae'd's cabinet fell and Mortezaqoli Bayat (Saham al-Soltan) was elected prime minister with Mosaddeq's support, and the Majlis passed a more detailed bill leaving no concessions for the Soviet demand, and Kaftaradze left Iran with bitterness. The Tudeh party got angry with Mosaddeq and some of them, including Qasemi and Maleki, started to attack him in their newspaper articles. Other leaders also went along with their views though they did not put them down on paper. In particular, Maleki's three successive articles entitled 'Sar o Tah Yek Karbas' (All of the Same Cloth) in *Rahbar*, though devoid of personal attacks, were critical of Mosaddeq and his attitude.

In his Majlis speech Mosaddeq, alluding to the sixty non-Tudeh deputies present, had commented 'sixty is more than eight' (Tudeh deputies), 'even if a few more artisans are added to them'. This provoked Maleki into writing that the future would show that 'the few artisans, porters and toilers who make up our social base would be able to run the country better than the sixty and their forces that you taunt us with'. Mosaddeq had refused to second a motion suggested by a radical deputy,

Gholamhossein Rahimiyan, that the 1933 oil concession to the AIOC be cancelled, privately explaining to the deputy that such a motion would be rejected, and this would provide a firm legal basis for that concession.[57] Being unaware of this sound logic, Maleki wrote that this showed that Mosaddeq's argument for refusing a concession to the Soviet Union while not supporting the cancellation of the British concession revealed his policy to be a maintenance of the status quo.[58] He also wrote other articles in defence of the concession.[59] Years later, when Baqa'i's *Shahed* was attacking Maleki for his articles in support of the Soviet demand, Maleki responded by saying that he did that as a matter of party discipline, but this does not justify his action. The fact is that both he and the other reformists still believed in Soviet goodwill, despite their criticism of the Tudeh leaders' uncritical attitude towards the Soviet embassy in Tehran.

AZERBAIJAN

This was a fateful turning point for the Tudeh party. Despite some external and internal setbacks due to the saga of the oil concession, in 1945 the party was quite strong and the only popular and well-organised party in the country. The party-affiliated trade unions spearheaded by the United Workers Central Council under Reza Rusta's powerful leadership were much stronger than the relatively feeble semi-official workers' organisation known as ESKI. The only genuine rival to them was the union organised and led by Yusef Eftekhari, the old communist and critic of Stalin whom the Tudeh now described as a Trotskyist and now as a British agent.[60]

Rusta's organisation had become so strong that it even ran its own detention centres where they took undesirable workers, including Eftekhari, for punishment. According to Eskandari, 'Rusta went so far that, I don't know whether it was a garage or something else [and] whoever he opposed they would take and hold him there'. He further added that Rusta and his union had once laid siege to a house which they had rented in order to forcibly reduce the rent, and, since the owner was not there, they abducted his brother and said that 'we have taken him hostage'.[61] Tabari confirms this in his memoirs, saying that Bahrami had once been detained there.[62] Note also Avnesian's highly critical view of Rusta and his behaviour.[63]

Azerbaijan had been a headache for the Tudeh leaders from the start. Being under Soviet occupation, the provincial party had been dominated by immigrants from the Soviet Union, some of whom behaved atrociously towards the people, were financially corrupt and guilty of sexual abuse, and yet at the same time they put the fear of communism into the hearts of ordinary people. The news from Azerbaijan was so worrying that the party decided to send Maleki there with full powers to purge and reform the local party.

Once there, Maleki expelled the undesirable elements (many of them immigrants) and managed to attract teachers, intellectuals and progressive business people to the party. He launched communal and cultural projects and in so doing he showed the human and Iranian face of the party. He noticed that non-Tudeh newspapers had been banned from Azerbaijan and ordered that all of them should be allowed in the province. He spoke in Persian in formal meetings and Azerbaijani Turkic only on informal occasions.

Six portraits of Stalin hung on the walls of the Tabriz city committee building. Maleki took down five of them himself and had them replaced with those of local heroes. He also ordered the portraits of Soviet generals to be removed from the walls of factories. Mohammad Biriya, the powerful, unscrupulous head of Tabriz's United Workers Central Council, had put a large portrait of Stalin above his head in his office. No matter how hard Maleki tried, he always refused to take it down. Maleki went to the lengths of convening a plenum of party activists with the express agenda being the removal of Stalin's portrait above Biriya's desk. In the end Biriya took it down and put it on the mantelpiece.[64]

This way Maleki made many enemies, not least among the Soviet occupying forces, the news of his activities having reached the Soviet embassy in Tehran. Maleki was summoned to Tehran to report; hoping to dislodge Biriya from Tabriz, little did he know that this was a subtle form of banishment, for he was not allowed to return.[65] Eskandari says that Maleki was 'banished' from Azerbaijan.[66] Maximov, the Soviet ambassador, was critical of Maleki's activities in Azerbaijan, especially regarding Stalin's portraits, and Eskandari had responded that Maleki had been acting on behalf of the central committee.[67] However, Maleki says the central committee had been summoned by the ambassador over the issue; he had spoken so forcefully to them that they had relented.[68]

There was much more to come. Pishevari, whose credentials had been rejected once by the Majlis and the second time by the Tudeh party congress, had moved to Tabriz in midsummer 1945 and left his newspaper *Azhir* (which translates as both siren and warning) in the care of a couple of his friends. He was in contact with the Soviet forces there as well as Mir Ja'far Baqerov, the powerful party boss of the Soviet Republic of Azerbaijan who dearly wished to separate Iranian Azerbaijan from Iran and join it to his own seat of power.

Early in September 1945 Pishevari launched his Ferqeh-ye Demokrat-e Azerbaijan, or Azerbaijan Democrat party. The choice of title was a shrewd one. It appeared to be a local Azerbaijan party in line with the old Democratic party led by Shaikh Mohammad Khiyabani in 1920. It has now been proved that Khiyabani was not a separatist at all and had actually suppressed the local Bolsheviks.[69] Indeed, Pishevari, who was a communist contemporary, knew more than anyone else about his suppression of the Bolsheviks. However, Khiyabani had led a revolt and had been defeated and killed in the process, but he left behind an enduring myth as a pro-Bolshevik revolutionary, much cherished as a lover of freedom.

Both Baqerov and Soviet officials in Iran had been behind the launching of the new party, though the Tudeh party had been caught unawares and felt that the new party would be seen as a rival to them, at least in Azerbaijan. But this did not last long and the Ferqeh soon took over the Tudeh party provincial committee and became one with it. This was in the wake of the revolt of the Ferqeh on 13 December 1945 when their gunmen disarmed the local brigade of the Iranian army and declared an autonomous Azerbaijan. Not only were Tudeh party members astounded but so too were most of their leaders.[70]

The Soviet presence was a double-edged sword, one of whose edges eventually turned out to be sharper than the other. On the one hand, the Russian army could at least be used as a countervailing force against the threat of armed intervention by the centre; on the other, the confrontation with Tehran required both the tacit approval of the Soviet government and protection by the occupying Russian troops – a situation which would inevitably make Ferqeh a pawn in international power games. The ultimate failure of the movement owed a great deal to this dependence on Soviet support.[71]

As mentioned earlier, there was no love lost between Pishevari and the Tudeh leaders. But Pishevari desperately needed control of the Tudeh provincial organisation in Azerbaijan in order to implement Ferqeh's policies. Not only did the Tudeh heads dislike Pishevari, but they were also concerned about the implications of his revolt for their reputation in the rest of the country. However, he demanded that the Tudeh central committee dissolve their organisation in Azerbaijan and deliver it to him.[72]

Maleki went to work. He passed a resolution in the central committee rejecting any attempt to dissolve the party organisation in the province, and the launch of the Azerbaijan Ferqeh outside the framework of an all-Iranian party. All this was put in a formal statement due to be published the same evening. He writes in his memoirs:

> [I] was ignorant of the spirit of Stalinist internationalism. The good and model internationalist was [Abdossamad] Kambakhsh who through his machinations postponed the publication of the central committee's statement, rushed to the Soviet embassy next morning and brought an order from them for the central committee to reverse their decision and dissolve their organisation in Azerbaijan. And so, next day, instead of critical comments, full-length photos of Pishevari and Gholamyahya were published in *Rahbar*, the party's newspaper organ.[73]

Eskandari says that he posted a very 'polite and fraternal' letter of the central committee from Paris addressed to the Soviet Communist Party saying that another party in Iran (i.e. Ferqeh) was not needed. But when he returned to Iran, his central committee colleagues told him that they had been summoned to the Soviet embassy and told that this was the wish of Comrade Stalin.[74] It is worth noting that, in his book, Kambakhsh maintains total silence about all this as well as the entire events of the year until the fall of Ferqeh.[75]

This way the Tudeh party was willy-nilly identified with Ferqeh and ended up sharing in its catastrophic failure. When Pishevari launched Ferqeh in September 1944, for a couple of months Mohsen Sadr (Sadr al-Ashraf) was prime minister; he was an unpopular conservative politician who was opposed by Mosaddeq, the Tudeh party and moderate Majlis deputies. His tenure lasted until 30 October, even before Ferqeh's revolt, and was replaced by that of the moderate conservative Ibrahim Hakimi (Hakim al-Molk). But he was not at all up to handling the Azerbaijan crisis on top of all the other problems that faced the country.

QAVAM'S CABINET

There was little choice but to call on Ahmad Qavam (Qavam al-Saltaneh), a shrewd, able and strong old-school politician whom the Soviets and Tudeh leaders looked upon with approval; indeed, Eskandari says that the Tudeh faction in the Majlis played a vital role in his gaining a majority.[76] He became prime minister before February and immediately went to work. Qavam had been already prime minister three times, twice under Ahmad Shah and once under Mohammad Reza Shah, though they were all typically short-term tenures. The shah disliked him intensely, mainly because of his strong and independent personality, and because he did not approve of the shah's active role in politics.

In the meantime, the press office of the British embassy in Tehran decided to send a few Iranian journalists on a visit to

Britain, among them Maleki representing *Rahbar*, the Tudeh party organ. There he had an interview with Ernest Bevin, the Labour foreign secretary, which had a very positive effect in Tehran and boosted the Tudeh party's morale. He told Bevin that he wanted democracy for Iran, but those Iranian authorities who were believed to be associated with Britain were opposed to it. And he added that democracy for him was when the deprived masses would be a party to it. Bevin wondered whether he wanted Britain to put matters right in Iran, to which Maleki replied that he did not and simply emphasised that what they wanted was that certain elements in Iran should not oppose democracy in the name of Britain.

Bevin pointed out that he himself came from a working-class background and wanted Iranian oil workers to live in comfort. Alluding to the Tudeh party, he said that the British did not wish people of Iran to act in the interests of a foreign country under the cover of democracy. Maleki emphatically denied that the Tudeh party worked in the interests of any foreign government and said that the party's sympathy for the Soviet Union arose from a sense of international solidarity, adding that any country that respected democracy would have the friendship of the Tudeh party.

It is a fairly long interview and the dialogue mainly concerns political conditions in Iran and the suppression of the press, and once again the hope that Britain would not encourage the anti-democratic forces in that country. It ended with Bevin claiming that Britain would like parties and trade unions to be free in 'the Near East' on the condition that they stand on their own feet and not be dependent on others, and Maleki replying that history has not shown the labouring classes of any country to be instruments of a foreign government. The labouring people stood on their own two feet and wrote their own destiny independently.[77] Maleki also talked to Morgan Phillips, general secretary of the

Labour party, and criticised the Labour government's foreign policy. Phillips expressed sympathy for his criticism and told him that soon India would have independence.[78] After the split the Tudeh hierarchy claimed that Maleki had been enrolled as a British agent during that visit, and Tabari indirectly repeats this in his memoirs.[79]

THE FALL OF FERQEH

The linchpin of Ferqeh's power was the persistence of Soviet occupation of Azerbaijan as well as other regions in the north, despite the fact that they had pledged to withdraw their forces at the end of the war. Qavam was therefore fully conscious of the need to somehow persuade Russia to end the occupation. First, he abolished many of the illiberal acts of the previous regime, restored freedom of the press and removed other restrictions, including those against the Tudeh party. There was a huge demonstration in Tehran on the occasion of the reopening of Tudeh headquarters, and, in general, the public took a favourable view of Qavam.

At the same time, Qavam decided to go to Moscow at the head of a delegation, to which Stalin warmly assented. While he was negotiating with Molotov and Stalin in Moscow, Seyyed Zia and his supporters were trying to extend the life of the fourteenth Majlis which was coming to an end. The reason for this was that the Majlis would otherwise have to go into a long recess, as it in fact did, because elections could not be held before the settlement of the Azerbaijan crisis, and this would obviously strengthen the hand of Qavam. The Tudeh and Qavam's supporters were opposed to the proposed extension and Qavam won the day.[80]

Qavam's negotiations in Moscow did not result in an agreement, though he continued them with the Soviet ambassador,

Sadchikov, in Tehran, which led to the Qavam–Sadchikov agreement. Briefly, this drew up a timetable for the Soviet forces' withdrawal and an amicable settlement with Ferqeh's government in Tabriz, in exchange for the pledge of north Iranian oil to the Soviets. However, this did not have any practical effect due to the bill that Mosaddeq had passed in the fourteenth Majlis, and when, in 1947, the relevant bill was submitted to the fifteenth Majlis it was rejected. It is likely that Qavam had anticipated this, but it is difficult to know why Stalin took the risk. There were other factors as well that persuaded Moscow to reach terms with Qavam, including Iran's appeal to the UN and, especially, pressure from America. The details of the Azerbaijan crisis may be found in several books to which the interested reader may refer.[81]

The Qavam–Sadchikov agreement did not at first affect the Tudeh party adversely. Indeed, the party went from strength to strength, attracting many teachers, workers, students and academics to its ranks. At the same time, in April-May 1946, Qavam invited a delegation headed by Pishevari for negotiations which ended without a definite conclusion being reached over Pishevari's insistence that Azerbaijan must keep its own army. Further negotiations in Tabriz by Qavam's political assistant led to an agreement but the thorny military question was left open. Nevertheless, both Ferqeh and Tudeh were pleased and solemnly declared their support for Qavam. It must also have satisfied the Soviets that Qavam was pursuing a peaceful policy vis-à-vis Azerbaijan. Maleki, however, did not share the Tudeh's belief in Qavam's goodwill and was, as ever, critical of events taking place in Azerbaijan.[82] Avanesian says that the Soviet embassy had persuaded them to enter Qavam's cabinet and that Eskandari, Yazdi and Keshavrz had gone along with it to fulfil their ambitions.[83]

The next episode in the Qavam scenario was the formation of a new party entitled the Democrat party of Iran with a left-leaning programme as an alternative to the Tudeh party. But the Tudeh leaders still maintained their optimistic attitude towards Qavam. For example, Tabari wrote in an article:

> we are well aware that some people wish to muddy the relationship between freedom-lovers and the founder of this party, the prime minister. But we are too intelligent to become an instrument in the hands of these provocateurs. Mr Qavam al-Saltaneh who has proven his goodwill ...[84]

The honeymoon led to the convening of 'the first congress of Iranian writers' between 25 June and 2 July on the initiative of Iran–Soviet Cultural Society in the presence of Qavam and Sadchikov with full Tudeh participation.[85] On 15 July, barely two weeks after the congress ended, a great general strike was declared in the oil province of Khuzistan. The Tudeh leaders clearly were not in favour of such an action but as events unfolded the matter was soon out of their hands. There was bloodshed after the intervention of the local police and army, and many workers were killed and injured. Qavam pleaded ignorance and sent off two Tudeh leaders together with two of his own lieutenants to pacify the workers with promises of reform and of punishment of those responsible for the bloodshed, and they thus broke the strike, its only tangible result being the release of the striking prisoners![86]

Shortly afterwards the Tudeh party joined Qavam's new cabinet in a coalition between them, Qavam's Democrat party and the small, top-heavy social democratic Iran party, with Eskandari as minister of trade, Yazdi as minister of health and Keshavarz as minister of education. The Iran party was represented by Allahyar Saleh as minister of justice. Maleki and many reformists were critical of this decision, arguing that Qavam was wily and would deceive them, a prediction which, as usual, turned out to be true. Nevertheless, Keshavarz made him under-secretary for education, Maleki having turned down the vice-ministership. According to Eskandari, to all intents and purposes Maleki was running the ministry of education.[87] And in the short period that the coalition lasted, he was especially successful in the provision and extension of school places in deprived areas.[88]

The coalition did not even last three months[89] and Qavam rid himself of it when he no longer needed it. In the middle of this period there was a rebellion by southern tribes led by Naser Khan Qashqa'i, which was intended to counter the Tudeh and the Azerbaijan Democrats. There is no evidence that the British plotted or supported this rebellion but, in view of the apparent rise of pro-Soviet power in the north, they must have kept their options open. It has even been suggested that the southern revolt had Qavam's tacit approval to enable him to shake off the Tudeh coalition and abolish the Azerbaijan and Kurdish autonomies. That is unlikely, but he certainly tried to turn it to his own advantage as much as possible.[90]

There was a peaceful settlement with the southern rebels which sounded the death knell for the coalition and turned the tide against the Tudeh party and Azerbaijan. A couple of months later Qavam sent troops to Azerbaijan ostensibly to ensure the freedom of the impending Majlis elections. Russia having abandoned Pishevari's government, and Soviet troops having already departed, the Azerbaijan resistance collapsed in December 1946 – a year after the revolt – and most of its civilian and military leaders and officers crossed the border to the Soviet Union.

This was catastrophic not only for Ferqeh but also for the Tudeh party and its leaders. Esknadari had told Khameh'i that not until the last moment had they expected this catastrophe, but were thinking that the Ferqeh would resist, unaware of the fact that the Soviets had advised them against it: 'when I heard the news of the flight of Pishevari and the Democrats and learned the Soviets had told them not to resist, it was so unexpected and insufferable that I sat down and cried hard for a whole hour.'[91] Eskandari himself says that 'for me personally this event was a great shock'.[92] Tabari was to write years after the event:

> All the heavy and generally humiliating consequences which led to defeat were products of the acceptance of the Tudeh leadership of the Soviet demands. The Soviets demanded that the [Tudeh] leadership surrender before their political will of the day. Stalin expected this. Berya and Baqerov would add other demands to his. There was a relationship of subject and sovereign between an independent country's party and the Soviet leaders.[93]

THE REVOLT IN THE TUDEH PARTY

There was a great anti-Tudeh backlash not just by the government but by the people at large. Maleki writes in his memoirs that he dearly wished to be arrested, so ashamed was he of having to face public hatred:

> ... although party friends and even ordinary party members knew that personally I did not share in the moral failure; on the contrary, ignoring the principles that I had seriously recommended [to the leadership] had resulted in the defeat. But non-party people were not aware of this.[94]

We may recall that Sadeq Hedayat was a party sympathiser and was especially close to the reformists who often held their meetings at his home. From a moral and intellectual viewpoint no one's reaction to these events is more telling than his. He wrote in a long letter to Fereydun Tavalloli, a well-known poet and satirist as well as party reformist, from Tehran to Shiraz:

> After the great test which we took – and which was apparently for the sake of freedom but in fact for its destruction – no one can do anything anymore ... And, one has to be truly a descendant of Daryush ... to be fooled by these silly antics. The story is long and puzzling, but the betrayal had many sides to it. And now the Tudeh are wallowing in their shit in order to cover up the truth. Anyway, we must eat our own shitty glories spoon by spoon and say how nice it is too.[95]

There was an outcry in the party and demand for the trial of the party leaders. A meeting of around sixty leaders and cadres was convened which looked like a revolt against the central committee. As Eskandari puts it 'the reaction of the cadres was vehement'.[96] Khameh'i quotes Maleki as having said that Tabari had suggested the reformists should split from Tudeh and form another party, but Maleki had turned down the suggestion.[97] Needless to say, large numbers of party members left it quietly.

The central committee resigned and an eleven-man provisional executive committee was elected to convene the second party congress within three months where all the issues concerning the party and its leadership would be discussed and a new central committee would be elected. The members of the new executive committee were made up of four members of the old central committee and seven of the reformists, including Maleki.[98]

Not long afterwards Eskandari, Kambakhsh, Ardeshir and Tabari escaped to Moscow through a Russian corridor. The first three were about to be arrested on charges of sabotage, but Tabari was safe and so was returned to Tehran. Eskandari went to Paris where he spent a few years and eventually joined his comrades in East Germany. Kambakhsh was sent to Baku.[99]

Maleki relates the events as follows:

> After a while, one evening they invited me to a meeting in Qolhak [village, north of Tehran]. When I arrived I saw that the entire members of central committee were there. They all rose as I entered the room, whereas this was not the custom in party meetings. But I realised that their extraordinary respect indicated the bankruptcy of their policies and the triumph of the policies I had recommended and they had not heeded ... Anyway, on the suggestion of Iraj Eskandari it was agreed that the central committee should resign and be replaced with a provisional executive committee ... with full powers to run the party ... They elected three secretaries and made me first secretary but as this involved certain duties and obligations which were very pleasant for some but very unpleasant for me [i.e. contact and liaison with the Soviet embassy and the government establishment] I did not accept it.[100]

Yet the underlying problems still persisted while four of the reformist members of the executive committee, Tabari, Kiyanuri, Qasemi and Forutan, having tasted power and prestige, defected and joined the party establishment. The immediate issue was the launch of the second party congress, which the committee kept postponing on one or another excuse, fearing that the congress would result in total victory for the reformists. Instead, they convened the Tehran provincial conference in July 1947 and that in fact confirmed their worst fears, given that, by the party constitution, Tehran had 75 per cent of the congress vote. Tabari admits that 'the organisational success was with the Maleki group. In the Tehran conference this group succeeded in gaining the majority.'[101] Kiyanuri also confirms this.[102] According to Kambakhsh, the reformists managed to win the majority of the seats in the newly elected Tehran provincial committee as well as seventeen representatives for the hoped-for second party congress.[103]

An outspoken critic at the conference was Eprime Eshag, known as Dr Eprime who, two years before, had finished his studies in England and returned to Tehran. He was an old student of Arani's who would have been arrested with the Fifty-Three had he not received a state scholarship to study in England a few months earlier (see Chapter 1). He had soon organised a group of young reformists known as the Avangardists, since he believed that the party needed a young vanguard for effective action. To this end, he published a pamphlet entitled *Cheh Bayad Kard* (What Should Be Done), followed by another, *Hezb-e Tudeh bar Sar-e Dorah* (The Tudeh Party at the Crossroads, under the pen-name Alatur) in which he was assisted by Jalal Al-e Ahmad. The party establishment responded to this in a pamphlet entitled *Dar Rah-e Yek Enheraf* (On the Way to a Deviation), written by Zakhariyan under the pen-name Yalda. It has been wrongly suggested that the reformists had a left and right wing, respectively led by Eprime and Maleki, but this is a palpable mistake.[104] Kambakhsh's claim that Eprime and his circle were under Maleki's leadership is also untrue, though it is understandable, as his purpose is to reduce the entire reformist movement to Maleki's 'long-term plan' to split the party.[105]

The executive committee went on resisting the pressure of the membership for convening the congress and this created an atmosphere of intense discontent and frustration in the party.

THE PARTY SPLIT

The pressure of the reformists for convening the party congress and the continuation of the party establishment to resist it brought matters to a head. Indeed, in a selective party meeting Kiyanuri went as far as saying that in view of the intra-party conflict 'the Soviet comrades' had forbidden the holding of the second congress.[106] This created a perpetual conflict within the party, especially led by the young reformists. Some of them, as we have seen, had organised themselves into the Avangardist movement. Three of them in particular spearheaded the movement, as Al-e Ahmad, who was one of them, writes:

> My acquaintance with Maleki became serious through the [party] split. Before then, I had listened to his talks in a [party] cell or a 'critique and discussion' meeting or had read something by him ... But after the Azerbaijan episode ... and the flight of the first rate leaders ... and when Tabari and Kiyanuri and Maleki rose to the leadership, and we the young reformists were running the [Tehran] provincial committee, Mohandes Nasehi, Hossein Malek and I had serious dialogues, on the one hand, with Maleki, and on the other, with Dr Eprime.[107]

He goes on to say that both because of his cooperation with Eprime in publishing *The Tudeh Party at the Crossroads* and due to a critical talk he had presented to the party's Rasht branch, he was summoned for trial by party leaders Kiyanuri, Radmanesh and Forutan who told him that they should stop making mischief:

> And that was the beginnings of the split ... And it went as far as creating a party within the party with cells inside cells, and selection of people, and unifying ideas and attitudes until late one night Nasehi invited us to his home and said that he had heard that if we did not move quickly they would expel all of us from the party since our party within the party has been discovered.[108]

Khameh'i says that he was in regular contact with the Avangardists and was encouraging them to prepare for a split.[109] At any rate, Al-e Ahmad writes that the very evening Nasehi warned them of the threat of expulsion the first declaration of the split was written by Maleki, Khameheh'i and others. At first Maleki hesitated but when he heard the arguments of the others he agreed to act. One important concern was whether or not the Soviets would back the split, since, though unlike the party establishment they were not 'lackeys of the embassy', they still had high regard for the Soviet Union and knew that it was very popular among young intellectuals and ordinary party members, only recently having defeated the Germans at Stalingrad and taken Berlin. But they could not believe that the Soviets would back the party establishment with full force, as in fact they did.[110]

About a hundred or more of the leaders and cadres of the party signed the two declarations of their split from the party. In the first few days most members of the Tehran provincial committee supported the move and if within a short period the Soviets had not condemned the event and described its leaders as British agents they would have won the day. But the Soviet pull was very strong and made its impact.

The most important document of the split is a sixty-page pamphlet entitled *Do Ravesh bara-ye yek Hadaf* (Two Approaches to the Same Goal). It was unsigned but written by Maleki and published in the name of 'The Tudeh Socialist League of Iran'. This is an historic piece of work in that it discusses the whole history of the intra-party conflict, criticises the position of the party establishment closely and with argument and evidence, and yet its language is soft and leaves the door open for reconciliation. A lengthy analysis of this work may be found in the introduction to Maleki's memoirs.[111] However, the response of the party bosses was that they should withdraw their declaration of 4 January or face expulsion. This led to the second and final declaration of 17 January 1948 and the party was split for good. As Maleki was to admit later, this was not 'two approaches to the same goal', but to two different goals.

The Soviet offensive accompanied by the barrage of the Tudeh's hostile, and in some cases libellous, charges against the splinters made the party splinter group give up the idea of founding the Tudeh Socialist League of Iran for the simple reason that they would not have been able to attract the Tudeh majority to themselves. However, this project was to be carried out later by Maleki and some members of the splinter group in a different format and under a different name (see Chapter 3).

3

POWER STRUGGLES AND OIL NATIONALISATION

The fifteenth Majlis elections following the fall of Azerbaijan Democrats and the Kurdish 'republic' in Mahabad were manipulated by Qavam's party[1] – the Tudeh having boycotted them largely because of its demoralisation over the Azerbaijan fiasco – resulting in the overwhelming electoral victory of his Democrat party and his return to office. But the appearance of parliamentary strength was deceptive, since, revolts and threats of disintegration having subsided, politics returned to its normal chaotic trends, with Democrat party deputies splitting into pro- and anti-Qavam factions. This was encouraged by the shah who was also busy trying to turn the British and American envoys against a strong, independent and triumphant prime minister.[2] The shah's strong and interfering twin sister, Princess Ashraf, also played an active role in toppling Qavam's government. Before his government fell in December 1947, Qavam took the bill for the Soviet concession of north Iranian oil to the Majlis in October, being virtually certain that it would be defeated, as in fact it was, adding to Soviet and Tudeh anger and delighting the Anglo-American powers.

This led to vocal demands for a better agreement with AIOC than the 1933 concession, especially when Taqizadeh, the finance minister at the time, said openly in the Majlis that he had signed it under duress:

> I had absolutely no role in this matter other than the fact that my signature is underneath the agreement. And even if I had refused to sign, someone else would doubtlessly have signed it … And the refusal of one person – if such a refusal would have been at all possible – would not have had the slightest effect on the result.[3]

The AIOC had not even adhered faithfully to the 1933 agreement.[4] It behaved like a colonial power in the Khuzistan oil province and suffered from bad labour relations. In 1944, there was a local workers' strike which was settled as a result of government intervention, but, as noted in Chapter 2, in July 1946 there was a full stoppage which ended in bloodshed.

The two consecutive ministries of Qavam from January 1946 to December 1947 – a long period by the standards of the 1940s – afforded an opportunity for ending the politics of chaos, and the establishment of long-term normal, constitutional government. As noted, however, the politics of chaos proved stronger after the immediate threat of disintegration had subsided. Following the abortive governments (December 1947–November 1948) of Ibrahim Hakimi and Abdolhossein Hazhir – the latter of whom was an able and unpopular politician and a close favourite of Princess Ashraf's – it fell to Mohammad Sae'd's second premiership (November 1948–March 1950) to try and renegotiate the 1933 agreement with the AIOC.

Both the Azerbaijan episode and the split had greatly weakened the Tudeh party, the former leading to a large exodus of members, the latter of the cadres. For example, Tabari writes that 'after the split, the small party organisation ... had lost a group of its members some of whom were prominent, but this catastrophe was at the time regarded as a victory'.[5] The second party congress that had been held up for more than a year for fear of the triumph of the reformists was convened in the summer of 1948 – as Tabari points out – amid jubilation and triumphalism, and endorsed all the party decisions which had been in dispute for years; 'and the general result of this congress was a false impression and trust towards the erroneous ways of the [party] leadership.'[6] Naturally, the strongest condemnations of the splinters in the congress were a foregone conclusion.

THE BANNING OF THE TUDEH PARTY AND THE FORMATION OF THE NATIONAL FRONT

The shah was anxious to curb the influence of the Tudeh party, extend his own power and reduce the parliamentary licence. The opportunity for banning the Tudeh party and amending the constitution to enable the shah to dissolve the Majlis arose after an abortive attempt on the shah's life on 4 February 1949. Nureddin Kiyanuri, a Tudeh leader later to become its first secretary under the Islamic Republic, was involved in the assassination plan, but the party as a whole did not have prior knowledge of it.

It was the work of a secret assassination group within the party led by Kiyanuri which had earlier assassinated the sensationalist journalist Mohammad Mas'ud.[7] Many, including Sa'ed, believed that General Ali Razmara, the chief of staff, had had a hand in the plot, despite the fact that the general himself arranged for the arrest of a number of suspects and the exile of Ayatollah Seyyed Abolqsem Kashani – a Tehran *mojtahed* and political campaigner – to Lebanon.[8] There is evidence that Razmara had friendly contacts with Tudeh through Kiyanuri and Khosrow Ruzbeh.[9] Decades later Kiyanuri praised Razmara in his memoirs.[10]

The Tudeh party was quickly banned by the Majlis, though this was not related to any suspicion of Razmara's possible role. Some of its leaders were arrested (later to escape to Russia), some fled shortly afterwards and some went into hiding. Thenceforth the Tudeh party went underground and turned into a monolithic Stalinist party, despite the acute personality conflicts at the top. The constituent assembly met in the following April. It provided for the establishment of an upper House which had been already anticipated by the constitution but had not been set up – a senate, half of whose members would be directly appointed by the shah, and the other half by an electoral college. More important than that, it empowered the shah to dissolve parliament. But this did not go unchallenged: a few deputies censured the government; Qavam wrote a letter to the shah and strongly criticised the move, to the latter's great annoyance; Kashani objected from exile; and Mosaddeq (a few months later) made critical remarks about it.[11] The amendments, however, did little to change the situation, which could only change by the use of military force as it in fact did after the 1953 coup.

Meanwhile, Mohammad Sa'ed's government was negotiating with AIOC for a better deal for Iran. A deal was eventually negotiated, known as the Gass-Golsha'iyan, or the supplemental agreement, the most important provision of which was to increase Iran's royalties from four to six shillings per ton of crude. The Majlis would have passed the corresponding bill had it not been for the vociferous opposition and filibustering of a small opposition group – including Mozaffar Baqa'i, Hossein Makki and Abolhasan Hayerizadeh – backed by the press and public outside parliament, in July 1949, only a few days before the life of the fifteenth Majlis came to an end.[12]

When the fifteenth Majlis came to a close, ranks were closed and battle lines were drawn on all sides. Outside Tehran, the elections were largely in the hands of the central and local powers, but the Tehran elections could not be easily rigged. Baqa'i and Makki had brought Mosaddeq out of his self-declared political retirement, and Baqa'i began to publish a daily entitled *Shahed* (Witness) on 12 September 1949, which looked more like a party newspaper even though the party had yet to be founded.

They accused General Razmara and Abdolhossein Hazhir, the minister of court, of rigging the Tehran elections, and twenty out of about five thousand protesters outside the shah's palace, led by Mosaddeq, were allowed to have a *bast* (sit-in), in the palace. They broke the *bast* a couple of days later but, gathering at Mosaddeq's home, they declared the formation of the NF.[13] This was on 23 October 1949. On the same day, the Tudeh party's secret newspaper organ, *Mardom*, described its leaders as agents of imperialism and of the royal court.[14]

Hossein Fatemi addressed the Tudeh in his newspaper *Bakhtar-e Emruz* (Daily West) on 30 November 1950:

> From day one till now what has the National Front done to deserve such a flood of anger and foul language ... In the last few months the Front has been fighting against the supplemental agreement and for the nationalisation of oil in the entire country. Why are you angry about this? Do you have a mission from AIOC to denigrate the work of our courageous representatives?

In fact, the Tudeh response to the formation of the NF was nothing short of hysterical, and one of their main concerns was the
fear that the Front would steal their show and pull the rug from
under their feet. As Amir Khosravi writes:

> ... since the Tudeh leadership regarded the democratic
> and anti-imperialist struggle as their own monopoly,
> they believed that this was their private domain and
> wanted to use all possible means to stop every 'interfer-
> ing person' from entering it. All that attack, insult and
> name-calling against the person of Mosaddeq and the
> National Front ... [and later] continuously organising
> strikes and wars of nerves in factories, the university,
> the schools and government departments, as well as
> demonstrations and shows of strength in the streets and
> city squares was to achieve the dream of hegemony over
> the national movement.[15]

However, it went much further than that because they believed
that the Front was an agent of America and for that reason it
had to be destroyed since it was more dangerous than those the
Tudeh believed to be British agents. The Tudeh's main concern,
after all, was and remained with America for reasons that had to
do with their complete loyalty to the Soviet Union.

Ten days after the formation of the Front a member of
Fada'iyan-e Islam shot and killed Hazhir in Sepahsalar Mosque
where he was distributing gifts among *ta'zieh* leaders in a religious congregation held in the name of the royal court. The
Society of the Devotees of Islam (*Jam'iyat-e Fada'iyan-e Islam*)
was a relatively small but highly vociferous and militant political group. It mainly consisted of young zealots who, at the

time, did not wish to overthrow the monarchical regime but to impose certain Islamic rules such as the veil, the banning of alcohol, the expulsion of women and Baha'is from the civil service, etc. They also had strong anti-British feelings. As part of their campaigns they occasionally resorted to assassination: before killing Hazhir, they had assassinated Ahmad Kasravi, the anti-Shia scholar.[16]

The Tudeh party split of 1948 had removed all 'dangerous' arguments from within the Tudeh party, ensured the leadership's grip over organisational and policy questions and affirmed and enhanced the party's Soviet connections. The banning of the party in 1949 and the subsequent arrest and escape of most of its traditional leaders completed this process. The ban worked in its favour in so far as it turned it into a tight-knit and highly disciplined organisation under a small leadership.

There were still factions and faction fighting, but this was now almost exclusively confined to differences in the character and personality of the remaining leaders in Tehran, the personal rivalry among them and their views on tactical questions. There was no more argument about party democracy, politics and ideology, or the relationship with the Soviet Union. The dominant faction was that of Kiyanuri, its rival being the faction led by the party's youth leader, Nader Sharmini, while the rest of the local leadership – including Mohammad Bahrami, the general secretary – was caught in the middle.

Within a short period, they managed to restart the meetings of party cells at private homes, and the very fact that they had been attacked by the establishment made them popular, and all about Azerbaijan was forgiven. They managed to acquire a secret printing facility and would soon begin to publish public newspapers which were not openly affiliated to them. Thus the irony was that the banning of the party strengthened it and this was enhanced by Razmara's tactically friendly attitude and, later, Mosaddeq's permissiveness towards them.

The splinter group, on the other hand, did not fare well in the atmosphere created by the Soviet denunciation and Tudeh libels and invectives. As noted, they had initially wanted to set up a socialist organisation but before it took off the ground at all the Tudeh denounced it as 'an organisation for spreading imperialist hypocrisy', and advised its members to seriously fight 'these enemies who are newly created by imperialism ... and are devils who are reciting the Koran'.[17]

Some of them such as Anvar Khameh'i and Hossein Malek continued to keep a small group together, so small that its 'congress' was attended only by twenty people.[18] They published a political-cum-intellectual journal called *Andisheh-ye Naw* (New Ideas) which lasted only for three issues.

THE CLASH OF IDEAS

Maleki, however, was politically inactive for about a year and a half when Al-e Ahmad, who was in contact with him, visited him one day and suggested he write for Baqa'i's *Shahed*. He went further and invited Maleki and Baqa'i to his home for supper and that is how Maleki began to write a series of articles for *Shahed* which were later published in a volume entitled *Barkhord-e Aqayed o Ara* (The Clash of Ideas).[19] In these articles he produced a thorough critique of the Tudeh party and the Soviet Union, inviting a barrage of personal abuse. It was the first time that the Tudeh and the Soviets had been evaluated from this angle.

The Tudeh party

After the abdication of Reza Shah the system of absolute and arbitrary rule was facing serious failure and its members and elements were frightened and destabilised. On the other hand, a large number of liberals as well as socialists and Marxists joined the Tudeh party so that, in the first couple of years of its formation, it became the main base for the struggle for freedom, democracy and social justice. But the Tudeh policies gradually led to the loss of those hopes and many of its members left the party, and the Tudeh leadership turned the party into an organisation whose members followed their leaders on the basis of blind faith in communism and the Soviet power.

The biggest mistake of the party was that instead of relying on the Iranian people it became dependent on Soviet power. The party leaders, excepting a couple of them, were not agents of the Soviet Union, but none of them had the courage to resist orders from the Soviets and their agents within the party. For example, because the Soviets were allied with Britain during the war, and to avoid British suspicions, they were not in favour of serious labour activities in Khuzistan, the oil province. And when the workers largely by their own initiative led a general strike, two leaders of the party went there and helped break the strike. Another example was Tudeh's support – due to Soviet pressure – for the Soviet demand for an oil concession against the real wishes of many of its leaders and most members of its rank and file. They managed to overcome the members' disquiet by resorting to the concept of 'democratic centralism', and promising that the matter would be discussed in the forthcoming congress which, however, was convened triumphantly only after the party split.

Another fundamental mistake the Tudeh party made was to support the revolt in Azerbaijan, going as far as delivering the provincial party organisation to Ferqeh. Many of the Tudeh leaders disliked Pishevari, had not admitted him to the first party congress and were opposed to the dissolution of the local Azerbaijan party. The pressure of the Soviet embassy and their agents inside the party, however, made them relent and go along with it. Therefore, when the Soviets withdrew their support from Ferqeh for the pledge of north Iran oil, the Ferqeh leaders fled and Azerbaijan was awash with blood, and the Tudeh party had to face the music.

And now that the idea of oil nationalisation had been put forward, the Tudeh declared that it was an imperialist ploy and regarded the NF leaders as agents of imperialism because they could not imagine that Iran would be able to implement this policy by depending on its own people without the support of an outside power. For this very reason the party would once again choose the wrong tactics and strategy, and would once again fail.

The continuation of the Tudeh mistakes was not only due to its leaders' lack of will or ignorance. They depended on their members' blind faith in communism and their belief that whatever emanated from the Soviet Union must be the gospel truth. Therefore there was no room for objective discussion and criticism. And even those who may have had doubts had not the guts to speak out both for fear of being charged with various crimes and losing their emotional attachment to their Soviet idol.

The Soviet Union

The Soviet Union is one of the most important as well as complex phenomena in world history. The October revolution was not inevitable but, after the February revolution in Russia, the will of the Bolshevik party leaders managed to lead a revolution in that country that had been predicted for more advanced societies. They had now made of Lenin's ideas something they called Leninism, and claimed that all socialists must accept it.

The Soviets expected all communist parties and countries to sacrifice their interests for Soviet interests, and they called this internationalism. Internationalist ideas would only be authentic and progressive so long as they were based on the equality of nations, rather than other nations giving up their rights to a world power. The Tudeh party accused those who believed in this as being anti-Soviet. But this was not right. The real meaning of friendship with the Soviets was the establishment of friendly relations with them and the prevention of the establishment of Western bases against them in Iran.

That apart, there was no democracy and no individual freedom in the Soviet Union. It was not only responsible for the death of millions of Soviet peoples, but had even purged hundreds of Bolshevik leaders, and was currently imposing similar policies on East European countries. It was a regime that was 'the historical embodiment of Ivan the Terrible'. Neither was there democracy within the Soviet nor other communist parties. Communists called the regimes of the Soviet Union and other Eastern European countries 'dictatorship of the proletariat'; in fact, it was dictatorship over the proletariat.[20]

The National Front

Despite the Tudeh propaganda, the NF is not a party representing one social class but is a front which is made up of various social forces. And its importance and political influence is not so much due to the strength and weaknesses of its leaders but to the fact that it depends on the Iranian people and puts forward the people's demands:

> This author, without being a registered member of the National Front, without simply admiring its leaders ... without believing in the sufficiency of its actual aims and programmes for social reforms, nevertheless regards the National Front as the progressive force in present-day Iran, especially as it has the ability to actualise the potential force that exists within our people.[21]

> The National Front's successes are not just due to its leadership, but more than that, to the fact that the Front leaders have taken the people's demands, their needs, and their trust seriously ... Under the leadership of the same leaders the Front has managed – at a time which has not been so opportune – to obtain a large amount of political freedoms. From the fifteenth Majlis [1947–9] onwards, and particularly since the attempt to assassinate the shah, the Front, by constant struggles against bullying and coercion, has eventually managed to ensure freedom of speech, and abolish the dismal laws that limited press freedom.[22]

> But all these efforts [libelling and mud-slinging against the National Front by the Tudeh party] were useless. A new era had dawned and the people who were not highly literate but possessed strong arms and healthy ideas saw that for the first time in recent times, a force which completely emanates from the people, without submitting to this or the other foreigner, can struggle against the establishment and succeed. To put it briefly, the National Front not only offered the people the policy of reform, but it had also shown how to achieve it.[23]

Conspiracy Theory

As early as 1949, and in the midst of public indignation against the AIOC, the raging Cold War and international anti-imperialist movements, Maleki launched a campaign against the conspiracy theory of politics as a most destructive barrier to the country's social and political development. He said that he did not at all wish to underrate the power, influence, interference and unequal position of the great powers past or present, in Iran or in other colonial and semi-colonial countries. But he opposed the view (a) that all the country's ills were due to colonialism and impe- rialism, (b) that all the (sometimes even minor) events in the country's affairs were due to the underhanded machinations of these powers, (c) that all the main actors in the Iranian govern- ment, politics and opposition were agents of one or another great power, (d) that it was *not* possible for the country to develop and progress except by joining one or the other Cold War bloc, and (e) that all seemingly independent efforts and achievements were bound to be smokescreens created by a great power so as to obscure the vision of the people and allow them a way in through the back door.

The contemporary reader without close knowledge and/ or experience of this Iranian conspiracy theory, and its length, breadth, depth and coverage at the time, might find Maleki's views and arguments commonplace if not altogether bland. They must refer to the country's political literature to be able to appreciate the extraordinary nature of his systematic argument against the conspiracy theory,[24] which in part helped reinforce his detractors' heavy charges against him and his ideas. If there was one thing on which almost the whole of the country's intellectuals, and virtually all the political trends and tendencies – ranging from the shah through to the conservatives and the Tudeh party – were

73

united, it was this theory, first as it affected the role of Russia and Britain, then Britain and the Soviet Union and, last but not least, the United States, although Britain was never quite lost sight of even until the revolution of 1979 and after.

It is difficult to find any other political thinker, intellectual, leader or activist who led a campaign (albeit a largely futile one at the time) against this conspiracy theory from the late 1940s through to the late 1960s. In his 1949 article 'The Nightmare of Pessimism', Maleki described the conspiracy theory as the main cause of pessimism among the intelligentsia about the country's future prospects:

> [They] have turned the British empire – which is in a process of decline, and is losing her bases one after the other – into an omnipotent, supernatural, and irresistible power. In our country's capital one can find intellectual politics-mongers who think it impossible to have a political movement independent from foreigners. If you mention India's freedom to them, they would immediately smile and express surprise at your naïveté not to realise that Nehru, Gandhi and the whole of the Indian freedom movement … are nothing but a farce. As we all know, some people also regard Hitler (certainly) and Stalin (probably) as stooges of the British.[25]

In a following article on 'Maraz-e Esti'mar-zadegi' (The Disease of Imperial-Struckness), where, for the first time in the language of politics, he made use of the Persian suffix *zadegi* to indicate a pathological affliction (cf. Al-e Ahmad's *Gharbzadegi*), he said that a terrifying spectre had been made of British imperialism, and this had resulted in the Iranian people's complete loss of self-confidence. The society was 'struck', he wrote, by the illusion of British omnipotence, and this had led to the belief that the Iranians were no more than puppets in the hands of foreign powers, utterly incapable of improving their own lot. The phobia had gone so far, he argued, that as soon as you suggested positive steps for social progress, most would react by saying, 'But they would not allow it', it being obvious that the third person plural refers to British imperialism:

> There can be no doubt about the strength of imperialism. But we must find out where that strength lies which has penetrated so well down the veins and stems of our society and has thus become the turn of phrase of these gentlemen, who are struck by imperialism.[26]

He went on to say that, in fact, much of this strength lay precisely in the illusion of its invincibility. It was a complex phenomenon consisting of two different – 'objective and subjective' – parts. The objective part corresponded to imperialism's real power, presence and ability to interfere in the country's affairs. But the subjective part was a figment of the imagination and 'has no counterpart in reality'. If those people who had given up all hope for fear of 'the *illusion* of imperialism' tried to overcome that illusion, assess its strength no more or less than it in fact was, and – at the same time – did not underrate the strength of Iranian people, then it would be possible for Iranians to overcome the real and objective strength of imperialism:

> Some ... individuals who suffer from imperial-struckness ... do not even think in terms of reform, let alone take any steps towards it. This group of politics-mongers and intellectuals who suffer from the paranoia of the omnipotence of imperialism and the impotence of Iranians (and

similar peoples), must justly be called imperial-struck. It is very difficult to argue with those who suffer from this sickness.[27]

'The aggrandisement of the strength of imperialism', he wrote in the subtitle to his article, 'today serves Britain's interest and tomorrow the Soviet Union's, but it will never serve the interest of Iran.'

As noted above, Maleki published these articles on the subject in 1949–50. He was to continue in the same spirit for the rest of his life, in theory as well as practice, saying that unreasonable fear of the great powers would work against the country's interest and its ability to improve its domestic and international situation. Hence, although he was critical of Soviet domestic and international politics, he nevertheless believed that the best policy towards the Soviet as well as the American bloc was to establish friendly but independent relations with both of them (see Chapter Four).

OIL NATIONALISATION POLICY

As a result of the campaign of Mosaddeq and the NF who enjoyed popular support, and due to possible American intervention with the shah, the rigged Tehran elections were cancelled and new elections were held. Six of the NF leaders – Mosaddeq, Baqa'i, Makki, Hayerizadeh, Mahmud Nariman and Ali Shaigan – were returned as deputies. Ayatollah Kashani, who was also on the Front's list of candidates, was elected *in absentia*, although he was never to take his seat in this or the following Majlis. Allahyar Saleh, the de facto leader of the Iran party which was affiliated to the NF, was returned as deputy from his native Kashan where a similar battle against election rigging had been fought. It was a small team; but it was one of the strongest opposition groups yet in the Majlis' history.

By their tactical retreat over the Tehran elections, the shah and the establishment had hoped to kill three birds with one stone: to appease Mosaddeq, the Front and their large following; to erect an outside barrier against Razmara who was getting help from the Tudeh party; and to keep Sa'ed in power in order to push through the supplemental agreement. This did not work. The NF saw Sa'ed as an irredeemably pro-British prime minister with whom there could be no real deal over oil and democracy. On the other hand, Razmara was quietly preparing the ground for his own premiership. Hence Sa'ed's new ministry did not even last a month. It fell on 19 March 1950, almost exactly a year before the Oil Nationalisation Bill was to be passed by the Majlis.[28]

Ali Mansur (Mansur al-Molk) replaced Sa'ed as an interim prime minister. The British embassy in Tehran brought pressure on him to get the supplemental agreement off the floor of the Majlis but he did not have the stomach to face a crusade against himself both inside and outside the Chamber. On the other hand, he did not want to cross swords with AIOC and the British government.[29] He found the solution in setting up an ad hoc oil committee to investigate and report on the proposed agreement to the full Chamber. It is an irony of history that the same committee was to become the instrument for the rejection of the bill and the nationalisation of Iranian oil.

When the NF was formed and for some time later it did not have a clear policy vis-à-vis the oil industry. It emphasised democracy and independence and it opposed the supplemental agreement, arguing for a better, though still undefined, deal. Implicit in their earlier campaigns was the possibility of the abrogation of the 1933 oil concession, but their experience of Reza Shah's abrogation of the D'Arcy concession and its results was present in their minds, and they knew that abrogation based on proof of the agreement's illegality was no easy task. Some Front leaders such as Baqa'i were even thinking of improving the terms of the supplemental agreement.

Once in January 1949 during the debates on oil in the fifteenth Majlis, Abbas Eskandari had dropped the word nationalisation but neither he nor anyone else had picked it up.[30] The next time when the idea of nationalisation was mentioned in the Majlis it was Hayerzadeh, a Front member of the oil committee, who, addressing Razama, said that he should nationalise Iranian oil.[31] Next day Hossein Fatemi, owner-editor of the popular daily *Bakhtar-e Emruz* and a leader of the NF, confirmed Hayerzadeh's view in a lead article and wrote that the NF would not agree with any other solution of the issue but nationalisation.[32] Yet it took about four more weeks for this to become the Front's official policy.

Maleki jumped at the idea and wrote an article supporting it and arguing why it was the best policy for the Front to pursue. Baqa'i was hesitant, incredible as it may sound, because he thought Fatemi was a British agent.[33] As a result, it was a month before he agreed to publish Maleki's articles. As Maleki was to write in his open letter to Kashani almost two years later:

Dr Baqa'i, like all the common people, regarded the oil nationalisation policy as a British formula. And as members of the National Front know, in several meetings [of the Front] he had opposed oil nationalisation on the argument that it was a British game. After several long discussions I convinced him that oil nationalisation was the best of all policies, so that at last he changed his mind over his lead

78

article – which had suggested another agreement with AIOC – and accepted the policy of oil nationalisation. The first principal articles in support of the nationalisation of Iranian oil published in the press were written by me in *Shahed* ... The articles were held up in the office of *Shahed* for a month until Baqa'i was convinced.[34]

As an example, Maleki wrote in his first article:

> The necessity of the nationalisation of this great industry has become clear ... Why does the British parliament have the right to nationalise the great steel and other indus-tries which belong to British individuals, and the Iranian people cannot do the same with their oil which against their will has been rented out to a foreign company by arbitrary decision makers ... Great Britain and Holland had important political and economic privileges in India and Burma and Indonesia which, compared to south Iran oil did not have greater legal bases. [When Great Britain and other countries] were compelled to forego those privileges, why should a national and social movement in Iran not end a privilege which has turned Iran into a semi-colonial country ...[35]

The shah and the conservatives, being behind the supplemental bill, naturally opposed it. The paradox is, however, that many of them, including the shah, suspected that Mosaddeq and the NF were products of Britain. The shah went on believing or at least pretending that Mosaddeq was a British agent till the end of his life.[36]

As noted, the Tudeh party also opposed the nationalisation policy. They believed that Mosaddeq and his colleagues were agents, not of Britain, but of America, planning to wrest Iranian oil from British hands and deliver it to American companies. They were also conscious of the Soviet claim to north Iran oil, and that is why at a later stage they suggested that only south Iran oil should be nationalised. On 17 January 1951, the Tudeh weekly *Nameh-ye Mardom* (People's Letter) wrote: 'In principle, how would it be possible to nationalise an industry which is in the hands of imperialism?' But in attacking the NF the Tudeh went much further than that and did not stop at insult and invective. For example, *Besu-ye Ayandeh* (Towards the Future), another public Tudeh newspaper, had on 14 October 1950 written:

> 'Melli' [national or popular] is a barricade behind which the demagogic enemies of the people, thieves, plunderers, base payees of imperialism, parasites and dirty insects continue their conspiracy, subversion, poisoning of minds, darkening of psyches, wheeler-dealing and insulting those who are fighting for freedom ...
>
> Melli is opposed to imperialism and yet carries the standard of imperialism; is an enemy of the foreigner and yet receives orders from the foreigner; is concerned about the people and yet bloodies the heart of the people; breast-beats for freedom, yet weaves a silk rope with which to strangle the people.

The same newspaper wrote on 22 November 1950:

> People know what kind of hotchpotch the National Front is, and how the hands of imperialism have created it in order to deceive the people. The people will never forget that the leader of this Front is a deceitful man who, in his

long life, has had all sorts of colourful tricks up his sleeve in order to deceive the people.

Again, on 23 November:

> The National Front, whose leader is an agent of British imperialist policy, and Dr Baqa'i, the official payee of the AIOC, Sergeant Makki who is the page boy of the British embassy's information department, and Dr Hossein Fatemi whose skin, flesh and bone belong to the oil company, today regard themselves as the heroes of breaking the oil barrel ...

The charge of being British agents here must have been due to the sheer intensity of mud-slinging since, as we have seen and shall see again, the official Tudeh view was that the NF was the agent of America:

> This so-called nationalisation is supposed to expel British imperialism from Iran in order to make room for the dominant American imperialism ... The National Front would like the people to be so *busy fighting British imperialism* that they could totally forget the exploitative imperialism of America ... American imperialism is also in favour of the oil nationalisation ... The National Front is a bungling propagator of nationalism in order to keep the people's struggle apart from that of other peoples, to spread hostility towards the Soviet Union ... [and] finally to serve American imperialism.[37]

This indeed was the crux of the matter. Of all the reasons why the Tudeh party was so angry and embittered about Mosaddeq and

81

the NF it was their confrontation with Britain, not America, that the Tudeh regarded as their greatest sin. They were not all that keen on improving Iran's lot from oil or even stopping British influence in Iran so long as America was not at the sharp end of the attack.

America was the Soviet Union's main global adversary, and confrontation with America was the principal task of communist parties almost regardless of local conditions. The fact is that America until then had not played any significant role in Iran and was generally popular among the people. But for the Tudeh, Soviet interests had a higher priority over Iran's. It was the same attitude and policy that impelled the Tudeh to fan the flames of anti-Americanism in post-revolutionary Iran and zealously celebrate the hostage-taking of American diplomats in 1979. They even resorted to spying for the Soviet Union.[38]

THE NATIONAL FRONT VERSUS RAZMARA

As noted, Ali Mansur set up the Majlis oil committee on the suggestion of a hardline conservative, to take the bill off the floor of the House. Mosaddeq was suspicious both for that reason and because he did not wish the oil issue to disappear from public view. Nevertheless, the NF faction agreed to cooperate and supplied five of the committee's eighteen members, including Mosaddeq, who reluctantly agreed to chair it. This was on 20 June 1950. Five days later General Ali Razmara managed to dislodge Mansur and – as prime minister – to come out into the open as the country's most powerful leader. On the day he introduced his cabinet to the Majlis, Mosaddeq and his followers made such a loud noise in the Chamber as had not been heard since the struggle against Reza Khan's republic in 1924.[39] Baqa'i's *Shahed* became the most vocal organ of the opposition, and when they hired men to interfere with its sale, he, together with a few other Front deputies, began to distribute it themselves on the streets of Tehran.

This was the time when Mosaddeq headed the opposition inside the Majlis and Baqa'i led the crowd out in the streets of Tehran. Although he still had to have a party of his own, he had kept his Action Group for the Freedom of Elections intact, and was being aided from the ranks of the movement. In December 1950, a group of toughs attacked the offices of *Shahed* to teach Baqa'i a lesson, who was spending his nights on the premises. According to Baqa'i they were helped and protected by the police. He barricaded the building, alerted the public, led the defence and the counter-offensive and became the hero of the hour.[40] From this moment he emerged as the movement's young and able heir apparent until his opposition to Mosaddeq's government in 1952.

The argument over oil had been going on for some time, but it was Razmara who acted as the catalyst for the rise of the Popular Movement in its full sense. He was forty-seven when he became prime minister, and by far the youngest lieutenant general, which was then the highest rank in the army. He was able, intelligent and extremely hardworking, and combined boundless physical energy and stamina with an unusually strong nerve.

He was an educated officer from the middle class, yet he was a replica of Reza Khan in almost every other respect: intelligent, tough, bold, ruthless, single-minded and politically astute. His style, approach and techniques also resembled those of Reza Khan. By sheer hard work and good diplomacy he had established a position for himself in the armed forces that made him seem almost indispensable for their existence and development, and so he was popular in the army. Just as Reza Khan had once got rid of Swedish officers in the gendarmerie, so Razmara took full command of that force from the US adviser, General Schwarzkopf, thus getting rid of a close friend of the shah and – his chief rival – General Zahedi, and increasing his own power and prestige at a stroke.[41]

The Tudeh party saw in him (much like the old socialists and communists had seen in Reza Khan) a kind of 'bourgeois demo-cratic' leader with whom they could ally themselves against the shah and conservatives, and the NF. This was in part because of his careful cultivation of the Soviet Union. There was even a new Iran–Soviet trade agreement, reminiscent of the one signed by Reza Khan in 1927. This was seen by many, and not just the NF, as a product of cooperation between the Soviets and Britain.[42]

While both the Soviet Union and Tudeh believed Razmara was a 'British agent', that was nowhere as intolerable as the pos-sible growth of the American influence in the country. Even as late as the day before the 21 July 1952 uprising (when Qavam was briefly prime minster), *Besu-ye Ayandeh* described Razmara as the British agent and Mosaddeq as the American agent. In any case, as long as Razmara was alive the Tudeh mud-slinging against the Front was in effect to help Razmara, for the Front was not responding to them in a like manner.

In fact Razmara was an agent of no great power; on the contrary, he cultivated the three powers in the service of his own interests, and the evidence suggests that (just like Reza Khan between 1924 and 1926) they saw him as the best avail-able alternative in Iran, and they all regretted his death.[43] The British believed that no one was better than Razmara, therefore they should support him.[44] On the other hand, John Wiley, the US ambassador, had admitted that he had directly backed Razmara.[45] The NF believed that he had been brought to power by America, to the extent that *Shahed* published a lead article that stated, 'America could not establish a black dictatorship in Iran.'[46] It continued harping on that theme for a couple of weeks. On 3 July 1950, it ran the headline: 'By imposing Razamara on the Iranian people, America has betrayed the American public opinion'. And on 22 July: 'Razmara's premiership, the biggest mistake of America in Iran'.

Regarding the home front, Razmara was helping the banned Tudeh party in many ways, the most important being his giving them permission to launch the Peace Club, a Tudeh front organisation, which was then part of the global Soviet strategy. He also let them establish the Democratic Youth Centre (*kanun-e javanan-e democrat*). They could publish newspapers and other publications, and organise meetings and demonstrations so long as they were not formally presented as Tudeh activities.

Both the Soviet Union and the Tudeh party accused the United States of having arranged the assassination of Razmara in March 1951. *Pravda*, the daily organ of the Communist Party of the Soviet Union(CPSU), wrote that he was 'killed by the circle who are close to the Americans ... It was Razmara alone who was trying to improve Iran–Soviet relationships ... the Americans alone were interested in destroying Razmara.'[47] Their theory was that Razmara was trying to settle the oil question in Britain's favour and to the exclusion of the United States; hence the Americans were behind his assassination. The argument was reproduced by *Besu-ye Ayandeh* a month later: 'As soon as it became clear that Razmara's being at the helm was not welcome to the Americans, a few shots were fired in the Tehran Mosque [sic] which ended the life of the Iranian prime minister ... The hand of the murderer had been guided by the American spying department in Iran.'[48] Furthermore, this also proved that Mosaddeq and the NF were 'agents of American imperialism' and had succeeded Razmara in order to deliver Iran's oil to American companies.

On 27 May 1950, Zahedi resigned as the country's chief of police following a quarrel with Razmara. That evening Ahmad Dehqan was assassinated. He was a Majlis deputy and a powerful businessman and newspaper publisher with eight Majlis deputies under his command, and was opposed to Razmara. He was also staunchly anti-Tudeh and anti-Soviet, and the convicted assassin was a Tudeh member. Many believed that the assassination of Dehqan was a product of cooperation between Razmara and the Tudeh party, which they also believed to be the case in the attempted assassination of the shah.[49] Baqa'i acted for the defendant in the court, arguing that he had been duped, and *Shahed* was repeating that Dehqan's assassination and that of Mohammad Mas'ud were related to each other.[50]

As noted, the attempt on the shah's life had led to an official ban on the Tudeh party and the arrest of ten of its leaders. On 15 December 1950, the prisoners broke out of jail and eventually fled to the Soviet Union. The shah, the conservatives and the NF all believed that Razmara had had a hand in their escape.[51] One week later, Baqa'i named Razmara to his face as the culprit in a formal Majlis meeting.[52] However, Gholamhossein Forutan, a Tudeh leader who was then in hiding, has written that it was he and the Tudeh secret military network who organised the jailbreak and that Razmara was not involved in it.[53] Razmara's secret cooperation with the Tudeh party was tactical and had no basis in ideology. But his suspected involvement in the Tudeh leaders' jailbreak was the last straw for some of his conservative friends, and alarmed the religious establishment. The increasingly dominant theory among the conservatives (echoed by no less a person than Jamal Imami, the majority leader, in the Majlis oil committee) was that there had been an explicit Anglo-Soviet accord over Iran which could divide the country into British and Soviet zones of influence as in 1907.[54] That was a gross exaggeration, but it did look as if the Soviets and Tudeh preferred the supplemental agreement to oil nationalisation, and, certainly, Razmara to Mosaddeq.

The shah was additionally – and much more realistically – afraid of losing his throne. There is extensive contemporary documentation of the antagonism between the shah and Zahedi, on the one hand, and Razmara on the other.[55] There were even rumours circulating about an imminent Razmara coup. On the other hand, NF leaders believed that, having obtained the passive support of the Tudeh party and having pacified the Soviet Union, Razmara was anxious to settle the oil issue with Britain, receive substantial aid from the US and establish a military dictatorship in the country.

So, as time went by, the shah and the conservatives seemed to be moving closer to the NF in the same way as Razmara was increasingly identified with the Tudeh party in the public eye. There had been no explicit deal between the NF and the conservatives. But when, for example, one compares Baqa'i's deliberately complimentary words about the shah (in his Majlis speech of 21 December just a few days after the Tudeh jailbreak) with his crusade against the constituent assembly a few months earlier, it becomes clear how fast events had been moving. The popular leaders had then seen the constitutional amendment as the work of the shah, the conservatives, Razmara as well as the British. But they could now see the genuine contest between the two sides, and they regarded Razmara as the more dangerous rival and adversary. The shah thought the same.

Exactly what the shah and the conservatives were up to for the elimination (physical or otherwise) of this dangerous enemy is not known. They are likely to have been plotting against him both inside and outside the army, with General Zahedi leading the campaign in the military sphere. Zahedi was an old 'Reza-Shah general'. He was appreciably more senior in age – and formerly in rank – to Razmara, 'the young upstart', and had personal ambitions of his own. Their conflict and quarrel went so far that they broke off relations in 1950.[56] He was self-regarding and no 'lackey' of the shah. But neither his natural abilities nor his personal ambitions were comparable to those of Razmara; and he saw his prospects as generally consistent with the shah's interests, though only up to the point that he would keep his independence.[57]

At any rate it was the rivalry with Razmara that had motivated Zahedi not to rig the second Tehran elections against the NF candidates, when for a brief period he became the country's police chief. And it was for the same reason that Razmara sacked him in that post. Just as Razmara's position in the army and his success in dealing with foreign powers had alarmed the shah, Mosaddeq's increasing public support began to alarm Razmara. Nevertheless, Razmara, like the shah, saw Mosaddeq as a less dangerous enemy, and they both began to try to neutralise (or enter an agreement) with him. But he could not be manipulated by either of them. Razmara had several private meetings with Mosaddeq, and even put a number of cabinet posts at his disposal, but the latter refused to take advantage of the offer. During the weeks running up to Razmara's assassination, the shah sent Jamal Imami to Mosaddeq three times, offering to sack Razmara if he was willing to become prime minister.[58]

The shah's calculation was correct. The conservative deputies would not easily have dismissed Razmara, given his strong military base and good relations with the foreign powers. The shah's trump card at the time was Seyyed Zia who had the backing of the religious establishment as well as Britain. In the circumstances, he could not have taken on both Razmara and Mosaddeq at the same time. Therefore, the shah had no choice but to try to dislodge Razmara through Mosaddeq, in the hope of later outsmarting Mosaddeq with Zia's support. But Mosaddeq would not budge. There were several reasons for this, the most important being that he suspected the same majority which would vote him into office would then refuse to pass the oil nationalisation bill. He would then have to resign, and the whole movement would collapse. When Mosaddeq refused to cooperate, the shah and his friends had to think of other ways of dealing with the fearsome general.

RAZMARA'S ASSASSINATION AND OIL NATIONALISATION

Razmara was assassinated on 7 March 1951 while attending a funeral service at the Royal Mosque in Iran. The self-confessed assassin was Khalil Tahmasebi, a member of the *Fada'iyan-e Islam*. But there was more to it than that. Immediately after the assassination, Seyyed Zia had confided to friends that the shah might have been involved in the incident. The Seyyed had related that he was with the shah when Asadollah Alam – the shah's close confidant and minister of labour who had witnessed Razmara's assassination – had hurriedly arrived at the palace and joyfully told the shah: 'they killed him and we are relieved.'

However, the belief in the shah's involvement in the affair was much more widespread and went as far as Mosaddeq himself who was neither a friend of Razmara nor of Zia. For example, in a Majlis meeting of May 1951, shortly after he had been named prime minister, Mosaddeq strongly hinted that the shah had been behind the general's assassination: 'His Majesty is extremely angry because yesterday Dr Mosaddeq had said in the Majlis … when the shah had told him he had issued orders for his protection, Mosaddeq had replied "[The guards] will not be more trustworthy than those of Razmara", meaning that the shah had been involved in the killing of Razmara. This has made the shah very angry.'[59]

At the same time, there had been rumours that the bullets fired at Razmara did not match, and that an army NCO in plain clothes had fired the fatal shots from a Colt at the same time as Tahmasebi fired his low-calibre handgun. However, Colonel Mosavvar-Rahmani's detailed discussion of the event in his memoirs has left little room for speculation that the plot had different sides to it.[60] For example, he relates his conversation with Colonel Deilami shortly after the event and the letter from Deilami to the shah which he had read out to him, ending with the following words (which Rahmani emphasises he is paraphrasing from memory): 'As your Majesty knows very well, no one had a greater role in getting rid of General Razmara than Mr [Asadollah] Alam and this servant.'[61]

Meanwhile, the Majlis oil committee had been meeting regularly under Mosaddeq's chairmanship. In the first couple of meetings the committee was still groping in the dark, trying to clarify its own specific function and terms of reference. At first, the deputy finance minister began to attend it in a 'consultative capacity', but as soon as the committee began to emerge as a powerful parliamentary and political instrument the finance minister himself joined its meetings. The opposition's attitude towards the supplementary bill was absolutely clear from the outset. It was the gradual change on the part of the conservative members of the committee which began to turn the table against the government for fear of an Anglo-Soviet accord, echoed by Jamal Imami, as noted above. It is important to note that Imami was both opposed to Razmara and close to the shah, so that the former had complained to the British ambassador about the shah receiving Imami regularly.[62]

When the new Iran–Soviet commercial treaty was concluded, Razmara himself attended the committee meeting of 4 November 1950 at Imami's personal invitation. He openly committed the government to the supplemental agreement, but also mentioned that 'further negotiations' were still going on with the oil company without specifying their nature. Two months later the AIOC offered him a fifty-fifty agreement which he did not disclose (see page 92).[63] In the next few meetings Imami spoke openly against the agreement on the grounds that Razmara had told them that he was negotiating for a better deal. More significantly, however, he made indirect references to the presumed Anglo-Soviet accord over Iran, saying, 'the British are bringing the Soviet Union forward in order to frighten us'.[64]

On 10 December, Makki, the committee rapporteur, reported to the full House on the committee's findings and presented the committee's unanimous resolution that the supplemental agreement 'is not sufficient for the vindication of Iran's rights and interests: therefore the committee declares its opposition to it'.[65] Five days later the Tudeh party leaders broke out of jail and in the next few days came the aforementioned attack on *Shahed*'s premises. Imami then began to give open support, in the Majlis, to Baqa'i and the NF against press censorship and the imprisonment of the Popular Movement journalists. Baqa'i in return thanked Imami – who, he specified, 'used to back Razmara's government'.

For good measure he also praised the shah, and put in a good word for Reza Shah as well. Clearly, then, there was an implicit (almost spontaneous) realignment of forces to get rid of Razmara.

In the meantime, following Makki's report to the full House, the government tried to withdraw the supplemental agreement bill in order to prevent its formal defeat. The tactic backfired, however, especially as the finance minister, in the course of the debate, emphatically defended the 1933 agreement. This was the final nail in Razmara's coffin. It was then, in January, that the oil company offered him the fifty-fifty profit-sharing formula (plus two million pounds) which, to their amazement, he asked to be kept confidential, and did not himself make public.[66]

The fact that the NF deputies were primarily concerned with the politics (rather than economics) of oil, shows up in the course of the debates in remarks made by different individuals. Thus Mosaddeq said at one point that 'the moral aspect of oil nationalisation is more important than its economic aspect'.[67] For Hayerizadeh, 'whatever happens in this country is the oil company's doing, and it would be better for the oil to be destroyed by fire than remain in the oil company's hands'.[68] Makki, speaking in the meeting of the full House, preferred to 'seal over the oil wells' rather than let the oil company remain in Iran.[69] And Baqa'i wished that Iran's oil deposits would be destroyed by 'an atom bomb' if the company was here to stay.[70] That is why (later under Mosaddeq's government) they were not prepared to enter into a settlement with Britain that included the company's return in one form or another.

The reason why Razmara hid the fifty-fifty offer is ultimately a matter for speculation. But given the circumstantial evidence it is likely that he was waiting for an opportune moment, perhaps a coup, to throw it dramatically down as a trump card. At any rate, there can be little doubt that had he survived and made the offer public it is highly unlikely that Iranian oil would have been nationalised.

The bill for the nationalisation of Iranian oil was passed unanimously by both Houses of parliament on 20 March 1951, the eve of the Persian New Year and almost three weeks after Razmara's assassination.

4

THE TOILERS PARTY

MOSADDEQ'S PREMIERSHIP

The immediate question the country faced after the assassination of Razmara was to find a prime minister. A number of candidates were put up by the Majlis deputies, including Qavam, Seyyed Zia and Hossein Ala. Ala was the only candidate whom the NF would not oppose; he also had the shah's support. Therefore he was voted in on 11 March as the new prime minister. He was a British-educated lawyer with a long diplomatic career, having been Iranian ambassador to the United Kingdom and the UN among other positions. He was a moderate conservative and had a good reputation within the establishment. His cabinet included a member of the Front and a few who were sympathetic to it.

Mosaddeq was still leader of opposition and the Front was especially keen that Ala help the Oil Nationalisation Bill pass through the Houses of parliament, as in fact he quickly did. On the other hand, it is difficult to imagine what else the parliament could have done in the circumstances. He had hardly begun his task when, on 15 March, the oil workers in Khuzistan went on strike. The reason behind it was the oil company's decision to reduce their pay by 30 per cent just as Norwuz (Persian New Year) was fast approaching.[1] Needless to say, this time the strike was fully supported by the Tudeh party.

The NF saw this as a deliberate provocation by the oil company in order to provide an excuse for the British government to send troops to the province, especially as the Royal Navy was quickly sent off to 'show the flag'. The government declared martial law in Khuzistan as well as Tehran, but the strike spread to a few other cities. Mosaddeq and Kashani jointly wrote to the oil workers that they should not let themselves be provoked and try to keep calm.[2] It did not work and at one stage there was bloodshed in Abadan. However, the strike was eventually settled on 22 April after further interventions by Mosaddeq and Kashani in and out of the Majlis, and government mediation between the company and the strikers.

Parliament had passed the principle of nationalisation but had not laid down the instruments by which oil would be nationalised. In other words, the sheer principle was open to interpretation, such as entering an agreement with another foreign company. To circumvent that, the NF proposed what later became known as the Repossession Bill (khal'-e yad) to the oil committee which was still standing. The committee passed the resolution on 27 April, and submitted it to the floor of the Majlis. This meant precisely nationalisation in the sense of repossession of the oil industry in Khuzistan by the government, including compensation to AIOC and priority for it to purchase national Iranian oil. It meant actual Iranian ownership and production of the oil which implied the cancellation of the 1933 agreement via a legal and internationally credible route.

This was too much for Ala who resigned despite the shah's attempts to persuade him to withdraw his resignation. In the fateful Majlis meeting that followed, the Repossession Bill was debated. Jamal Imami, who was a senior conservative deputy and member of the oil committee and had not voted for the repossession resolution, argued against it, since he believed that it would mean the interference of the legislature in what was the domain of the executive. Therefore, he suggested to Mosaddeq that he assume the premiership and then submit the Repossession Bill to the Majlis. In practice, this could have resulted in the Majlis rejecting the bill after he became prime minister in which case he would have had to resign. On the other hand, it was not unlikely that Imami expected Mosaddeq to refuse the offer and be accused of shirking responsibility.

After all, Imami had three times offered Mosaddeq the premiership on behalf of the shah when Razmara was in power, and each time Mosaddeq had turned it down (see Chapter 3). As Mosaddeq himself said several times in public, this time he accepted the offer, thinking that otherwise Imami would propose Seyyed Zia for the job. However, Mosaddeq agreed only on the condition that the Majlis would there and then also pass the Repossession Bill. A straw vote (*ra'y-e tamayol*) was taken and the majority voted in favour. The bill had been passed and Mosaddeq had become prime minister after the favourable vote in the senate.

Meanwhile, Maleki and Baqa'i were in regular contact and Maleki continued to write in *Shahed*. At the same time he had kept in touch with the majority of the Tudeh party splinters who no longer had faith in the Soviet Union or were committed to Marxism-Leninism, contrary to the few who had set up a small organisation led by Anvar Khameh'i.[3]

The NF as such did not have an organisation and was identified with its committee and deputies. The groups affiliated to it were made up of the old Iran party, its small religious splinter group called the people of Iran party (or God-worshipping socialists), the small but highly active nationalist Iranian people's party and the bazaar guild. Of these, relatively speaking the largest and most important was the Iran party which was nevertheless a small, top-heavy organisation whose importance lay mainly in the fact that its leaders were reputable public figures, university professors (then a prestigious position) and technocrats. However, small as these parties were, none of them answered to the description of a modern political party, which the Tudeh party alone did at the time.

THE TOILERS PARTY

This party was founded by Baqa'i and Maleki on 18 May 1951. Babak Amir Khosravi, a prominent leading member of the Tudeh party who had broken away from it, writes:

> Maleki who has now re-entered the arena in a sensitive moment of Iranian history is no longer content with his 'clash of ideas' column in *Shahed*. Although these writings and analyses of his had a remarkable role in providing the basis for the leading idea of the freedom-loving, democratic Iranian left and the early formulation of the Third Force theory ... We must frankly admit that Maleki's initiative for founding the Iranian People's Toilers with Dr Baqa'i was extremely courageous, selfless and risky. Since the political background, attitude and character of these two were so different that would have made their political cooperation seem difficult.[4]

The foundation of the Toilers party – its full name being the Toiling People of Iran's party – was a response to the need for a modern political party behind the Popular Movement. The

NF, as we have seen, had become little more than a name which soon went out of fashion and was replaced by the term Popular Movement (*Nehzat-e Melli*). This went beyond the mere oil nationalisation programme and included the campaign for full independence, democracy and freedom – a term cultivated, if not coined, by Khalil Maleki. The other Popular Front parties mentioned above were not up to the task of creating a modern organisation which would provide an alternative to the Tudeh party in terms of organisation, publications, political campaigns, policy and programme; a party which would provide a home for large numbers of Popular Front supporters who would otherwise have joined the Tudeh party or stopped being active.[5]

Maleki, who was both an acute political thinker and intellectual, and an able organiser, was neither a politician in the narrow sense of the word nor one who would care for popular acclaim. Therefore, if, at the time, he had founded a party just with his Tudeh splinter friends it is likely to have become more of a leading political intellectual circle. On the other hand, Baqa'i was a charismatic and popular politician, and a skilful public speaker. But he would not have been able to organise a modern party with the characteristics described above. Their combination proved very fruitful for quite some time until Baqa'i decided to leave the party with his personal followers, by which time the party was well established and, popularly known as *Niru-ye Sevvom* (Third Force), went on from strength to strength as the largest modern Popular Movement party (see Chapter 5).

Maleki and the former Tudeh intellectuals organised and ran the party cells, published the weekly *Niru-ye Sevvom*, edited by Ali Asghar Hajj-Seyyed-Javadi, and the monthly intellectual journal *Elm o Zendegi* (Science and Life), edited in turn by Al-e Ahmad, Nader Naderpur and Amir Pichdad; they also wrote most of the articles of *Shahed*, which had become the party's daily organ. The old splinter intellectuals included Al-e Ahmad, Naser Vosuqi, Mohammad Ali Khonji, Fereydun Tavalloli (famous poet and satirist), Naderpur (famous poet), Hossein Malek, Abolqasem Qandehariyan, and a few others, almost all of whom became well known in their time.

There were, however, others who were not party members but were active in party publications such as Simin Daneshavar (famous writer and Al-e Ahmad's wife) and Gholam'ali Sayyar (writer and essayist). Maleki himself was active in all these spheres and wrote virtually all the party's theoretical and intellectual political books and pamphlets. Al-e Ahmad translated André Gide's *Return from the USSR*, which is a thorough critique of Stalinist Russia. He also translated Jean-Paul Sartre's play *Les Mains Sales*, which, although not quite explicit, is a scathing critique of internal assassination in a European communist party. He also translated (with Ali Aghar Khobrehzadeh, another Tudeh splinter) Arthur Koestler's *Darkness at Noon*, the celebrated fictional account of the Stalinist purges of old communists in Russia.

EARLY CAMPAIGNS AGAINST MOSADDEQ

Meanwhile, inasmuch as the premiership of Mosaddeq had led to great public satisfaction, it had also resulted in certain undesirable developments. The Tudeh party's hostility and vicious campaigns were nothing new, but shortly after Mosaddeq assumed office, *Fada'iyan-e Islam*, which had earlier supported the NF, fell out with both Mosaddeq and Kashani and turned into their deadly enemies. The reason for this was that the two leaders had not turned the country into an Islamic state, something that neither of them had promised nor even desired. Indeed, Kashani's response to some partial demands towards Islamic rule was so succinct that is worth quoting them directly:

> [The British colonialists] are now using other tactics in order to weaken our struggle. I am currently receiving signed letters asking why we do not ban the sale of alcohol, expel women employees from government departments, or order the ladies to wear chador. The authors of these letters are either direct agents of Britain, or have their own axe to grind, or are stupid.[6]

Fada'iyan-e Islam's hostility towards Kashani did not cease, even after he broke with Mosaddeq, until the 1953 coup in which both participated and which they supported afterwards for some time.

At the other end of the spectrum, the shah worried lest he should lose his throne. That is why he sent Ala, now court minister, to seek assurances from Mosaddeq that the country would not be turned into a republic – an assurance Mosaddeq gave by writing on the first blank page of a copy of the Koran that he hoped the holy book would curse him if he ever contemplated such an idea.[7]

Nevertheless, the shah was secretly working against Mosaddeq despite public expressions of support for him. In particular, he was collaborating with Britain to ensure Mosaddeq's early failure. As early as 15 March 1951, when he had just heard the news of the Majlis unanimously passing the oil nationalisation bill, he had expressed regret to the British ambassador that it had not been possible to stop the NF's policy.[8] That was before Mosaddeq took over the government.

A few weeks after he became prime minister, the British ambassador reported to the Foreign Office that the day before the Majlis had passed a vote of confidence in Mosaddeq, despite the fact that some influential people, 'including the shah and Seyyed Zia', had tried to encourage the deputies not to attend the meeting; a few of them did not show up, but the rest attended 'from fear [of a public backlash]'.[9]

Furthermore, the shah, Seyyed Zia and others were constantly emphasising to the British diplomats that, to prevent Mosaddeq from succeeding, oil shipments should stop, the Abadan refinery should be shut down, British technicians should be withdrawn, and, in any case, they should not settle with Mosaddeq under any circumstances. This was the summer of 1951, in the wake of Richard Stokes's mission to negotiate with Mosaddeq, and before its failure led to actual repossession of the oil fields and refinery in September.

Mosaddeq's first cabinet was broadly based and included a few conservatives and uncommitted politicians. But the shah was still unhappy. Many appointments, such as those of provincial governorships, had been made without his consent. Foreign policy had slipped out of his hands and ambassadors no longer reported directly to the royal court as before, although neither this nor the shah's approval of provincial governors was constitutional. He was also worried by the extensive and increasing Tudeh activity, as well as their open press and publications under other names.

This was a Razmara legacy, but it continued and was intensified under Mosaddeq for two reasons: there was not an easy way of curtailing such activities legally because they were not conducted under Tudeh's name (which had been already banned); and the banning of any political party was not consistent with Mosaddeq's ideals. On the other hand, the fact that his government did not use the full force of the law to stop campaigns of defamation, disruption and destruction against itself was equally true of both right and left. This was a major defect of Mosaddeq's government and one of the main reasons for its eventual downfall. However, to make the shah happier, Mosaddeq had not only appointed General Zahedi minister of the interior but, on the shah's advice, had also made General Hasan Baqa'i (no relation to the other Baqa'i) chief prefect of the police.[10]

This provided the means for Mosaddeq's opponents of both right and left to make their first major move against him. On 16 July 1951, Averell Harriman, President Truman's intermediary in the Anglo-Iranian negotiations, arrived in Tehran. The US government, in principle being opposed to old-style imperialism and wishing to extend its power and influence in Iran as well as stem the tide of universal communism, and having nothing to lose (if not something to gain), was hoping to steer a middle course and find a solution acceptable to its British allies as well as the Iranians. Dr Henry F. Grady, the US ambassador in Iran, and George McGhee, the young assistant secretary of state, played an important role in formulating this policy. Harriman's mission was to smooth the way for the British delegation, led by Richard Stokes, who would shortly arrive for negotiations with Mosaddeq.

The Tudeh party was persistently leading campaigns and street demonstrations – full as they were of verbal and physical violence – against Mosaddeq, and tacitly or explicitly cooperated with the right against him. For example, the documents discovered at the house of the AIOC's chief representative in Tehran, N. R. Seddon, revealed that the company was aiding the Tudeh press explicitly to render their opposition more effective.[11] They were also using the Peace Club, a Tudeh front organisation which included members of the conservative establishment.

The moment Harriman's visit was announced the Tudeh party denounced it as proof of a complete sell out to the United States, and planned street demonstrations for the day of his arrival. These were banned by the government but the party decided to go ahead and break the law. Mosaddeq had personally instructed

General Baqa'i to stop the demonstrations but not to use firearms without his prior permission. That is exactly what Baqa'i did and there were a number of injuries.

Baqa'i and Zahedi were sacked, and Baqa'i was committed for military trial which, predictably, cleared him of any misconduct. Mosaddeq did not resign (as might have been hoped by the architects of the event), but this was a serious blow to his prestige. However, the Tudeh party – the organisers of the demonstrations – went completely unpunished. This led to many a repeat performance right up to Mosaddeq's downfall.

THE FAILURE OF STOKES'S MISSION

The provisional board of the newly formed National Iranian Oil Company, headed by Mehdi Bazargan, had gone to Abadan in June to a hostile reception by AIOC officials. But Mosaddeq had instructed them not to take any action yet, and to be careful not to cause the slightest provocation to justify British military intervention in the name of defending British lives and property. Iranian oil workers were likewise advised to avoid creating any incidents.

We saw earlier that, just as preparations were being made for the arrival of Stokes's mission, the British embassy was busy plotting the downfall of Mosaddeq through the shah and the Majlis. The British ambassador had been anti-NF from the very beginning, and despised Mosaddeq personally to the extent that, as early as 6 May 1951, he described him as looking like a cab horse, and unjustly accused him of being an opium addict.[12]

The government, however, was still hoping for a quick and amicable settlement, though this seems to have been rather naïve. In fact, AIOC had made an attempt at negotiation in June

1951 – the Basil Jackson mission – but it clearly envisaged the continuation of AIOC's activities under the nominal umbrella of oil nationalisation which was certainly a non-starter and was rejected.[13]

The British negotiating team led by Richard Stokes, Lord Privy Seal in Clement Attlee's Labour government, arrived in Tehran on 3 August, and Mosaddeq went out of his way to receive them as the country's honoured guests – which might have been one reason for Stokes's kind gesture in sending him a Christmas card in jail two and a half years later.[14] Before the arrival of Stokes, Mosaddeq had obtained – with Harriman's active support – a formal acceptance of the principle of oil nationalisation from the British government 'qua itself, and on behalf of the Anglo-Iranian Oil Company'.

There were intensive negotiations until 22 August involving Harriman as well as senior members of the Iranian government, including Mosaddeq himself. To cut a long story short, the gist of Stokes's and Harriman's proposal was that the National Iranian Oil Company would own the entire oil under the ground and take over AIOC's assets on the condition that a British purchasing company would run the export of Iranian oil at an (implicit) fifty-fifty agreement for twenty-five years, although the 1933 oil concession would have come to an end in 1993. There was no argument about the price but the differences were on the management issue best described in the following passage:

> The breakdown of the negotiations was announced both by Dr. Mossadeq and Mr. Stokes on Aug. 22, after a second tripartite meeting at the Saheb Gharanieh palace between the Persian Prime Minister, Mr. Stokes, and Mr. Harriman. In a statement issued after this meeting, Dr. Mossadeq declared that the crux of the Persian Government's differences with

Mr. Stokes lay in the proposed form of British management under the National Iranian Oil Company; that he
(Dr. Mossadeq) wished to have British heads of technical departments, who would report only separately and
individually to the board of the N.I.O.C.; that Mr. Stokes
had insisted that there should be a British general manager
(if a British managing agency, as originally proposed, was
unacceptable to the Persians) to whom heads of departments should be responsible, and through whom they
should report to the N.I.O.C's board; and that the Persian
Government 'could not accept the British demand for
a British manager at Abadan.' Mr. Stokes declared after
the tripartite meeting that there was 'no point in going
on with the talks,' and added: 'The essential thing is to
assure continued production of oil. This means keeping
a staff, and this in turn means keeping a British manager.
As Dr. Mossadeq refused to do this, I regretfully had to
conclude that there was nothing for me to do but go home
immediately.'[15]

In other words the disagreement was on the conflict between
British control and Iran's complete independence, something
which, as noted above, was more important to Mosaddeq and
his team than mere revenue. Nevertheless, both Stokes and
Harriman stressed that they had departed from Iran in a friendly
atmosphere and that the negotiations would continue later, a
promise the Conservative government which came to power in
October failed to keep.

Attlee's government was tired and in disarray, and the successful handling of this blow to British interest and prestige
was beyond its capability. The Conservative opposition and the
British press, both quality and popular, were demanding strong

action and – in Anthony Eden's later words – wanted to 'restore the stolen property'.[16] Beyond the sheer legal and technical arguments, the British were seriously worried about the spread of the disease of Mosaddeqism in the Arab Middle East which they still controlled, and a similar threat to their position in the Suez Canal, especially in view of Mosaddeq's immense popularity in those countries.[17] The nationalisation of Iranian oil appeared to be a serious blow to the British Empire's position and prestige the world over, and it undoubtedly hurt national pride.

REPOSSESSION

The failure of Stokes's mission must be seen against these Iranian and British perspectives. The Iranian government saw no choice but to activate its repossession operations in Khuzistan. In an address to the British technicians and skilled staff, Mosaddeq invited them to stay at their posts with the same pay and conditions, but they refused the offer. Eventually, they were served notice to leave the country, and late in September the oil zone was occupied by Iranian troops. By this time the battle lines were clearly drawn. Attlee's government was divided over possible military intervention but it was probably American influence which stopped them from taking military action.

Britain had already applied for and obtained an injunction from the International Court at The Hague (on 6 July 1951) to forestall repossession, pending the result of its litigation against Iran. The Iranian government rejected the Court's injunction, however, on the grounds that, since the 1933 agreement had been concluded, not between the two governments, but between the Iranian government and an independent company, the International Court lacked jurisdiction in the case, an argument which was to be confirmed in July 1952 by the Court itself. On 28 September, Britain complained to the UN Security Council about Iran's disregard of the injunction. Meanwhile, AIOC was refusing to pay its outstanding debts and royalties to Iran, and Iranian assets at the Bank of England were frozen.

In Britain the general election in October brought the Conservatives to power, with Eden as the new foreign secretary. A letter from President Truman to Mosaddeq gave him the impression (falsely as we now know) that he wanted to talk to him personally in Washington.[18] That is why the prematurely old and ailing prime minster led the Iranian delegation to the Security Council, although this did not pass without incident. Baqa'i, who had been included in the delegation, was refusing to join it because he had objections to the inclusion of another person.[19] He told Maleki, who told him that – Baqa'i being virtually the heir apparent of the Popular Movement at the time – this would make a very bad impression both in Iran and abroad. He suggested Baqa'i go and see Mosaddeq himself, and Mosaddeq somehow convinced him to relent.[20]

At the Security Council, the Iranian delegation presented their legal case as well as documents showing their grievances against AIOC and won their case: the Council decided to postpone a decision, pending the Court's ruling on its jurisdiction in the case. In the United States, meanwhile, Mosaddeq met President Truman, Dean Acheson (secretary of state) and, several times, George McGhee. McGhee came up with a brilliant formula which Mosaddeq accepted.

Acheson then took the proposal to Paris to obtain Eden's approval, while Mosaddeq waited in Washington for the result. But Eden turned it down and told Acheson that 'the Persians are good at coming again' and that he should 'send him home'. More specifically, he said that American fears of communism as the only alternative to Mosaddeq's government were unfounded (even though that was exactly what the British government and press were suggesting in public), and that there were other, better alternatives to both Mosaddeq and communism in Iran which would become evident, given time and support, especially if Mosaddeq was boycotted by the West. For good measure he dropped a hint as to America's possible participation in Iranian oil in a future settlement which Acheson graciously declined.[21] It is worth noting that although in his memoirs Eden describes the Paris discussion on other matters at some length, the only reference to the proposed American formula, and Mosaddeq's acceptance of it, is that 'they were anxious to complete an agreement with him if it were possible'.[22]

THE INTERNATIONAL BANK'S INTERVENTION

Mosaddeq returned home via Egypt, where his tumultuous welcome by the Egyptian people reaffirmed to the British Foreign Office the soundness of their strategy towards him. He was then at the height of his popularity both at home and abroad: he had won the argument in the UN Security Council, the Popular Movement had not split, the shah publicly supported the Movement and Iranian oil had not yet been boycotted. At this time, the International Bank for Reconstruction and Development (later the World Bank) came forward with a temporary solution.

They offered to act as an intermediary for two years between the Iranian government, AIOC and the British government, by taking over the running of the oil operations at their own expense, and dividing the net earnings into three parts: a part to be paid to the former company, a part to the Iranian government and a part to be divided by the two parties after they reached a final settlement.

Britain was not very happy with the idea since the Conservative government at any rate was reluctant to deal with Mosaddeq. But they had to consider America's favourable attitude towards the Bank's proposal, so they accepted it with some reluctance. Mosaddeq was at first open to the suggestion and, after some preparatory work, the Bank sent a high-level mission to Tehran led by its vice president, Robert L. Garner. The Bank's representatives had hardly set foot in Tehran than the Tudeh party led a hysterical press campaign against it, declaring the whole thing treasonable and, inter alia, wrote in its Teaching Pamphlet No. 12: 'When ... the wheeling and dealing with the International Bank proved our views about Mosaddeq and his demagogic gang, then the mask of the enemies of the people was torn apart and his [sic] treacherous face was seen by all.'[23]

The government nevertheless entered into earnest negotiations with the Bank's representatives. There were some queries about the Persian Gulf price of $1.75, and the 58 cent 'discount for the major buyer' (i.e. Britain). A more important difficulty was that Iran was reluctant to let the Bank employ any British technicians in its operations, but this, too, was not something which would have stopped the agreement.

The agreement failed mainly because Iran suggested that in its preamble they would write that the Bank was acting 'for and on behalf of the Iranian government', which would contravene the Bank's neutrality and would never be acceptable to Britain. It was on this petty legal point, indeed, that the whole scheme collapsed and the Bank delegation left Iran. But just before they left, senators Mohammad Soruri and Abolqasem Najm al-Molk – both of them government supporters, Soruri

becoming president of the Supreme Court a few months later –
went to plead with Mosaddeq to accept the Bank's intervention. Mosaddeq told them that he personally was in favour,
but if he accepted it (without the insertion of the words 'for
and on behalf of Iran'), the people of Iran would accuse him
of treason.[24]

This was the greatest missed opportunity in the whole of the
Anglo-Iranian oil dispute. It would have been tantamount to a
ceasefire declaration. Oil production would have resumed and
there would have been plenty of time to find a final settlement
of the dispute in a peaceful atmosphere, which was likely to
have been more favourable to Iran than any of the solutions later
offered by Britain and America.

Fouad Ruhani writes in his detailed account of the subject:

... the main cause of the failure of the negotiations ...
was precisely ... that the Iranian government wanted the
Bank to act as its agent and representative, whereas the
Bank regarded itself as an independent mediator, and
pointed out that, as far as they were concerned, both sides
of the dispute had equal rights, and that the Bank could in
no way act such that it would support the legal claims of
either side ... Thus [Robert L.] Garner [who led the Bank's
mission] explained to the Iranian representatives that the
Bank's intervention was possible only on the agreement
of both the Iranian and the British government, and that
any deviation from this position would contradict its neutrality. The Bank's point was obviously right, and as it later
became clear, Dr Mosaddeq himself had no qualms about
it, but, his advisers [told him] that it would be damaging
to Iran's interest and so he changed his mind about the
Bank's intervention.[25]

The failure of the Bank's intervention led to the international boycott of Iranian oil, leaving Iran with no choice but to resort to the policy of non-oil economics. This they managed fairly well by taking appropriate, if unpopular, measures.[26] But it could only last for a short period because the country was poor, foreign exchange scarce, the cost of running the oil industry with hardly any oil income high, with no hope for economic development. When, a year and a half after the failure of the Bank's intervention, Mosaddeq decided to close the seventeenth Majlis by referendum, one of the reasons behind it was that he feared the discovery by the Majlis that he had secretly printed money to help relieve the economy in the face of the international boycott of Iran which followed the failure of the Bank's intervention. The measure had been sensible but would not have been necessary had the Bank's mission not failed, resulting in the oil boycott.[27]

Khalil Maleki was in favour of the Bank's offer and, as he was to write later:

> The solution suggested by the International Bank, although not ideal, was in some ways very beneficial to the Popular Movement, since, being a provisional two-year solution, the Movement could settle its political and economic situation; and after strengthening the internal situation and establishing social and economic discipline it could continue with any solution or struggle which it thought expedient.[28]

However, non-oil economics meant government deficit and austerity and so Mosaddeq issued a number of public bonds (known as Qarzeh-ye Melli) and appealed to the public to buy them to help government finance. Zahmatkeshan and their newspaper

Shahed led a campaign in favour of the government appeal, asking patriotic people to respond positively. The Tudeh party, on the other hand, denounced the appeal and campaigned against purchasing the bonds. For example, in its issues of 12 and 13 March 1952, *Besu-ye Ayandeh* wrote, among other things:

> *Shahed* expects the people of Iran to respond warmly to a government which is not trusted, a government that fights against the toilers and the liberation movement of our country much more harshly than Razmara and Qavam.

And the Tudeh satirical weekly, *Chelengar*, wrote in verse, in its issue of 20 May 1952:

> Führer! Open up your reason's eye
> Have a quick look at the country; You have issued bonds for the people
> Truly you have performed a miracle; Do not deceitfully milk the people any more
> Pick up the bucket and sell the oil; And he who affords it would not easily buy
> because he does not trust the government; You are a special slave of America
> You are a hard-headed enemy of our people.

PARLIAMENTARY ELECTIONS

The International Bank's mission having failed, Mosaddeq faced two major issues: the state of the economy in the absence of oil revenues, especially as the US would not grant him foreign aid before a resolution of the oil dispute with Britain; and the

113

impending parliamentary elections for the seventeenth Majlis. This was an awkward corner. The provincial magnates – many of whom were opposed to the government – would interfere in the elections with the help of the provincial army and gendarmerie chiefs who still took their orders from the shah;[29] and the Tudeh party would resort to any means to return its deputies mainly for Tehran and a few other cities.

Mosaddeq discussed the whole election issue with the shah who asked him, 'What about the Tudeh party?' He replied that they, too, had a right to their vote but predicted that they would not manage to get any of their candidates elected.[30] The shah was seemingly unconvinced. But the real issue was that both men wanted to send their own candidates to the Chamber: Mosaddeq, by free vote, and the shah, via interference. However, because of the vastness of the country and the poor means of communication in many areas, elections in Iran were always a long and arduous process, though they were conducted relatively quickly in the major cities. The results were therefore announced as they came in.

In the event the Popular Movement candidates won in many of the major cities. All twelve seats for Tehran were won by their candidates, the Tudeh vote being way down and the conservatives coming last. Baqa'i and Ali Zohari, the Toilers party candidates, were elected from Tehran. Why Maleki did not let himself be nominated, even for Tabriz, is not a mystery since he always shunned political power for himself.

However, the situation in smaller towns and rural areas was different, and the contest between supporters of Mosaddeq and the conservatives led to violent conflicts and even bloodshed. In the circumstances the names of eighty deputies-elect (out of the total of 136) had been announced, when Mosaddeq was to lead the Iranian delegation to The Hague for the International Court's hearing of Britain's lawsuit.

He decided to stop the rest of the elections until his return, but the worsening of strife in the remaining constituencies was to prevent the completion of the process. Still, two-thirds of the total number of deputies had been elected and if they had asked him to complete the elections he would have had to oblige. Only thirty out of the eighty elected deputies were Mosaddeq supporters, but they made up the strongest minority faction in the new Majlis.

Mosaddeq personally opened the case at the International Court and then hurried home for the formal opening of the new Majlis. By the time the majority of the judges voted in Iran's favour – i.e. that the Court did not have jurisdiction in the oil dispute – Mosaddeq had begun his second term in office, then resigned, then swept back to power by a public uprising.

THE JULY UPRISING

When the seventeenth Majlis began its business, Mosaddeq resigned by convention to allow the new parliament to choose its own government. In both Houses of parliament the straw vote went in his favour unopposed, but many in the senate abstained. Mosaddeq himself was looking for an excuse to quit but his advisers swept aside his protests about the insufficiency of the senate vote, saying that it would be a grave political mistake to quit on such a flimsy issue. However, by an irony of history, the shah provided Mosaddeq with a better excuse to resign.

Having accepted the premiership, Mosaddeq saw the shah to discuss the composition of the cabinet – something that constitutionally was not necessary – and there he suggested that he himself would 'supervise' the ministry of war. Convention decreed the shah proposed a general for that post, but that was unconstitutional. However, the shah had reacted angrily by saying he 'should let [him] pack his suitcase and leave the country first'.[31] Here was an opportunity for the shah to get rid of Mosaddeq. What he did not know, and was never to learn, was that Mosaddeq himself was looking for a way out. This came to light in the 1980s through the pages of Mosaddeq's memoirs, and even then in the shape of a fleeting remark within a totally different context.

When leaving for The Hague a couple of weeks earlier, he says, he had been convinced that Britain would win its case at the Court. He had therefore decided to resign the minute the unfavourable decision was announced and never to return to Iran.[32] However, he had had to return to Iran for the formalities of the new parliamentary session and had returned to office virtually against his own will. Therefore, the minute the shah opposed his suggestion of running the war ministry himself, he made for the door. The shah was frightened into thinking that he would rally his forces against him inside and outside the Majlis. There followed the comical scene of the prime minster wishing to leave the room and the shah blocking his way by leaning against the door. Having failed to persuade the shah to get out of the way, he fainted, either because of the pressure on his nerves, or because it was a diplomatic way out of the impasse.[33]

When he came round, the two men agreed that unless Mosaddeq heard from the shah by 8 p.m. he should send in his formal resignation. He resigned on 16 July without consulting any of his colleagues and advisers, lest they should try to persuade him to put up a fight. In his secret circular of 12 July to the senior members of the Toilers party, Baqa'i had openly said that Mosaddeq was looking 'for some excuse to shirk his responsibility, and be relieved of the problems which it has created'.[34] But he cannot have known the reason behind it.

The shah turned to Qavam whom, as has been noted above, he disliked, but counted on his strength as a politician and his acceptability to Britain and America. Next day the news of Qavam's appointment stunned everyone, and the thirty Popular Movement deputies were thrown off guard. Their first reaction was to think of an alternative government of their own (Abdollah Moazzami's name was being mentioned) when Baqa'i shook them all by shouting, 'Our prime minster is none other than Dr Mosaddeq'.[35]

Things went wrong for the shah and Qavam for various reasons, but Qavam's radio broadcast was the most fatal of them all. In it he threatened to 'court-martial' his opponents and deliver them into 'the heartless and pitiless hands of the law'. Furthermore, he promised to 'keep religion apart from politics, and ... prevent the spread of superstition and retrogressive ideas'.[36]

The message was received and understood by the whole of the Movement, and not least by Ayatollah Kashani, who published a reply putting Qavam down in commensurate terms, and calling on the people to prepare for resistance. Qavam, backtracking fast, offered to let him fill half the cabinet, but his envoys returned empty-handed. Worse still, Kashani wrote to the shah via Ala stating that he should restore Mosaddeq to office or he would personally lead the revolt.[37]

Meanwhile, the bazaar and the Popular Movement parties prepared for a counter-attack and *Shahed* became the most effective medium for the struggle. A general strike began to spread on 20 July and became complete the next day. The ground had been prepared both by press campaigns and by the *bast* of the Popular Movement deputies in the Majlis. But the strike and public demonstrations were almost spontaneous, although the Toilers party played an important role in organising and leading the crowd once they were out in the streets. Baqa'i wrote a lead article in *Shahed* that day, headed by the following verse: 'Although the arrow goes through the bow / The archer's finger behind it is seen by those who know'. It was the most audacious dart yet thrown at the shah by a Popular Front leader.

The police failed to control the situation the previous day, and so the troops were called out on 21 July. In Tehran alone there were seventeen deaths and many more casualties. The shah got cold feet and at about 4 p.m. asked Qavam to resign and reinstated Mosaddeq.[38] The Tudeh party did not issue a statement in support of the revolt or command its members to join it, but it has been claimed that some of its members had joined the crowd of their own volition.

All this time, the Tudeh party played a peculiar role. On 18 July *Besu-ye Ayandeh* wrote that whatever the outcome of 'the two wings of the regime' (i.e. Mosaddeq and Qavam), after fourteen months of Mosaddeq's premiership it had been proved that neither was a friend of the people. 'They all are enemies of the people and defenders of exploitation [of the people] by the Iranian establishment.' On 20 July it claimed that in the Majlis elections Mosaddeq had in the first instance wanted to get American agents elected 'but in practice, in order to prevent the election of the real representatives of the people [i.e. the Tudeh candidates] he collaborated with the court and agents of Britain'.

However, having been restored to office in triumph, Mosaddeq was then at the pinnacle of his popularity and power, especially as the next day the news came of the International Court's decision in Iran's favour.

THE ZAHMATKESHAN SPLIT

If the events leading to the 21 July uprising had not taken place it is possible that Baqa'i would have broken up the Toilers party sooner than October 1952. As noted, he had almost come to blows with Mosaddeq as early as a year before over the composition of the delegation led by the latter to the UN. Regarding himself as an early founder of the Movement on account of his campaign against the supplemental bill in the fifteenth Majlis, he expected a special place in the Movement and a special treatment by Mosaddeq. He was, after all, still the Movement's heir apparent. Instead, he felt that Mosaddeq listened to others such as Fatemi, Shaigan and some Iran party leaders more than him.

Baqa'i had been closer to Ayatollah Kashani almost since the campaign for oil nationalisation began. And soon after the 21 July revolt Kashani had written to Mosaddeq bitterly complaining about three of his appointments to his government and the army, and threatened to leave town, and even the country, which showed the seriousness of the position. Mosaddeq had been somewhat more restrained in his reply, defending the appointments, and saying that he would rather resign than let the Ayatollah leave town. Kashani had similar grievances about some of his recommendation to government departments being ignored.[39] And two of his three sons who had stood for the Majlis election had not been elected.[40] Nevertheless he was elected speaker of the Majlis with Mosaddeq's support in preference to two members of the Popular Movement faction in the Majlis, Shaigan and Moazzami, the latter of whom was later to replace him.

Still, Baqa'i was somewhat ahead of Kashani in bringing the conflict out in the open. In September he was treated in hospital for a mysterious illness. Yet he later claimed that, while in hospital, he had been summoned by the shah to his palace, offering him the premiership which he did not accept.[41] This is extremely unlikely, if only because it was a few weeks after the 21 July revolt and Mosaddeq's triumphal return to power. However, his long stay in hospital afforded time and privacy to meet his own confidants in the Zahmatkeshan leadership, and some of the leading

opponents of Mosaddeq, including General Zahedi. Maleki and
the rest of the Zahmatkeshan coalition became alarmed. They
were by no means averse to criticising Mosaddeq's government
and they said so at the time of Baqa'i's break with them, but they
regarded a confrontation with the government as detrimental to
the whole Movement.[42]

At the end of September Baqa'i asked Maleki to see him in
hospital, and there he raised the issue of 'presenting Dr Mosaddeq
with an ultimatum' and that he must be attacked in the party
organs:

> I pointed out to him that Dr Mosaddeq's government
> will not last more than a few months. If he succeeded
> against your opposition, your share in the victory would
> be reduced. And if he did not succeed you would at least
> take some of the blame for his failure.
>
> However, my firm arguments did not manage to change
> his mind about the deals which he had already made [with
> his visitors] in the hospital. When I realised that in fact
> some dangerous wheelings and dealings had been made,
> after consulting the executive committee and the party
> organs, explicitly pointed them out and declared the sup-
> port of the Toilers party for Dr Mosaddeq. Today it is as
> clear to me as daylight that this very support of the party
> organs for Dr Mosaddeq, and my efforts to prevent the
> denigration and weakening of the government determined
> Dr Baqa'i to resign [from the party].[43]

After Baqa'i left hospital, he called the council of party activists
for 10 October to test the ground. However, he quickly realised
that he was in a small minority. When, amid the arguments, he
was asked if on 20 July he had sent his old friend and a party

leader, Isa Sepahbodi, to see Qavam, and if so for what purpose, he refused to comment. Then, in Al-e Ahmad's words there was a loud cry of 'expulsion'.[44] Nevertheless the argument continued and at one stage Baqa'i managed to provoke Maleki by deliberately insulting Hossein Malek (his brother) who was absent from the meeting.[45] In the end, Baqa'i said that his idea of a party was like a garden where he could sit, smoke his pipe, and get up and leave.[46]

Baqa'i then offered his resignation from the party and got up to leave. As Maleki continued in his letter to Ayatollah Kashani:

> Since in my view and those of the council of activists and the great majority of the party his resignation was a great blow to the Popular Movement, all the party members and I did our utmost to make him change his mind. On the evening of his resignation, I begged him to let me go to his home but he did not agree, and he even brushed aside the begging and weeping of some of the most committed activists of the party harshly. And all the efforts of our party comrades to bring us two together were unsuccessful. I even suggested that the other Tudeh party splinters and I would resign and leave the party to him but he said that the whole of the party was my 'cabal'.[47]

Furthermore:

> I do not regard [the leadership of] a General Negib [re Zahedi] acceptable for Iran even assuming that it would be good for Egypt. Dr Mosaddeq's personality has relieved us of the need for the General Negib types who might even be truly 'noble and dignified' [the meaning of the word *negib*] and no noble and dignified Iranian general would take any steps towards Dr Mosaddeq.[48]

Baqa'i submitted his written resignation two days later, but the party continued as usual and *Shahed*, the party newspaper, was duly published. It is clear that Baqa'i had already made up his mind even before the meeting of the activists. His idea of a party that was acceptable to him was a group of personal devotees who would receive and carry out his orders without a fuss. At first, he did not clarify the real reason for his resignation – namely the party's refusal to assault Mosaddeq's government – and simply pretended that the party and Maleki had proved too left wing for him:

> From the very beginning a small number of people led by Mr Khalil Maleki had deviationist ideas ... Many a time they discussed communism in the party cells ... They were planning to turn Zahmatkeshan into a communist party which was not connected to Moscow.[49]

Still, Baqa'i said in the same speech that his original resignation was because he had been told that 99 per cent of the party members were behind Maleki.

Baqa'i had some personal cronies in the party, tough nuts like Ahmad Eshqi, Amir Mubur (the Blonde), Habib Siyah (the Black), etc., who often attacked Tudeh demonstrations with knives and clubs. More thugs came to Baqa'i's aid when, two days after his 'resignation',[50] a group attacked the party headquarters, beat up all those present and kicked them out, smashed office equipment and furniture and locked the building. The man who organised the raid was Shams-e Qanat-Abadi, a turbaned mob leader and head of the Muslim Devotees Group (*Majma'-e Moslamanan-e Mojahed*), which was in effect Kashani's arm. He was also a pro-Kashani Majlis deputy, who was later to abandon him after Kashani had been himself abandoned by the shah and Zahedi. This was done under the watchful eyes of the police, whose chief prefect, General Kamal, was a Baqa'i friend.[51]

The book entitled *Khalil Maleki According to SAVAK Documents* (*Khalil Maleki beh Ravayat-e Asnad-e SAVAK*) is mainly a compendium of SAVAK secret documents regarding Maleki's activities. Although not entirely reliable, it is useful for research purposes as long as it is used carefully. In it, there is a fascinating account, based on Qanat-Abadi's memoirs, on how they organised the assault on the Toilers party headquarters. He begins by saying that 'When Dr Baqa'i confronted Mosaddeq, Khalil Maleki and his cabal stood up to him ... Suddenly Dr Baqa'i realised that Khalil Maleki and the party members were on one side and he, Ali Zohari and one or two others were on the other side ... The great leader [Baqa'i] had been reduced to an ordinary member of the party.'

Baqa'i, 'moaning and red in the face', enters the Majlis. Qanat-Abadi asks him what is wrong and Baqa'i (and Zohari, who was with him) reply that they had been 'expelled' from the party. In the amusing conversation that follows Baqa'i asks Qanat-Abadi to 'think of something'. The latter replies that he has. Baqa'i asks what it is, and he replies: '*coup d'état.*' Baqa'i asks him to stop joking and he replies he is not. He adds that he will telephone members of the Muslim Devotees Group 'at Mr Kashani's house' and ask them to come to the Majlis:

> Baqa'i asked what shall we do next. I said after the boys arrive you will immediately take your walking stick and lead them, and they will ... follow you shouting slogans and *salavat* [praising the Prophet Mohammad]. And then they will take the leader of the Toilers party – with pomp and ceremony – to the party headquarters and throw Khalil Maleki's boys out of it, shouting slogans and *salavat* for an hour.
>
> You will then lock up and come to the Majlis with the keys. And tomorrow you will write in *Shahed* that Khalil

Maleki and his cabal who are used to party splits had conspired to split from the Toilers party. This was reported to
Dr Baqa'i who raised the issue in the central committee
and they unanimously decided to expel Khalil Maleki and
his cabal ... Zohari laughed and told Baqa'i 'Doctor aren't
you and I the party's central committee?' Baqa'i agreed.
Zohari said we should put Qanat-Abdi's plan into effect
then. Qanat-Abadi then made the necessary phone calls
and a group of Muslim Devotees, about two hundred
of them, came and took Baqa'i for the coup at the party
headquarters. And once again Dr Baqa'i became leader of
the Toilers party.[52]

After Baqa'i had resigned from the party and smashed its headquarters with the aid of a mob, Maleki's enemies and detractors
gave him the title of (among others) 'split-monger' from then on.
Besu-ye Ayandeh's response to the conflict in the Toilers party was
that 'the bankruptcy of the Toilers party exposes the baselessness
of the Third Force theory and shows that in the present world
such a force can only exist in the minds of the masked paid agents
of imperialism'.[53]

It is worth noting that on the very days when these events
were taking place, the government uncovered a plot by General
Zahedi and General Hejazi and the three Rashidiyan brothers
who were agents of MI6 'with the aid of a foreign embassy'. Hejazi
and the Rashidiyans were arrested but, as a senator, Zahedi had
parliamentary immunity. However, the government broke off
diplomatic relations with Britain. It is now known that the charges
were correct but the government did nothing to investigate the
plot and bring its perpetrators to justice. It is not unlikely that
Baqa'i had known about it, as this was pointed out a couple of
days after the 'coup' against the Toilers party, in the pages of

the first and second issues of *Niru-ye Sevvom* (daily), 15 and 16 October 1952.

The news of the 'coup' in the Toiler's party spread widely the same day and by the evening a couple of hundred party activists, shocked and dismayed, gathered in and outside Maleki's home wondering what to do. A few of the leading figures were almost in despair saying that they had once had to leave the Tudeh party, and now they had to face another conflict, so they might as well quit. Maleki typically said that they should do whatever the young party members suggested.

Al-e Ahmad, himself a leading figure, then got up and said that nothing had changed and they should be thankful to have been relieved by Baqa'i and his gang. The decision was then made, becuase Baqa'i had occupied and smashed the party headquarters, that they would rename themselves the Toiling People of Iran's party (Third Force); and from then on they became popularly known as the Third Force party. The weekly *Niru-ye Sevvom* had been published for some time but, on the very day after the 'coup', the first issue of the daily *Niru-ye Sevvom* was published and continued to be published until the 1953 coup.

5

THE THIRD FORCE

Maleki had set himself two main missions: to offer an intellectual and theoretical alternative to the Tudeh party and to organise a modern party to support the Popular Movement. It was he and his close colleagues who had organised the Toilers party. No wonder, then, that after his split with the party, Baqa'i said that 99 per cent of the party members were behind Maleki.

In fact they doubled their efforts after Baqai's departure, and the Third Force grew fast, launched a new and daring Progressive Women's Movement (*Nehzat-e Zanan-e Pishrow*), which published its own journal; increased their publications and other activities; continued their highly effective 'discussion and criticism' weekly meetings which Maleki had founded in his time in the Tudeh party (see Chapter 2); and gave unwavering support along with policy advice and solid (though loyal) criticism to the government. Their moment of glory came on 28 February 1953 when they helped win the day for Mosaddeq.

Baqa'i, on the other hand, soon began to reveal his opposition to Mosaddeq, and gradually became the most outspoken member of the opposition in the Majlis. Indeed, he went much further and secretly plotted a coup with Zahedi, and together with the latter was recommended by the shah to the American embassy as the only people they should trust.[1] He was also involved in the kidnapping and murder of General Mahmud Afshartus, the chief prefect of the police (see page 162).

THE THEORY OF THE THIRD FORCE

Maleki developed his Third Force theory at the peak of the Cold War in the late 1940s and early 1950s. A couple of years earlier, the world had held its breath during the Berlin Crisis. In 1949, Mao and the Chinese communists had driven Chiang Kai-shek out of mainland China and turned America into its bitter enemy. Shortly afterwards, the war in Korea was raging and that in Vietnam (then against France) creeping. In 1948 the communist takeover in Czechoslovakia had added that country to Stalin's war prizes with little fuss. India's independence had brought hope to the colonial and semi-colonial countries of Asia and Africa, but both the United States and the Soviet Union regarded Nehru and his team with suspicion. Tito's Yugoslavia had already broken free from the international communist movement. The West was naturally pleased about this as far as it went, but otherwise had no more enthusiasm for Tito than it had for communism in its own territories. On the other hand, Moscow and its international brotherhood denounced Tito – 'Marshal of the Traitors' – Milovan Djilas and the rest of the Yugoslav leadership in terms which are almost unprintable.

Ever since 1943 two main political camps had emerged in Iran: the pro-Soviet camp represented by the Tudeh party and the pro-Western camp represented by the political establishment.

But when, from 1946, the Cold War winds began to blow – and this was reflected by the revolt in Azerbaijan – attitudes hardened such that each side literally believed that its opponents were paid agents of the West or the East. Moreover, they regarded anyone claiming independence from both as naïve at best, but more often as an undercover agent of the other side. Indeed, Loy W. Henderson, the American ambassador, speaking to the shah after the coup, heavily criticised Nehru's policy of independence from the two blocs and positive neutrality.[2]

Maleki's Third Force theory must be studied against this domestic and international background. He presented various parts of the theory first through his 1949–50 series of articles ('Barkhord-e Aqayed of Ara') in the weekly *Shahed* which he then formulated into a coherent theory in 1951 and 1952. He introduced two principal concepts: 'The Third Force in General' and 'The Third Force in Particular'. The 'General' concept referred to the desire and/or efforts to break free from the two stereotypes everywhere in the world outside the US and USSR. 'The Third Force in Particular' described the specifically socialist road to social and economic development, which was independent from the Eastern bloc and discovered by each country on the basis of its own culture and historical experience.

At the time the world political map was divided into two blocs: the 'socialist' and the 'imperialist' camp; 'the iron curtain countries' and 'the free world'. Maleki divided it into three: the West, the East and the countries which many years later became known as the Third World. These were countries 'which neither feel free in Mr Truman's free world nor do they see any sign of socialism in the Soviet Union's socialist camp. These masses of people in Asia, Europe, Africa and elsewhere wish ... to cooperate with each other and ... protect their own national and social character and identity.'[3] It was clear at the outset,

then, that the Third Force theory went beyond a mere articula-
tion of the foreign policy of non-alignment, though this itself
was quite a novel idea at the time and formed a small part of
Maleki's theory. According to this theory, the apparently solid
and homogeneous front put forward by the West was misleading. Western Europe, in particular, was an advanced cultural
and historical entity of its own which would soon recover its
separate identity from the US, but without crossing over to
Soviet communism:

> The western [European] civilisation with its deep histori-
> cal, economic, industrial and scientific roots will eventually
> recover from its present weaknesses, and will not surrender
> to either of these two simple civilisations which themselves
> have sprung up from Europe, but which have developed in
> the less advanced circumstances of Russia and America.[4]

This he described as the Western European Third Force in
General, which was represented by Western European liberal
democracy, and was likely to lead to the formation of a Western
European social and economic union. But he also defined a
European Third Force in Particular:

> In Europe 'the Third Force in Particular' finds expres-
> sion in a socialist approach which is consistent with the
> progressive tenets of European democracy ...[5] Vis-à-
> vis American capitalism and its numerous European
> fellow-travellers, and Soviet state capitalism (which claims
> to be socialist, but which has destroyed economic, politi-
> cal and personal freedoms in Russia), a European road
> to socialism in the particular sense of the Third Force is
> now developing.[6]

Similar tendencies also existed within Eastern bloc countries, wrote Maleki, but Soviet suppression prevented their public expression and development:

> Whenever the Third Force has dared raise its head in eastern bloc countries it has been condemned and destroyed as deviationist, and as an agent and spy of imperialism. The only exception to this rule among Balkan countries is Yugoslavia, because that country has not been conquered or – as the Cominform would have it, liberated – by the Red Army.[7]

It is worth noting that five years later, in 1956, the Soviets put down Hungary's revolt by military force and seventeen years later, in 1968, gave the same treatment to Czechoslovakia's attempt at liberating itself from the Soviet yoke.

Maleki's regard for Yugoslavia was both because of its break with Stalin and (as part of that) because of its own independent approach to socialism. But he did not necessarily agree with the Yugoslav system even for that country, let alone for Iran, and he became more acutely critical of constraints on political freedom when the regime began to persecute Milovan Djilas, the anti-Stalinist theorist and ex-party leader who was embarrassingly outspoken in his critique of Soviet communism. Indeed, long before then, and as early as 1949, Maleki wrote:

> I am not concerned with the details of Tito's policies, nor even his major policies which may well be open to criticism and about which I know very little. [I am only concerned with the view] that having regard to one's national self-interest is not in conflict with healthy and proper international relations.[8]

The special reference to the Balkan countries in the above quotation was not accidental, for, surprisingly, Maleki also predicted a rift between Russia and China, despite the apparently solid bond that existed between them at the time, and for many years to come:

> The movement that Dr Sun Yat Sen began on the basis of his three fundamental principles, and which Mao Tse-tung now continues, will not in the end remain a satellite of the Soviet Union. Indeed it can be confidently predicted that similar developments to those of Yugoslavia will also take place in China. The forms which these developments will take will doubtless be different from what happened in Yugoslavia. But their substance would be similar resistance against [Soviet] pressures and expansionist behaviour.[9]

In short, Western Europe's Third Force in General was an attempt to protect its great traditions, identity and independence from Russification and Americanisation. Its Third Force in Particular was expressed through the development of democratic socialism based on Europe's own advanced experiences in both fields. Within the Soviet orbit, the Third Force in General and in Particular were one and the same thing, namely efforts to break free from Soviet domination and build an independent road to socialism on the basis of each country's peculiar culture and tradition. Yugoslavia was the actual and China the potential example of this movement, even though they left much to be desired in regard to personal freedoms and democratic control.

There remained the colonial and semi-colonial countries. Here, the Third Force in General had emerged in the form of anti-colonial movements, which wished to throw off the shackles of colonialism, but did not wish to replace them with Soviet domination. On the other hand, the West's notion of 'freedom' for these countries meant little more than the continuation of the status quo, which included their own overriding influence.

Meanwhile, Soviet communism and its supporters in the third world argued that all efforts should primarily be put to the service of the Soviet Union, 'the headquarters of the world proletariat'. According to this theory, the destiny of the world proletariat was directly bound up with the fortunes of the Soviet Union. The progressive and democratic forces in every country – big and small, rich and poor – must therefore give complete priority to the domination of the Soviet power in its global contest with the United States.

Thus in both Western and Soviet eyes, any movement in colonial countries which did not toe their own particular line was bound to be an agent of the other side. They were both wrong, however: in spite of the local ruling establishments and communist parties, which together made up a small (though powerful) numerical minority, there existed the independent force of the people of these countries – including their culture and history – harnessed by indigenous leaders and intellectuals who were not committed to either of these global powers, nor did they subscribe to their particular ideologies. This was the Third Force in General – the non-communist movement for freedom and independence – within colonial and semi-colonial countries.[10]

But there was a Third Force in Particular, composed of the left wing of these popular movements, which wished to bring about political progress and economic development via their own peculiar roads to socialism. It would be best to discuss this tendency in the context of Iran.

The Third Force in Iran

The Popular Movement was Iran's example of Third Force in General, and its left wing was Iran's Third Force in Particular:

> All those who have no hope in the decadent ruling establishment and no expectations from leaders of the Tudeh party ... belong to the Third Force. All those who support the nationalisation of Iranian oil everywhere in the country [i.e. not only in the south, as the Tudeh demanded], that is the nationalisation of all the resources and industries which either Britain or Russia hopes to possess at one and the same time, are part of the Third Force. All those who find it possible to maintain Iran's political and economic independence without its attachment to the Western or Eastern Bloc who believe in the power of their own people, and the ability of their own leaders, and who think it possible for the people of Iran to hold their own destiny without blindly following this and that foreign power, belong to the Third Force ...

But there were those who did not belong:

> The gentlemen of the Tudeh party as well as those in the ruling establishment ought to be taught to overcome their sense of weakness and inferiority, and recognise their own existence and the power of their own people; that is, the Third Force. Those who have not managed to recognise their own existence and independence have failed to understand the reality of the Popular Movement of Iran.[11]

The Third Force in Iran was not just a movement independent from the two international blocs; it was at the same time an alternative approach to national self-realisation and development. It was an alternative social model, 'a mode of national and social living distinct both from the American and Russian models which they try to impose on us'. The Third Force is the modern manifestation of freedom-loving men and women of Iran, itself reflecting a great deal of historical experience through the centuries of Iranian civilisation.[12]

Despite the Tudeh party propaganda, the NF was neither an instrument of imperialism nor even a 'bourgeois' or 'petit-bourgeois' movement. It was a broad coalition of various political tendencies who shared in the objectives of independence and democracy, and whose left wing had put forward a specifically Iranian road to economic development and social justice. The model did draw on Europe's experience of industrialisation, democracy and socialism, but it was not an imported blueprint, and it was firmly based on Iran's resources and capacity, past and present, for

> it is conscious of the fact that real social progress finds its source and origin in the capacity and potential of the people themselves, and uses that potential to produce a programme which is consistent with the country's resources and with its stage of social development.[13]

The Zahmatkeshan (Toilers) party, being representative of the Third Force in Particular in Iran, argued that

> it seeks its social base among the great masses of the people, and the labouring and productive classes of this country ... It is conscious of the fact that real social progress must find

its source and origin in the capacity and potential of the people themselves, and use that potential to produce a programme which is consistent with the country's resources and with [Iran's] stage of social development.[14]

Apart from this vision of democracy and socialism, Maleki's main contributions in this period centred on two themes: one, the philosophy of history, socialist theory and the phenomenon of the Soviet Union; two, the Popular Movement policies and programmes.

HISTORY, SOCIALISM AND THE SOVIET UNION

Historical necessity and the Tudeh party

At the time, Soviet Marxism was the only interpretation of Marxism with wide currency in the realm of political theory and practice in the world. An important aspect of this interpretation (even in its Trotskyist version) was the belief in an iron historical necessity, a determinism which was almost indistinguishable from fatalism. In a word God had been replaced by History, and man was merely its instrument. Maleki, by contrast, emphasised the importance of both the individual and social consciousness in shaping events. What would have happened if Razmara had not been assassinated? he once asked. Here he was explicitly responding to St Beuve's question: What would have happened if Robespierre had died and Mirabeau had lived, instead?[15]

The concept of historical necessity was not invented by Marx. In modern political thought it goes back at least to Vico, Herder and Montesquieu. Other thinkers – Maleki mentioned Hegel, Monod, Guizot, Mignet and Spenser – later developed the same idea in the eighteenth and nineteenth centuries into hard determinism. But 'realistic socialists' 'corrected' their excesses:

> For a progressive and socially-conscious individual, history is a description and analysis of the present based on past experiences, in the hope of creating a better and more advanced future.[16]

There might be natural laws and historical constraints, but these did not in themselves condemn any individual or society to a certain destiny:

> Those who understand the laws of nature can impose their own will on them. Those who know past history and are familiar with its laws ... are able to govern future history.[17]

Britain's control of Iran's industry might have been a historical necessity, that is, a product of its industry and empire. But so was the Popular Movement of Iran and its reaction against it:

> So long as individuals and peoples are not conscious of social laws and social relations, they would be enslaved by the system which rules over them. But when the masses of people understood those social laws ... and realised that they are not due to celestial forces, it would be possible to undo the laws themselves. Hence, they move from the realm of necessity to the realm of freedom.[18]

There were two concepts of necessity: scientific and historical. The metaphysical concept was not only found among followers of traditional religions, but was shared by some modern ideologies as well. The elementary principles of democracy required that social change be based on the needs of the great masses of the people; and 'socialism is unthinkable without democracy', therefore, socialist necessity arose from democratic choice, not the dicta of impersonal history.[19]

Maleki's theoretical attack on the notion of 'historical inevitability', like his other theoretical analyses, had a firm basis in political practice and experience. Four years earlier, at the time of the Tudeh party split, in *Two Approaches to the Same Goal* (see Chapter 2), which was the splinter group's manifesto for launching their abortive Tudeh Socialist League of Iran, Maleki had firmly rejected the Tudeh leadership's fatalistic arguments in the hope of justifying their own mistakes as well as reassuring their membership that victory would inevitably be theirs:

> In the executive committee's statement, and as part of a long argument intended to prove the inevitability of past mistakes, it has been said: 'The party leadership is part of this same [Iranian] society, and its shortcomings cannot be isolated from the larger society and its limitations'... Those who – for the sake of justifying a few leaders – wish to base future decisions on the same mistaken methods of the past do the party no service at all ... In their view, historical inevitability would, willy nilly, take us to socialism. They therefore neither believe in an able and intelligent leadership nor in a conscious and active struggle. As they themselves put it, they have 'faith' in the International Democratic Front [i.e. Soviet Union] which is apparently supposed to succeed mechanically, and without the effort of the national movements.[20]

On the other hand, freedom of choice should not be confused with naïve as well as dangerous voluntarism which was the other side of the coin. The programme of every popular movement for social change 'must be consistent both with the existing social constraints and with the actual forces with which to bring it about'.[21] Voluntarism and political romanticism were doomed to failure, in part because they would choose any means to achieve their ends, whereas both for moral and scientific reasons ends and means could not possibly be separated from each other:

> In principle, the only standard by which the aims of a political party ought to be judged is the means which it employs. And if these do not correspond to its declared aims, we must conclude that that party does not pursue its alleged objectives. On the contrary, its real objectives are those which are placed at the end of the path which it treads.[22]

Soviet Union and state capitalism

Maleki discusses the anti-socialist characteristics of the Soviet Union with regard both to its domestic and foreign policies. In short, domestically the Soviet system was state capitalism, not socialism; and in its foreign policies it was a colonising, not a liberating, power.

The Soviet Union was a complex phenomenon. Stalinism had almost managed to destroy every fundamental tenet of socialism, and every democratic vestige of the Russian revolution. In its foreign relations, the Soviet behaviour towards its 'allies' and 'fraternal parties' was no less exploitative than that of Western imperialism towards non-European countries. Stalin's interpretation of socialist internationalism was that the world proletariat and their parties should sacrifice their own interests for the sake of 'the citadel of socialism', 'the headquarters of the world proletariat', the Soviet Union. Hence they now had an ideological justification for exploitation whereby the volunteers should let themselves be sacrificed in the hope of realising the millennium at an indeterminate time in the future.

Furthermore, Stalinism was not just a foreign policy or a pro-Russian theory of imperialism. 'The hypothesis that the Soviet Union is a socialist country cannot justify or absolve the anti-socialist realities of the Soviet state.'[23] Since, apart from the colonial relationship between Soviet Russia and its satellite countries and parties, the Soviet workers and peasants were also exploited, there were extreme inequalities in the standard of living, and the Soviet state ruled the society with an iron fist:

> First, the Soviet State apparatus contains capitalist characteristics; and, second, its means of production are owned by the state. Therefore all the existing phenomena in the Soviet Union can be explained by the hypothesis of 'state capitalism'. State capitalism in its present form in the Soviet Union is without precedent in history ...[24] In Soviet Russia the economy, production and productive relations are monopolistically based on the principles of state capitalism. The class that in the Soviet Union benefits from this socio-economic regime is a growing class which we call 'the party and state bureaucracy'. A group of influential party members, state mandarins and heads of firms have attained the position of command in the Soviet economy, polity and society ...[25]

It is doubtful if anyone had used the diagnosis of state capitalism for the Soviet regime before Maleki: Milovan Djilas's famous book *The New Class* was published in 1957.

Furthermore, the Soviet system was state capitalism because, while the state owned the productive resources, the workers were exploited on the same Marxian lines of creating surplus value for their employers. It might have been possible to explain this on the basis of Marx's theory of capital accumulation and economic development had there been a tendency towards industrial democracy and redistribution of income in Russia. But here as well the trend was the other way round. The state bureaucracy was expanding to the point of 'overmanning' within it, and there was a growing gap between its standard of living and that of the ordinary people.

Regarding the Popular Movement of Iran, the Soviet Union applied the same 'General Line' as it did everywhere else. Both Russia and the Tudeh party described Mosaddeq as an agent of American imperialism simply because the movement he led was independent of themselves. Even the Movement's objective struggle against British imperialism was not good enough for them, partly because the nationalisation of oil everywhere in the country had robbed them of the opportunity to get north Iran's oil concession, and partly because they preferred to deal with Britain in the Middle East, rather than the possibility of its replacement, the United States. In fact, the Soviet Union's global strategy, its international network, its seductive ideology and its local organisation in the shape of the Tudeh party posed 'the greatest danger for the Popular Movement':

The Soviet Union … has a global strategy for the implementation of which the parties which call themselves communist and their fellow travellers are its executive branches. As we know, every popular movement and every attempt at establishing social justice and struggling against imperialism which is not within the general framework of the Cominform is described … as an instrument of imperialism. Since our Popular Movement is not part of this whole, the headquarters of the Cominform regards the fight against this Movement as one of its most fundamental duties, which it conducts by means of its Iranian branch, i.e. the Tudeh party ...

By misusing and deforming socialism ... the Cominform has turned it into an instrument of the Soviets' expansionist policy. Thus, for the first time in history, an expansionist and aggressive power is using a weapon which has no rival of its kind. Tens and thousand – even millions – of simple-minded people believe that they are struggling for the greatest and most sacred ideal; whereas in reality, they have fallen into the trap of a state which does not hold the slightest value for their freedom and independence.[26]

The above is a short account of Maleki's ideas at the time from which he never departed. But he was to continue his thoughts and activities beyond the 1953 coup, and we shall discuss them in the later chapters of this book.

THE POPULAR MOVEMENT POLICIES AND PROGRAMMES

On the Oil Dispute

We saw that apart from some very early British suggestions before repossession, the first serious attempt by Britain to reach a settlement was the negotiations of Richard Stokes's mission in August 1951(see Chapter 4). It did not succeed ultimately because it insisted that the proposed operating company should have a British manager, despite the fact that it would reduce the operating period to twenty-five years (instead of the forty and more that were left of the 1933 concession) and would be based on a fifty-fifty agreement. Therefore its failure was precisely due to the fact that an element of British control of Iranian oil would have remained. This, rather than the Iranian share of the oil revenues, was the major obstacle, since the most important principle behind oil nationalisation had been full independence, or total liberation from undue British influence and interference in Iran's political affairs (see Chapters 3 and 4).

However, the failure of the International Bank's intervention was due to a very different factor. As noted in Chapter 4, the issue was not the control of Iranian oil, but the unreasonable and impractical Iranian demand that, *as a mediator*, the Bank act as its agent. Clearly this would have been unacceptable to Britain since legally it would have been tantamount to the Iranian ministry of finance acting as the mediator! This was mainly because of the hysterical attack by the Tudeh party on Mosaddeq, saying that the Bank's mission was proof that he was an American agent. It frightened a number of Mosaddeq's entourage into thinking that the people would describe it as a sell-out if they went along with the Bank's proposal. Ali Shaigan and the Iran party's Kazem Hasibi were most active in changing Mosaddeq's mind, though in the end it was just Hasibi and no one else.[27] When Robert Garner, vice president and head of the Bank's mission, had asked Hasibi what alternative to the Bank's proposal they envisaged, he had told him of a dream in which a holy man had told him they would definitely succeed.[28]

Maleki was firmly in favour of accepting the Bank's proposal since there was no harm and much good in it. The consequence of its rejection, as noted, was the boycott of Iranian oil and the austerity of non-oil economics. When a year and a half later Mosaddeq dissolved the seventeenth Majlis by referendum, one of his motives for doing so was that he feared the Majlis discovering that he had secretly printed money in the face of the oil boycott. And that provided the ground for the 1953 coup.

After Mosaddeq's unprecedented triumph in July – the July uprising and the International Court's decision in favour of Iran – the Iranian government reopened the oil issue (on 7 August), saying it was ready to negotiate, and demanded the repayment of AIOC's debt of 'several millions of pounds' to Iran, and that the British government release Iran's sterling balances at the Bank of England. Britain responded by making a fresh proposal backed by the US – hence 'the Truman–Churchill proposal'. The proposal's principal point was that Iran should agree to the referral of the question of compensation to the International Court's arbitration – now that the latter had denied its own jurisdiction without Iran's consent – with the British claim *including AIOC's loss of profit until 1990*. The remaining items – AIOC's sale of any oil already produced and stored, Britain's release of Iran's sterling balances and American aid to Iran to the value of $10 million – were relatively marginal.[29]

The Iranian counterproposals (of 24 September) were, briefly, as follows: (a) that Iran would consent to The Hague's arbitration *so long as the amount of compensation to AIOC was determined on the basis of the market value of its property at the time of nationalisation* (this was the principal point); (b) that the claims of both parties should be heard at the International Court, including the damages so far caused by the British boycott of Iranian oil, etc.; (c) that AIOC should pay in advance its total debt of £49 million to Iran. Once again it was point (a) that was the bone of contention. Britain rejected it.[30]

The last Anglo-American proposal to Mosaddeq, known as the Henderson proposal since it was presented by the American ambassador (Loy W. Henderson) to Tehran, was an improvement on the Truman–Churchill idea. It proposed either referral to the International Court as before with improved offers, or that compensation be determined by The Hague on the basis of the compensation paid to a British nationalised industry. This was interpreted by the Iranians as meaning the same as compensation for loss of profit until 1990, thinking that a nationalised British industry would be chosen which had been thus compensated. However, the proposal envisaged that *'the Iranian government would have total right in running its own oil industry'*.[31] Mosaddeq had been close to accepting the Henderson proposal but a couple of his advisers, and particularly Ali Shaigan, torpedoed it.[32]

Yet Mosaddeq did not give up searching for an acceptable solution. An American document which has very recently come to light shows that, in early May 1953, almost three months after the collapse of the Henderson proposal, Mosaddeq told Henderson that he was prepared to refer the arbitration on the oil dispute to President Eisenhower and accept whatever decision he came up with. Thus, in his dispatch of 4 May 1953 to the State Department, Henderson wrote:

> [The] Prime Minister apparently on impulse said 'I am willing [to] have this dispute settled by someone whom Britain and I can trust. I [am] agreeable [for] President Eisenhower [to] act as arbiter. I [am] ready [to] give him full power to decide [the] issue. Will you be good enough to ask President Eisenhower if he would undertake [to] settle this matter for us?' I replied I had no (repeat no) authority [to] convey any additional messages re settlement [of the] oil dispute.[33]

Mosaddeq asked him to at least convey their conversation to his superiors. Henderson agreed but pointed out that the president was extremely busy and that Britain might not agree to his arbitration: perhaps Mosaddeq would sound them out through their Interests Section at the Swiss embassy in Tehran. Mosaddeq said he must first be sure that Eisenhower would agree to be the arbiter, pointing out that the decision should not allow the British to come back to Iran: the president would be asked to decide solely on the amount of compensation. If this was agreed he would ask for full powers from the Majlis to go to America and present Iran's case, and from America he would 'send [a] message requesting [the] Majlis to permit him [to] transfer his full powers to [the] President'. Henderson wondered if, in the case of British agreement to the scheme, the Iranian public might think that British compliance would mean the result would go in their favour. '[The] Prime Minister said he [was] sure he could manage [the] situation [in] Iran if UK Government could manage [it] in London.' Henderson said that he 'would report our conversation to the US Government but not (repeat not) in form of [an] offer'.[34]

However, there is no evidence that the matter went any further than that.

If Iran had been a strong country with a strong economy the dispute would have been settled more or less justly for all concerned. But it was a weak country, suffering from an acute domestic as well as international crisis, and had an even weaker economy in view of the oil boycott, having taken on Britain and now America as well. With Eisenhower as president, John Foster Dulles as secretary of state and his brother Allan Dulles as the CIA chief, and at the peak of the Cold War, Iran simply could not afford not to settle the oil dispute. The Americans, encouraged by the British, were acutely afraid of the prospect of Iran falling into the Soviet lap. And the Tudeh party was increasingly doing everything in its power – secret military organisation, accumulation of arms, shows of force, strikes, unauthorised demonstrations, widespread publications, anti-American propaganda, and most of all the promise of imminent revolution – to confirm America's worst fears.

It has recently been suggested that the Anglo-American powers would not have settled the oil dispute short of regaining control of Iranian oil.[35] That is not tenable especially as it flies in the face of the fact that both the Truman–Churchill and the Henderson proposals would have left the control of Iranian oil in Iranian hands against the compensation that they demanded. The irony is that right from the moment that the nationalisation policy was launched, Mosaddeq and his colleagues emphasised that the principal aim of the Movement was full independence and democracy but they ended up wrangling over the amount of compensation. If the Henderson agreement had been accepted, there would have been neither the 28 February coup attempt (see page 158), nor the closure of the seventeenth Majlis, nor, above all, the 1953 coup. Full independence and democracy would then have been achieved by paying probably a higher price for compensation, though even this is not certain if only because the International Court had once ruled in Iran's favour.

The conservatives would lose much of their foreign support and encouragement the minute the oil dispute was settled. The Tudeh party would also be neutralised as soon as the government assumed a fair and cordial relationship with the Soviet Union – as proved to be the case when the shah and the Soviets established friendly relations after the coup and in the early 1960s. But in the meantime the government should apply the full force of the law (as it did not) to put a stop to secret plots, disruptions, agitations, anarchical behaviour, defamatory propaganda, etc.

Maleki was very much in favour of settling the oil dispute in the best possible way, writing several times that any settlement by Mosaddeq would be much better than one made by his successor. This prediction also turned out to be true.

Land reform, women and other issues

From the very beginning Maleki had regarded oil nationalisation as the first step towards independence, democracy, economic development and social reform. That is why he did not see the oil issue as an end in itself, but an instrument in a general social transformation. An honourable settlement of the oil dispute would remove international pressure, normalise the country's economic situation, increase the government's financial power and enable it to spend on projects for social and economic development. This would start a virtuous circle in favour of the Movement, and against its domestic enemies.

Land reform was and remained one of Maleki's two favourite themes for social reform. He advocated a comprehensive reform of Iran's system of land tenure, both for reasons of justice and morality and in the interests of social and economic development. He welcomed Mosaddeq's scheme for partial redistribution of income from landlords to peasants but viewed it as no more than a temporary measure.

On the question of women, Maleki did not miss an occasion to advocate (a) the full franchise and integration into civil society of the 'one-half of the society which brings up the other half on its lap', and (b) the need to mobilise the country's full capacity and potential by bringing women into the sphere of public economic and social activity. He wrote to Ayatollah Kashani:

> I am proud of what I have written about women's rights, and I assert with utmost courage that in the present circumstances it is not possible to keep more than half of the society in a state of paralysis. Today all the world's nations use their maximum human capacity in peace and war. If we could not or would not use women in social life – regarding

the administration of the entire aspects of the society – we would not be able to defend our independence.[36]

A couple of months before the Third Force's long and vigorous campaign for women's suffrage, about thirty 'women and girls' wrote a signed letter – from Mashhad – to *Niru-ye Sevvom*, copied to Maleki, thanking the party and newspaper profusely for their support of the cause of women.[37] However, as soon as the government raised the issue of a new general and local elections bill, Maleki wrote a long lead article entitled 'our neglected mothers, sisters and wives', of which this is a very short example:

> Half of the Iranian people suffer eternal prohibition ... If the rights of Iranian women are not restored, it will not take long before they would rise and retake their usurped rights and freedoms. The new elections bill gives us another chance to raise the issue of the restoration of the natural and usurped rights of women. As far as we know ... once again this bill does not include the securing of the rights of women, and that the prohibition of Iranian women will continue ... The usurped rights of women are both political and economic. By political rights we mean those rights which men enjoy in society and governance; in the sphere of economic rights [a series of obstacles] have deprived women of receiving equal pay for equal work and production, and the ability to participate in all social activities ...[38]

A week later, when the bill excluded women's franchise, *Niru-ye Sevvom* ran a big headline saying that 'in the reactionary law', women along with murderers, thieves, etc., have been deprived both of electing and of being elected. There followed another long lead article demanding change in the later readings of the bill. There was also a long and highly critical parliamentary report on the issue.[39]

The campaign continued right until early January, through which several members of the Third Force women's section – including the renowned educationalist Hajar Tarbiyat – all but pleaded for a change in the law, but to no avail. A delegation of the Third Force women's section was then received by Mosaddeq sympathetically who in effect told them that he was in favour of women getting the vote but that there was strong – not least clerical – opposition to it.[40] Some powerful ulama were indeed strongly opposed to the move.

Apart from land reform and women, there were almost continuous articles in *Niru-ye Sevvom* arguing that domestic reforms would not have to wait until the oil issue was resolved, and that such reforms would in fact strengthen the hands of the government. For example, once *Niru-ye Sevvom* addressed Mosaddeq in its headline asking him to use his powers, or his and the Movement's enemies would use theirs: 'The hungry, millions of toiling, homeless and deprived people, the people who lose their lives under torture by big landlords and their underlings are awaiting Dr Mosaddeq and his reforms.'[41]

On the whole the Iran party leaders and some other close advisers of Mosaddeq were not very enthusiastic about these ideas. Some of them were opposed to any settlement of the oil dispute short of total victory, elusive though this was, for fear of losing popularity. They did not advocate socio-economic development and said nothing about the liberation of women. Indeed, according to Ahmad Razavi a Popular Movement leader and vice speaker of the seventeenth Majlis, 'there were weeks when we were wondering what to do and tell the people in the absence of a strong negative current'.[42] However, they were not too keen on the efficient enforcement of the law either, because they were extremely averse to making enemies, conservative, Tudeh or any other.

The programme outlined above could best be applied as a package. In particular, a comprehensive land reform would not have been possible without the prior settlement of the oil dispute, although certain reforms of agricultural tenure would still have been possible. However, the enforcement of the law was not only possible, but absolutely necessary while the government faced hostile powers both inside and outside the country. This should not have involved ham-fisted or illiberal policies. It would not have been necessary to ban conservative parties and clubs, or the front organisations and publications of the Tudeh party. It would have been enough to bring suspected lawbreakers to justice, keep order in the streets and enforce the libel laws.

Maleki and the Third Force emphatically advocated the application of the law to protect the Movement. And that aside, when from April 1953 everyone was convinced that a coup was imminent, the Third Force party suggested the formation of Popular Movement district committees and a Popular Movement guard to defend the government, and managed to set up two such committees themselves.[43] But the government did not agree with their proposal or support their voluntary action. The government's inertia in enforcing the law and preparing to defend itself was one of the principal reasons behind the defeat of Mosaddeq and the Popular Movement when they were seemingly in power.

THE TUDEH'S RESPONSE

There was a myth repeatedly put forward by the shah and his regime, the British, the Americans and the Tudeh party that, after the July uprising, the Tudeh supported Mosaddeq. For the first three of them, it provided a justification for toppling Mosaddeq's government. For the Tudeh it was useful to claim that at least halfway they had supported Mosaddeq, rather than leading press campaigns, street turmoil, industrial strikes, etc., against him (which they in fact did), and providing every excuse for the hostile powers to believe that they would gain the upper hand in Iranian politics.

That indeed was a myth. The fact is that the Tudeh toned down its attacks on Mosaddeq and stopped some of the worst invective they used to employ against him, but its hostile attitude remained intact. For example, after the July uprising, Mosaddeq had asked and obtained from the parliament some delegated powers (*ekhtiyarat*) for six months so that he would be able to pass and enact reform bills and submit them to parliament for acceptance or rejection at the end of the period. There were many reasons for this which I have discussed elsewhere,[44] and Mosaddeq would justifiably have resigned – as he said he would – if he had not been granted these powers. The delegated powers act came up for renewal in January 1953 and Kashani, Baqa'i, Hayerizadeh, Makki and Qanat-Abadi in particular led a vociferous and vehement campaign against it.[45] From 12 to 21 January, when, after long debates, the bill was passed, *Niru-ye Sevvom* led a continuous campaign in its favour. In the end only one deputy voted against while six, including Baqa'i and Hayerizadeh, abstained.[46]

Beh Su-ye Ayandeh (Towards the Future), the leading open Tudeh publication, wrote in a lead article in its issue of 22 January:

Would it be logical to put the destiny of this country's fifteen million people in the hands of an ailing and despotic man who regards himself the fount of wisdom and possessor of every virtue and laudable quality [and] who does not hold the slightest value for the masses of the

people? ...Would it be right to delegate power to a man
who does not hesitate for a moment to trample underfoot
the people's rights in the interest of American imperialists?

And then addressing the Majlis deputies, i.e. the conservative
majority and Baqa'i, etc.:

If you voted for the delegated powers bill, and kept silent
against this demand of the destroyers of freedom, [and]
if you gave Mosaddeq a free hand to compromise with
the imperialists and join the Middle East Treaty[47] and if
you placed yourselves in the imperialist unions against
the Union of Soviet Socialist Republics, our great neighbour, tomorrow you would be bearing every possible
responsibility.

Shahbaz, the second leading open Tudeh newspaper, wrote in
its issue of 13 January on the same subject: 'There are no ifs
and buts about dictatorship. The shop that Dr Mosaddeq has
opened is the most scandalous form of Fascist dictatorship.'

In January 1953, the Soviet concession for the monopoly
of fishing in the Iranian part of the Caspian Sea came up for
review. The concession had first been granted to a Russian citizen
(Lianozov) up to 1925. Later the concessionaires were given a
longer term and in 1927 Reza Shah transferred the concession
to Soviet Russia for twenty-five years – a measure opposed by
Mosaddeq in the Majlis.[48] However, before its lapse at the end
of January 1953, the Soviet government asked for its renewal for
another term. Mosaddeq turned down the request, telling the
Soviet ambassador that Iran should not be expected to renew a
Russian concession which had fallen due, while it had nationalised a British concession decades before it was due to lapse.[49]

The day after the Caspian Fishing Company passed into Iranian hands, Maleki wrote in a leader in *Niru-ye Sevvom*:

The Iranian government's refusal to renew the Soviet fishing concession must not be put down to an unfriendly attitude [towards the Soviet Union]. The Iranian people wish to have a friendly relationship with the Soviet people, and maintain their political, economic and cultural links with them ... The Soviet government can be absolutely sure that the Iranian people have no wish to break up their friendship with the Soviet Union. But this friendship must not be based on the old lines. If the Soviet government does not respect the freedom and independence of the Iranian people, it should not expect a friendly attitude from them.[50]

On the same day, *Beh Su-ye Ayandeh* attacked the decision and wrote that 'to defend the Soviet Union is to defend peace, freedom and national independence'. The day after, it went much further. Having declared that 'the Third Force [party] spies and paid agents' intend to disrupt Iran–Soviet relations 'and prepare the ground for an even greater expansion of the destructive influence of American imperialism in our country', it had the following to say about Mosaddeq and his government:

The truth of the matter is that the Iranian government represents feudals, large landowners and big capitalists who are dependent on imperialism; and it does not reflect the interest of Iranian people. That is why it cannot be in agreement with Soviet policy, which is the policy of peace, freedom and happiness of the masses of all nations.

Both *Beh Su-ye Ayandeh* and *Shahbaz* at first denied that the Russians had asked for the renewal of the concession, but they had to retract their denials after Tass (the Soviet news agency) confirmed that the demand had indeed been made. Then *Mardom* (the official organ of the party's central committee), which was published clandestinely but circulated with little difficulty, put the party's official view on the matter on 13 February:

> On 21 January, because of the lapse of the activities of the Iranian Fishing Company [sic] the Soviet government made a proposal [to the Iranian government] for the renewal of the Company's activities [sic] for a further period [which was] fully and entirely in the interest of our people, and beneficial to our country. Yet, and despite these obvious truths, Mosaddeq's government – against the interest of our people and country, and in keeping with the orders of its foreign masters – formally responded to the Soviet government's proposals by declaring that his government had decided not to renew the activities of the bi-national Iran-Soviet Company because the period of its activities [i.e. the concessionary period] had lapsed. The Iranian people regard as an ugly decision this anti-popular [*zedd-e melli*] action of Mosaddeq, and believe that it has been motivated by hostility towards the people's interests, and the pursuit of the wishes of the imperialist masters of those who run Iran's present politics.

The above was a small example of Tudeh attacks on Mosaddeq on specific subjects when it was supposed to have supported Mosaddeq. Regarding his government and policies in general,

Beh Su-ye Ayandeh surpassed even itself in its lead article of 30 January 1953:

> The further Mosaddeq went on the road to carry out imperialist policies the more he had to face the harder resistance and struggle of the people. It was during the hardening of this struggle that Mosaddeq cooperated with the blackest and most reactionary anti-popular forces and resorted to blood-letting. Mosaddeq tried to strangle the Popular Movement because this was at the top of the American agenda ... Mosaddeq in line with the most reactionary circles of Iran's ruling class entered a widespread conspiracy against popular rights and freedoms. Massacre, imprisonment, arrests, collective banishments, organising attacks by professional thugs and knife-men was in order to carry out this plot ...
>
> And once again against the flood of the people's protests and protest movements the conjuring shop of oil was opened. But no reputation was left for the conjuror ... When the time of delegated legislation was up, the discredited conjuror opened his shop once again ... But the conjuror could not deceive the people again. The popular parties, organisations and press opposed delegated legislation and uncovered this high treason. The people are immortal but the old conjuror whose life is about to end cannot resist against them.

Much further evidence can be brought against the old myth of Tudeh support for Mosaddeq after the July uprising but enough has been said to explode it within this limited compass. The Tudeh in the past and its few sympathisers in recent times have criticised Mosaddeq for not agreeing to their slogan of 'united front' (*jebheh-ye vahed*) – i.e. a coalition of the Tudeh party and the Popular Movement – after the 21 July uprising.[51] One wonders how they would justify such criticism in the face of this evidence. Besides, the Tudeh party was openly dependent on the Soviet Union. How could a movement that prided itself in being independent of the two blocs become united with that party at the peak of the Cold War? All this is not to mention that the Tudeh had a secret military organisation, the existence of which was known though its network was uncovered after the 1953 coup. It also accumulated extensive arms caches during Mosaddeq's premiership.[52]

Maleki's share of the Tudeh character assassination – both written and verbal – is large and predictable, and for that reason not worth dwelling on. We shall just mention the Tudeh pamphlet dedicated to mud-slinging against the person of Maleki as well as the Third Force entitled *Niru-ye Sevvom, Paigah-e Ejtema'i-ye Amperialsim* (The Third Force, the Social Base of Imperialism) which was published by the Tudeh press in 1952; and the *Teaching Pamphlets* (*Nashriyeh-ye Ta'limati*) numbers 23 and 24, which were packed with libels and invectives against Maleki and the Third Force, to say nothing of what they wrote in their newspapers, *Beh Su-ye Ayandeh, Shahbaz, Chelengar*, etc. In his only extensive response, Maleki pointed out that

> in their open and secret publications and in their teaching pamphlets, and in the two pamphlets which they have recently dedicated to vituperation ... against the Third Force, attempts have been made to produce 'an abominable picture' of Khalil Maleki. And in every page of the *Teaching Pamphlets* 23 and 24 which completely and without exception are dedicated to 'Maleki's cabal, the band of paid agents of imperialism', one can see Maleki's name

accompanied with the vilest invectives ten times, and the name of Third Force with descriptions which is worthy of themselves, fifteen times.

In the recent pamphlet [i.e. social base of imperialism] ... they have pretended to put forward arguments as well, but here too they have flavoured their writing with abusive and indecent words against Khalil Maleki.[53]

28 FEBRUARY

On the morning of 28 February 1953, a rumour was suddenly spread that the shah was about to leave the country for a visit abroad, the impression being given that Mosaddeq was forcing him to leave the country. For the first time Kashani and Baqa'i joined forces with the right-wing military and civil opposition to take violent action against Mosaddeq.

Hossein Ala, the court minister, had once surprised Mosaddeq by saying that the shah had been thinking of going to Europe for some time because 'he was bored with having nothing to do'. Mosaddeq had responded with reassuring words and had advised against the idea.[54] Abdollah Mo'azzami was a senior Popular Movement leader and deputy who combined an independent mind with an unusually moderate political behaviour. He saw the shah and Ala several times in an effort to reduce the differences between the shah and Mosaddeq. These contacts led to a decision by Popular Movement deputies to send a delegation, including Mo'azzami and six others, to the court in pursuit of a rapprochement between the shah and the prime minister.[55]

Meanwhile, Ala had given Mosaddeq a hint about the shah and Queen Soraya's thoughts of paying a visit to Europe. The court minister told Mosaddeq that the couple were unhappy about their apparent infertility and wished to seek possible treatment abroad. Mosaddeq had suggested that perhaps the queen could go on her own and the shah would join her if there was any real need for it.[56]

On 24 February the seven-man parliamentary team was invited to lunch at the court. This time the shah himself joined the party and the deputies were pleasantly surprised to see him in a friendly mood towards Mosaddeq and the Movement. After leaving the palace they decided to go straight to Mosaddeq's house, which was nearby, to give him the good news. There are three versions of what followed – by Mo'azzami, Mosaddeq and Sanjabi – with some differences in detail, but concurrence on the main points.

Mo'azzami's recollections of the event have been presented in greater detail, and, for a variety of reasons, they are likely to be the most accurate. At the royal luncheon the shah's thinking of visiting Europe had been mentioned as a vague possibility. Then Mo'azzami had been called to the telephone at Mosaddeq's house and informed that the shah had decided to go on a trip soon. Back at the meeting, he had first informed a couple of colleagues of the matter in French, then (having sworn everyone to secrecy) he had broken the news. He added that Ala and another court official were on their way to the prime minister's house to discuss the matter.[57]

When the court officials arrived the deputies moved to another room. Mosaddeq advised them against the idea, but was told that the shah's mind was made up. He promised to cooperate in helping to organise and finance the trip as well as keeping the decision secret since the shah had insisted on secrecy 'lest there should be public anxiety and unrest'.[58] Years later, in his book *Mission for My Country*,[59] the shah claimed that the idea had been Mosaddeq's, but did not explain why he had agreed to go along with it. Whereas, in response to Mosaddeq's full and frank statement on 6 April after the collapse of the event, an official court statement had claimed that it had been suggested by 'three [sic] Popular Movement Deputies' whom it had not named.[60] However, both the direct and circumstantial evidence show that, assuming the decision had been serious, it had been taken by the shah himself.

On 25 February Ala surprised Mosaddeq by calling on him to say that the date of departure had been set for three days later, Saturday 28 February, when Mosaddeq was to have lunch at the palace at 1.30 p.m., and the cabinet would attend afterwards for an official farewell. Meanwhile, General Zahedi was taken into custody on 25 February in a security operation on suspicion of conspiring against the government. Typically, however, he was released without being charged.[61]

On the morning of 28 February, the powerful anti-Mosaddeq Ayatollah Behbahani had telephoned Mosaddeq enquiring if the rumour of the shah's imminent departure was true, and if so why he had agreed to it. Mosaddeq, greatly surprised that the news had leaked, confirmed it to Behbahani and said that he could not stop the shah's own decision. However, he was even more surprised when the shah personally rang and told him to go to the palace at twelve noon instead of 1.30 p.m.

At the palace, Mosaddeq found the shah's conduct strange and disorganised. There was neither lunch nor the full official ceremony with the cabinet, all of whom were present. Then a delegation from the Majlis arrived to try to dissuade the shah but he turned down their request. Meanwhile, Mosaddeq noted the arrival of Ayatollah Behbahani and another cleric on a similar mission. Kashani wrote two letters to the shah and issued two public statements. He wrote in one of the statements:

People, be warned! Treacherous decisions have resulted in the intention of our beloved and democratic [*demokrat*] shah to leave the country … You should realise that if the shah goes whatever we have will go with him. Rise up and stop him and make him change his mind. Because today our existence and independence depend on the very person of his majesty Mohammad Reza Shah Pahlavi and no one else.[62]

Baqa'i was also very active that day, and both his and Kashani's toughs had been sent to join the mob gathered outside the palace ostensibly to stop the shah from leaving the country. Other anti-Mosaddeq groups and parties – including the Retired Officers Centre, and the Zolfaqar, SOMKA and Arya 'parties' – also sent their troops to join the crowd outside the palace.

While still at the palace, Mosaddeq received a phone call from his office (which was in his own residence) saying that the American ambassador wished to see him urgently. Having nothing else to do he decided to leave the palace but when he got near the main gate he heard the noise of the mob outside and slogans against him. Then by chance he came across a member of the court staff who opened the palace back door for him. His car pulled up, and the minute the mob was alerted it began to run after it since Mosaddeq's house was nearby. By the time they got there Mosaddeq was inside, but they circled his home shouting 'death to Mosaddeq'. The notorious mobster Sha'ban the Brainless, accompanied by an army colonel, drove into the iron gates of his house in his jeep.

Maleki heard the news while he was teaching at school. He telephoned Al-e Ahmad at his school and urged him to gather the party activists and lead them to Mosaddeq's defence. They arrived just as the mob was attacking his home and attacked them from the rear. A street battle ensued and they put the mob to flight. On 29 February one of the long headlines of *Niruy-e Sevvom* ran as follows:

> Sha'ban the Brainless attacked Mosaddeq's home to massacre his family. In front of Mosaddeq's house the cries of abuse and invective by Colonel Rahimi and the knife-wielders were reaching sky-high. The defenceless young people by shedding their own blood put the knifemen to flight.

In time Mosaddeq heard about this and invited Maleki and thirty Third Force party activists one afternoon for tea. Some photos were also taken with the two leaders standing in the middle to commemorate the event.

THE MURDER OF AFSHARTUS

On 21 April 1953 Afshartus, the chief prefect of the police which then included the civilian intelligence departments, was kidnapped and later murdered. He was first lured to a private meeting at the house of Hossein Khatibi, a close associate of Baqa'i, where he was kidnapped and taken to a cave in the north-west of Tehran.[63] The accused were Khatibi, Baqa'i, four brigadiers, one major and a couple of NCOs and civilians. Afshartus's visit to Khatibi's house was part of his effort to bring Mosaddeq and Kashani together with Baqa'i's help, although Baqa'i was not present when he was kidnapped. General Zahedi was suspected of having been involved but Ayatollah Kashani, who was still Majlis speaker, welcomed him to take *bast* – as his 'dear guest' – in the Majlis to avoid arrest.[64]

Within days the plot was uncovered, but before the brigadiers were arrested one of them on Baqa'i's suggestion was sent to arrange the murder of Afshartus, so the star witness would not be found alive. After their arrest, all the generals confessed to the above accusations, but the one who had arranged the police chief's murder denied it, although he too confessed to the rest of the story. All the confessions were written and signed in their own hands. There were no complaints of mistreatment, only the brigadier who was accused of murder saying that his treatment had not been consistent with his status.

Baqa'i could not be arrested due to his parliamentary immunity, and he did not miss the opportunity to accuse the government of having tortured the accused, whereas they themselves did not make such a claim. The idea had been to kidnap a number of government leaders and politicians to force Mosaddeq to resign. Baqa'i was arrested two days before the final coup in August, since he was no longer a deputy. While *Niru-ye Sevvom* was constantly warning that procrastination in punishing the culprits would mean repetition of the same events,[65] the legal process was observed so well that the dossier was not yet complete when the government fell four months later. There was a sham trial after the coup where all the defendants were cleared of the charges, and no further effort was made to bring the 'real' perpetrators to justice. Baqa'i never told his side of the story, not even in his long interview with the Harvard University Iranian Oral History of Iran Project, despite being asked to.

The above account is largely based on the published documents, including the manuscripts, of the confessions.[66]

One more point. There had been precedents for basts in the Majlis to protest or be protected from a mob. But Zahedi's *bast* was most peculiar, because he was accused of murder, and the murder of the police chief at that. He was not only immune while in the Majlis but he was receiving visitors daily who would discuss the conspiracy plans with him. For example, one of his confidants who had had a long conversation with him inside the Majlis about his plans to topple the government presented a full report of their conversation to the American amnbassador Henderson the day after. Zahedi had even emphasised that 'sooner or later America will have to take action with the Shah because Iranians cannot save themselves'.[67]

However, in the run-up to the public demonstrations on the anniversary of the 21 July uprising, Zahedi was allowed to leave the Majlis and go into hiding for fear of the demonstrators breaking into the Majlis. It is not clear why he was not arrested and put in jail. Here is another example of the reasons behind Maleki's insistence on the implementation of the law.

THE REFERENDUM

Mosaddeq's decision to dissolve the Majlis was a grave mistake, prompted by a miscalculation. A slender Majlis majority had appointed Makki – now a leading member of the opposition – to the watchdog committee for issuing notes at Bank Melli (then the central bank) of Iran. Mosaddeq became anxious that Makki might reveal the fact that notes had been issued on his order confidentially, though with his delegated powers this was not illegal. But he was afraid of a row breaking out and shaking the already ailing economy as well as embarrassing the government for having kept it secret.[68]

Then came a motion of censure by Ali Zohari on Baqa'i's allegations of the torture of the suspects in the murder of Afshartus. Mosaddeq suspected that the same slender majority that had voted for Makki's appointment would vote for Zohari's motion and he would be overthrown by seemingly legal means. In fact, Mosaddeq commanded the absolute majority of the Majlis; and there was no comparison between the two cases, witnessed by the fact that once he decided to hold a referendum two-thirds of the deputies resigned voluntarily on his recommendation so that the Majlis lost its quorum.[69]

Many of his advisers, notably Sadiqi, Maleki, Sanjabi and Mo'azzami opposed his decision but to no avail. Sanjabi related that, after they had talked to Mosaddeq separately, Maleki suggested to him that they and Dariush Foruhar go to see Mosaddeq, this time as representatives of the Popular Movement parties.[70] According to Sanjabi, Maleki was the main speaker but when he failed to change Mosaddeq's mind he came out with these prophetic words: 'The path that you are treading will end up in Hell. But nonetheless we will accompany you to it.'[71] However, the decision was supported in the pages of *Niru-ye Sevvom*.[72]

As noted, two-thirds of the Majlis deputies voluntarily resigned, leaving it without a quorum, proving that Mosaddeq's anxiety that the Majlis would vote for Zohari's censure motion was unfounded. It was then quite unnecessary to hold a referendum since, given that the Majlis could not function with the twenty-eight remaining deputies, it should have been dissolved and preparations made for fresh elections. The opposition, including Baqa'i, Kashani, Behbahani, etc., had a field day declaring the decision illegal as well as forbidden by the Sharia. In fact, the decision was not illegal for there was nothing in the constitution or the Sharia that would forbid the closure of the Majlis by referendum followed by fresh elections.

The referendum was held in – to put it mildly – questionable circumstances. The rural areas were excluded in order to avoid the long process of counting their votes twice – once for the referendum, a second time for the new elections.[73] Also, the polling stations for 'yes' and 'no' votes were separated which did not reflect well on a democratic government. The result was a huge 'yes' vote, and the government issued the dissolution order. But before it received royal assent, 'the royalist coup' (in Anthony Eden's words) of 15–16 August was set in motion thirteen days after the polling.

Towards the end of June 1953, the kiln (brickmaking) workers of Tehran went on strike for better pay and conditions. The Third Force went on their knees to the ministry of labour to support them but the ministry insisted that the strike should be broken. However, a few days later, for some unknown reasons, they accepted the intervention of the Tudeh party and the kiln workers succeeded. As a result, 20,000 kiln workers joined the demonstration organised by the Tudeh for the anniversary of 21 July. The Third Force were indignant about the behaviour of the ministry of labour, but in the 3 July issue of *Niru-ye Sevvom* they congratulated the kiln workers on their victory.

6

THE 1953 COUP AND AFTER

THE COUP

The history of the *coup d'état* of 19 August 1953 has been written about at length and in much detail in numerous books and articles.[1] After the 21 July 1952 uprising when the British efforts at the constitutional removal of Mosaddeq had proved futile, they began to think of a military coup and to make contact with Zahedi and his circle. As noted in Chapter 4, an early plot was uncovered in October which implicated Zahedi, Hejazi, the Rashidiyans and the British embassy, and Iran broke off diplomatic relations with Britain.

In November, towards the end of Harry Truman's presidency, MI6 agents met with their counterparts in the CIA and tentatively decided on a military coup and began to make contact with Zahedi and other potential plotters.[2] In January 1953 President Eisenhower took office with the Dulles brothers running the State Department and the CIA. This was a conservative government at the peak of the Cold War, while the Tudeh behaviour in Iran was daily adding to American fears that Iran would go communist.[3] The American anxiety about the role of the Tudeh and fear that they might take over from Mosaddeq can be extensively observed in the set of documents most recently released by the American government.[4]

After Iran's rejection of the Henderson proposal for the settlement of the oil crisis, both Britain and the US declared that they would no longer pursue the matter with Mosaddeq's government.[5] The shah was also in contact with the American embassy, encouraging them not to reopen the dialogue with Mosaddeq, insisting that the oil issue must be settled after the latter's fall.[6] Therefore, America, backed by Britain, made a firm and final decision to overthrow Mosaddeq's government by force. Baqa'i, Hayerizadeh and some other former Popular Movement deputies were involved in this.

The shah had sent word to the American embassy that they should listen to Zahedi and Baqa'i and no one else.[7] Kashani is also likely to have known about the planned coup, at least through Baqa'i. The Americans have said that Ahmad Aramesh received $10,000 from them to give to Kashani for expenses, but it is not certain that Aramesh had told them the truth.[8] Meanwhile, America was implementing a vile press campaign against Mosaddeq through their agents in Iran. Rumours of an imminent coup were rife in Tehran.[9] The Tudeh was repeatedly issuing the slogan: 'We shall turn the *coup d'état* into a counter *coup d'état*.' The rumours were echoed in a lead article of *Niru-yr Sevvom* (weekly) on 13 August:

> the suspicious activities in Tehran of foreign agents during the past two weeks together with their internal counterparts show that a secret organisation is hopelessly working against Dr Mosaddeq's government, and the American and British imperialists have not yet lost faith in the use of their last card [i.e. Zahedi].

Various plans had been envisaged but the referendum to close the Majlis played right into the hands of the putschists. In the absence of the Majlis they managed to convince the shah to sack Mosaddeq and appoint Zahedi to the premiership. The shah was afraid of failure, especially as he suspected a British plot against himself. But in the end he relented. The move was made at 1 a.m. on 16 August. While the shah was waiting for news in a Caspian hunting lodge, the commander of the royal guards in the midst of a secret military operation presented the shah's notice of dismissal to Mosaddeq. Hossein Fatemi, the foreign minister, and a couple of other government leaders had already been arrested, but General Riyahi, the chief of staff, had given them the slip. However, news of the coup had leaked the day before and the government was ready for them. The coup failed and the shah, having heard, fled to Baghdad and thence Rome, and Zahedi hid in an American house close to the American embassy.[10]

Once the coup attempt was announced thousands of people gathered in the parliament square addressed by several Popular Movement leaders, one of whom, Fatemi, harshly attacked the shah and his court. Shaigan, Razavi and others were also somewhat scathing, but 'Maleki spoke moderately and said nothing except urging support for Mosaddeq'.[11] Riots broke out with harsh slogans against the shah – 'The shah is on the run / He is fleeing on a cart'[12] – followed by the attacking and looting of shops in the central parts of the city. The Tudeh were very active in the riots, but so were the black crowds that the CIA and MI6 agents had organised to swell the Tudeh ranks and help create panic among the people.[13]

Mosaddeq received the news that the Tudeh planned to tear down Reza Shah's statues. As he was later to tell his interrogator, General Hossein Azmudeh, he reasoned with himself that if he stopped it the people would be upset because they disliked Reza Shah, and, if he did not, they would be accused of giving free rein to the Tudeh.[14] So he decided to ask the Popular Movement to do it themselves, though inevitably the Tudeh got involved as well. Karim Sanjabi writes in his memoirs that Mosaddeq told him to 'go and talk to the parties and bring down the statues':

> I went to the Iran party and telephoned Mr Khalil Maleki who came along. I also telephoned [the other Popular Movement parties] and some bazaaris who also came along and we sent a group to carry that out ... In fairness I must say that Khalil Maleki said this action is not right ...[15]

The Tudeh issued the slogan of 'democratic republic', and the Third Force demanded a republic, though not a 'democratic' one. The practical activities of the Third Force had fallen into the hands of two of its leading figures, Mohammad Ali Khonji and Mas'ud Hejazi, who claimed immediately after the coup that Maleki was a traitor for a number of reasons, and especially because he had opposed the referendum. Predicting the likely outcome sooner or later, Maleki was neither jubilant nor demanded a republic.[16]

The rioting got even worse the next day, 18 August. Mosaddeq decided to act the following day, so he advised the Popular Movement parties, by phoning their leaders, including Maleki, personally to tell them to keep their members indoors.[17] However, the CIA and MI6 agents who had been busy reinforcing the Tudeh and other riots turned the tide and, by renting crowds led by such notorious thugs and racketeers as Teyyeb Hajj Reza'i and Hossein Ramezan Yakhi, who normally listened to Ayatollah Behbahani, mobilised a mob against Mosaddeq. All the small groups hostile to Mosaddeq – Baqa'i's Zahmatkeshan,

Qanat-Abadi's Mosalmanan-e Mojahed, the Nazi group SOMKA, etc. – also joined the mob that attacked Mosaddeq's house.[18]

Parts of the army as well as the police went to their support, and the radio station fell into their hands in the afternoon, from which a number of Mosaddeq's enemies, including Seyyed Mostafa Kashani (the Ayatollah's son) and Qanat-Abadi, made jubilant speeches. Mosaddeq's guards defended his home to the last bullet, and he was persuaded by those of his friends present in his room to climb over the wall and hide in a neighbour's house; he surrendered to Zahedi the next day, 20 August. Mosaddeq's home was ransacked, looted and left in ruins.[19] It was visited the very following day by Zahedi, Kashani and Baqa'i.[20]

The Tudeh party with their famous slogan that they would turn the *coup d'état* into a counter *coup d'état* simply took no action on 19 August or in the following days and weeks. Kiyanuri claims that he had telephoned Mosaddeq directly twice on 19 August via his wife Maryam Firuz who, he says, was an acquaintance of Mosaddeq's wife; and that the second time Mosaddeq had told him that he was 'alone, alone', and that they were free to do whatever they saw fit.[21] However, Nosratollah Khazeni, Mosaddeq's chief of staff, who was present at his house, maintains that Mosaddeq's wife had left for Shemiran early in the morning.[22] Later, Kiyanuri claimed that they had sent a delegation to see Mosaddeq at midday, but Khazeni rejects this as a figment of the imagination: 'The imagined delegation of Kiyanuri would first have had to come to my office ...'[23] However, even assuming that Mosaddeq had told Kiyanuri to do whatever they thought fit, no action was taken that day. Indeed, no action was taken even in the days, weeks and months that followed until Zahedi's regime destroyed their civilian as well as secret military organisations piece by piece. However, according to Amir Khosravi, tens of thousands of its civilian members had been ready to receive orders to swarm onto the streets on 19 August, not to mention their military organisation.[24]

MALEKI IN JAIL

In the early morning of 20 August Maleki went into hiding. All night in his hideout he could not sleep, pacing up and down, first feeling suicidal then dreaming of a sudden overnight uprising which would topple the leaders of the coup. On the radio they were constantly announcing the names of the people, including Maleki, whom the Martial Law Administration office wanted to surrender.

However, before the night was out Maleki had regained his composure and the first thing he did was to issue a long statement analysing the situation. This was typical of the man: no other Popular Movement leader or party ever did such a thing. He always believed that political leaders should take responsibility and, in all circumstances, discuss the political situation above all for the benefit of their followers. Contrary to expectations, Maleki's view of the situation was not pessimistic: immediately after the coup and for quite some time the regime was not as well settled in the seat of power as it would become three or four years later, and so it was not too optimistic to hope that the Movement could continue.

He believed that the Popular Movement had been visited with a major failure, but this should not cause its supporters to despair, and they should continue the struggle even in those difficult circumstances. He denounced the coup-makers, the foreign powers as well as the Tudeh party and wrote that, despite them all, it was possible to struggle for independence and progress. 'A resistance movement must be created from the heritage of the

Popular Movement. It must not be imagined that those who have replaced Dr Mosaddeq can do whatever they wish ... and if a rational and well-directed resistance movement comes into being, it is quite possible even in the darkest moment, to protect a large part of the Popular Movement's achievements and prepare it better for the near future'. However, he pointed out:

> In the present circumstances we can achieve the revolutionary aims of the Popular Movement and even the domestic reforms within the regime of constitutional monarchy by means of peaceful political, social and, at the same time, serious and decisive methods ... By peaceful methods we do not mean collaborationism, but the same way as we repossessed our oil industry from Britain without war and bloodshed. The same method could be used in other situations as well.[25]

Two weeks later Maleki delivered himself into the hands of the Martial Law Administrator and within days he was dispatched to Falk-al-Aflak, the medieval prison citadel in south-west Iran. Here most of his fellow inmates were Tudeh members and he believed that this had been done deliberately in order to subject him to constant psychological torture. He did not mind the presence of a few secondary, corrupt Tudeh leaders such as Mahmud Zhandi, chief editor of *Besu-ye Ayandeh*, whom he knew did not believe a word of the Tudeh accusations against him. Indeed, a Popular Movement deputy who was something of a poet and also an inmate uttered the following verse: 'Zhandi watch the Wheel of Destiny / Which has put you next to Khalil Maleki'.[26]

Maleki's mental torture was due to the fact that he knew all the ordinary members of the Tudeh party in that jail had no doubt that he was the vilest possible traitor and, as told by their leaders, was there only to spy on them. Maleki seldom stopped referring to this mental torture, and years later he wrote in an open letter addressed to the political establishment: 'You sent me all on my own with a large number of civilian and military Tudeh members to Falak al-Aflak prison, and made me taste the worse mental torture which is an invention of modern times and cannot be imagined by those who have not experienced it.'[27] He also wrote in his long letter of 20 February 1963 to Mosaddeq:

> What was waiting for me in Falak al-Aflak was a novel mental torture that has no precedent in history and is an invention of the twentieth century. There, I was caught in an environment full of spite and hatred. To be all on one's own among a group who had been his comrades-in-arms and now see him as an enemy and traitor is an insufferable torture that only those who have experienced it would appreciate its devastating effect.[28]

As things turned out later, they could have gone further than mere infliction of mental torture. Mehrdad Bahar, the twenty-four-year-old son of the famous poet laureate, who had been a member of the Tudeh youth central committee, was also an inmate in that citadel, thought that Maleki was the worst traitor to the cause of Iranian people. Sometime after his release, however, he began to doubt his old beliefs and especially his faith in Tudeh leaders. He decided to go and see Maleki and apologise for the doubts that he had had about him. He then told him about the Tudeh plot in Falak al-Aflak to murder him. This Maleki spoke of several times, but he documented it in his letter to Mosaddeq:

Years after I was released from prison, the son of the late Poet-Laureate Bahar – who was a prominent Tudeh member in Falak al-Aflak – turned away from that party and was coming to see me every week. He told me that his party comrades had drawn up the plan of my murder in the following way: Khosrow Qashqa'i was due to rise and capture Khorramabad [the town where the citadel is located]. At the same time, the Tudeh officers who were in a section of Falak al-Aflak would rise and take control of the prison. A three-man committee would then try and execute me there and then before the arrival of the Qashqa'is.[29]

About a year later Maleki, who had been held without trial, was transferred to a temporary police jail in Tehran, a sign that he would be released fairly soon. Maleki was accustomed to prisons and knew how to survive in them, except his last jail when the system had taken a turn for the worst. That, however, was years away and as he once wrote: 'I have got used to torture, and in jail I feel as if I am at home.'[30] Jalal Al-e Ahmad, who was regularly visiting Maleki in the police prison, related how Nima Yushij, the leading pioneer of modernist Persian poetry as well as his close friend and neighbour, was once arrested on some nonsensical political suspicions and taken to the police prison. Nima was not a political activist and seldom left home so Al-e Ahmad rightly believed that he would find prison insufferable. He visited Maleki in jail and asked him to take good care of Nima whom, in any case, Maleki had met before. Maleki had looked after Nima so well that when they released him a couple of months later he had said to Jalal 'What a banquet it was; as if I had been taken to a sanatorium'![31]

REBELLION IN THE THIRD FORCE

Maleki was highly principled but he was also a realist. As noted, before the coup he was worried about the consequences of the Tudeh show of force on the anniversary of the July uprising, and the referendum. Even in his speech in the parliament square on the day of the first coup's failure he had spoken moderately. Some of his comrades in the party were restless and expected more radical talk and action. He also had a couple of enemies in the party – notably Mohammad Ali Khonji and Mas'ud Hejazi – who bore him personal grudges. The interaction of these events in the last few days of Mosaddeq's government led to the small but noisy party opposition taking matters into their own hands, especially as Maleki was not prepared to behave too radically. One consequence, for example, was that not only did the Third Force issue the slogan in favour of a republic, but the headline of Khonji's lead article in *Niru-ye Sevvom* on 17 August read: 'So much for the turn of the court and the traitor Mohammad Reza Shah. The traitor Mohammad Reza Shah must be tried and punished.'

And just after the success of the second coup, Maleki's responsible statement mentioned above added fuel to their fire, especially as he recommended open and constitutional opposition. Eleven activists led by Khonji and Hejazi declared Maleki a traitor and added a few trumped-up charges from the more distant past. And while Maleki was in the prison citadel in Khorramabad, they began to campaign for Maleki's expulsion from the party. Although the party headquarters had been ransacked and set on fire on 19 August, the party cells were regularly meeting in private homes. The bulk of the party activists put up a fight against the claims of the rebels. They even begged them to lead the party until Maleki was released from prison, so that he would have a right of defence. But Khonji and Hejazi and their nine followers were adamant that Maleki must be expelled without delay. Caught in this tragi-comical situation, little was left of the party members within less than a year.[32]

Maleki received the bitter news in prison from Gholamhossein Golesorkhi, a party activist who had recently been arrested for his activities. We noted Maleki's descriptions of his mental torture in the midst of Tudeh members in Falak al-Aflak. It is not difficult to imagine how he must have felt on hearing this, a blow to his hopes and ideals. Yet he did not give up and, shortly after he was released from jail, a couple of meetings were held at Zia Sedqi's home for him to listen and respond to his accusers. According to Sedqi, Hossein Malek and Abdollah Borhan, these quickly deteriorated into sinister personal attacks on Maleki and became a fruitless exercise. Khonji had even told Maleki and Malek that they had been bribed. Subsequently, the new central committee issued a statement and expelled the eleven rebels from the party.[33] But by this time both the political circumstances and the Khonji–Hejazi campaigns had had their demoralising effect and the party was reduced to a large circle of faithful intellectuals.

Maleki himself was convinced that the Khonji–Hejazi campaign had been encouraged if not organised by General Farhad Dadsetan (head of the regime's internal security at the time) in order to destroy the Third Force party from within, and he cited a published statement by Dadsetan implying this.[34] It is virtually certain, however, that Khonji could not have known about any plot and was motivated by the psychological problems from which he suffered most of his life.

Meanwhile, Mosaddeq had been put on military trial and sentenced to three years' solitary confinement on the charge of having rebelled against the constitution between 16 and 19 August by ignoring the shah's dismissal notice, though he turned the table on his accusers and placed the prosecutor in the dock, which made him immensely popular. A number of Popular Movement deputies and ministers were also arrested, tried and given various jail sentences. Hossein Fatemi held out in hiding for a few months but was discovered by chance. He was first attacked by knife-wielding thugs led by Sha'ban the Brainless, but people intervened and he ended up in hospital. He was then put on secret military trial, sentenced to death and sent to the firing squad on a stretcher.

The secret cells of the Tudeh party, which was not quite a legal party even before the coup, were meeting regularly. Many of its ordinary members were arrested but most of them were released after signing a recantation statement in the press. The regime was, however, bent on destroying the party: first they arrested many of its activists and cadres as well as a couple of its leaders, then they uncovered their secret military network, arresting up to 600 officers and NCOs, executing more than twenty of them and sentencing most of the others to various jail terms. They also discovered their arms depots and secret printing press. And all this time the party did not lift a finger to defend itself, while its cells were being promised action from one week to the next.

Hamid Enayat, then a leading young Tudeh member, told how once the dealership was put under pressure to take action. The leadership sent word that early one morning before seven o'clock they should gather in the Kakh (now Felestin) Circus, which was then at the northernmost part of Tehran and remained only half built. They were to shout 'Death to the Shah' three times and then scatter. A couple of hundred of them went along. There wasn't another soul in the Circus. They shouted the slogan and began to run away. Not a single person chased them; only a few windows of the apartments were opened, their residents looking down upon them rubbing their eyes.[35] However, in one of its last issues, *Mardom* welcomed the Soviet invitation to the shah, describing it as necessary for the cause of peace.[36]

A few months after the coup the Tudeh central committee had secretly circulated a pamphlet entitled *Darbareh-ye 28 Mordad* (On the 19th of August) in response to rising criticism of their leadership by party members. Maleki had seen a copy of this and written a long response to it (now in 275 printed pages) which was found and published together with the Tudeh pamphlet in 2015 (in an eighty-seven-page appendix).[37] There is no scope here for a full-length description and analysis of these works, especially as the Tudeh party later significantly changed its analysis of the coup and its own policy under Mosaddeq. Very briefly, the Tudeh takes very little blame for its actions and inactions while putting virtually all the blame for the Movement's failure squarely on Mosaddeq's 'compromising attitude' towards the shah and American imperialism, encouraged by 'the reactionary wing of the National Front, such as the reactionary leadership of the Third Force (Maleki's cabal)'.[38] Maleki, on the other hand, is critical of Mosaddeq's lack of proper enforcement of the law against illegal activities of the right and the Tudeh party. He also criticises the government for ignoring the Third Forces' 'pleas' for setting up Popular Movement committees for its own safeguarding long before the coup. However, he defends Mosaddeq against the Tudeh's attacks and, among other things, he attacks the Tudeh for trying, and to some extent succeeding, to divert the Movement from its struggle against the British oil company towards a confrontation with America and frightening America into the belief that Iran would soon fall into the Soviets' lap; for its radicalisation of the political atmosphere, and its campaign against any possible solution to the oil dispute.[39]

A semi-clandestine organisation, the National Resistance Movement (NRM) (*Nehzat-e Moqavemat-e Melli*) was beginning to take shape shortly after the coup. The initiative came from the brothers Ayatollahs Reza and Abolfazl Zanjani, Mehdi Bazargan, Seyyed Mahmud (later Ayatollah) Taleqani and a few others, mainly from the religious wing of the Popular Movement. The Third Force joined them in Maleki's absence in jail, but they withdrew after his release and the expulsion of Khonji and Hejazi since they had been representing the party in the NRM in the interim. Others such as the Iran party the People of Iran party, and the party of Iranian People also joined more slowly, and for about a year the Movement managed to organise occasional small street demonstrations, and for a longer period circulated a small clandestine leaflet called *Rah-e Mosaddeq* (The Line of Mosaddeq), but on the whole it did not manage to make a significant political impact. Within a couple of years only its religious wing remained and that was not very active.

The University of Tehran and Alborz High School had been restless since the beginning of the academic year 1953–4, and armed troops were stationed in both. On 7 December, the day of Vice President Nixon's visit to Tehran, there was a spontaneous demonstration by a group of university students shouting slogans against the regime. The troops were under orders to shoot, not only to teach them a lesson in general, but also to forestall a repetition of the event while Nixon was still in Tehran. Three students were shot dead in a corridor of the Faculty of Technology. One of them (Bozorgniya) was a Tudeh member, another (Qandchi) was a Third Force member and the third (Shari'at-e Razavi) was a Popular Movement supporter who did not belong to any party.

MALEKI AND THE CONSORTIUM

When Mosaddeq fell the Majlis had not yet been dissolved because the dissolution notice had not yet received royal assent. Apart from that, the new regime had declared the referendum unconstitutional. That meant that the seventeenth Majlis was still in business, but if the regime had acknowledged that fact, then it would have had to face a Majlis, two-thirds of which had displayed their support for Mosaddeq by voluntarily resigning, including the Popular Movement deputies, most of whom were in jail. Therefore, in 1954, they decided to hold fresh elections for the eighteenth Majlis.

The Popular Movement was not allowed to publish a list of candidates. But their supporters would have known who to vote for despite the fact that a full list had not been circulated, even through unauthorised leaflets. In any event the votes cast for the Popular Movement candidates were not counted. Landlords or their candidates were returned from their estates as was the case in the fourteenth to sixteenth (and, less so, seventeenth) Majlis. For the larger towns and cities an official list of deputies was concocted, although some of them were not quite the kind of 'yes men' who were later to occupy the Majlis seats, especially from 1963 onwards. They even included a few independent deputies such as Mohammad Derakhshesh – leader of the country's Teachers' Association – who were to cause a few headaches for the regime in that parliamentary session.

The new regime's greatest test of strength was when Ali Amini, then minister of finance, submitted the Consortium Oil Agreement Bill for parliamentary approval. It meant the grant of another concession to foreign companies, which was precisely what the oil nationalisation had been intended to avoid. Apart from that, the terms of the concession were worse for Iran than

Stokes's initial proposal of August 1951. There was resistance both inside and outside the Majlis. Maleki talked to Derakhshesh, whom he had known for many years, and convinced him to deliver a speech against the bill. As he was to write to Mosaddeq years later:

> When the Consortium Oil Agreement was proposed, apart from other secret publications, another secret publication in stencilled form was issued, a copy of which is enclosed. In addition to secret publications, we thought it was necessary to find a tribune in the improperly established Majlis to let the world hear the voice of the Iranian people. Mr Derakhshesh was especially suited for this task. In the past, we had had some contacts with him [through the Teachers' Association] and while there were some disagreements between us we nevertheless helped him up to a point. At any rate we talked to Mr Derakhshesh and he too declared his opposition to the Consortium Agreement, and [he gave the technical material which he had received from other sources] to me to write his speech for him. A copy of this [very long] speech is enclosed.[40]

The NRM also published two long clandestine statements against the bill which in the circumstances were not widely circulated.[41] At the same time, a letter of protest addressed to the Majlis deputies and senators, signed by Saleh, Maleki, Zanjani, Mo'azzami, Shapour Bakhtiar and Mehdi Bazargan among others was circulated. It emphasised the history of NIOC's interference in Iran's internal affairs, argued that the new oil agreement would once again compromise the country's 'freedom and independence' and pointed out that it violated the Nationalisation Act. It went unacknowledged and was not reported by the media. The regime reacted by dismissing twelve distinguished university professors who had put their signatures to the document.

NABARD-E ZENDEGI AND THE PROPOSAL FOR A SOCIALIST LEAGUE

The decade following the 1953 coup was a dictatorship comparable to the decade that had followed Reza Khan's coup in 1921. The coup did not quickly result in personal and arbitrary rule, although within a couple of years – certainly after his dismissal of Zahedi in April 1955 – the shah became by far the most powerful player in the country. Apart from its foreign sponsors, the coup had been the product of a coalition of social and political forces. Therefore, all of the shah's allies shared the power – although at a decreasing rate – until the White Revolution of January 1963 when the shah inaugurated his final phase, the period of absolute and arbitrary rule (*estebdad*). Three phases may be distinguished in that decade: 1953–5 was the period of consolidation of power and elimination of both the Popular Movement and the Tudeh party from politics; 1955–60 saw the concentration of power and a rising economic boom which ended up in bust. This was followed by economic depression and power struggles between 1960 and 1963.

Before the conclusion of the consortium agreement and consequent lifting of the British oil boycott, substantial amounts of American aid were provided to keep Zahedi's government afloat. US aid continued throughout the 1950s even after earnings from oil were restored. In his first move to consolidate his own power, the shah dismissed Zahedi in April 1955, and all but in appearance sent him into exile to his villa in Switzerland where he died in the 1960s. He appointed the mild, meek and loyal court minister Hossein Ala to the premiership, his government lasting for a year until Manuchehr Eqbal replaced him. Eqbal was not just loyal but totally submissive to the shah to the extent that he once described himself as the shah's 'house-born slave'. His government lasted until August 1960 when an economic and political crisis had made it necessary to find major scapegoats.

The religious establishment had been behind the new regime as it had played a significant role in the coup and its legitimisation. Kashani, who had supported the new regime at first, fell out with it largely over its restoration of diplomatic relations with Britain and the consortium agreement. But the religious establishment remained quiet until the revolt of 1963, although it had already begun to become increasingly less happy about the situation from the late 1950s.

Iran dropped its policy of neutrality and non-alliance. In 1955, with strong American support, it joined a military pact with Britain, Turkey, Iraq and Pakistan, initially described as the Baghdad Pact, later the Central Treaty Organization (CENTO), after the 1958 coup in Iraq when that country left the pact. The flow of American military grants and advisers helped expand and reorganise the Iranian army. In 1957, the CIA sent a five-man advisory group to Tehran who, in the course of the next four years, helped organise and train an internal security organisation that became known as SAVAK. The principal function of this organisation – which in time became large and notorious – was to identify, control and persecute political opposition of any kind. In the mid-sixties and seventies, SAVAK extended its functions to the suppression of any and all dissident views, however mild, unorganised and even loyal. It also assumed a counter-intelligence role, although the army intelligence and counter-intelligence went on existing as parallel organisations focusing on the military side.

Before all that, when it had been much easier to conduct peaceful social activity in a quiet way, Maleki persuaded a young eighteenth Majlis deputy to obtain a licence to publish a serious monthly journal. Mahmud Afshar was the permit holder as well as nominal editor, and Maleki edited and published the journal virtually without there being a note of his name even above the lead articles, most of which he wrote himself. That is how *Nabard-e Zendegi* (Battle of Life) came into being. Maleki had first proposed the title *Elm o Zendegi* (Science and Life), which he had published up to the coup, but the authorities had turned that down without being aware that Maleki was behind the new journal. It was first published in February 1955, but after the tenth issue it was banned and Afshar blamed his lack of 'election' to the next Majlis on his association with that journal. Sometime later, the authorities agreed to tolerate the occasional publication of *Elm o Zendegi* (now thinking that the title Battle of Life was too radical) as a book, not a journal, although 'the book' was made up of articles written by different people.

Nabard-e Zendegi was a theoretical-cum-intellectual journal quite similar to *Elm o Zendegi* but with a slightly more cautious approach. Its articles were written by experts in their own fields, including university professors of a reformist bent, but the central role was played by Maleki who normally had more than one (unsigned) article in every issue, though he did not take responsibility for the signed articles. Inevitably, this was a journal addressed to the elite, including the Popular Movement leaders, assuming any number of them would care to read it at all. The articles were on history, sociology, science and scientists, socialism and democracy, economy and society, international affairs, poetry, book reviews, etc.

Maleki was particularly keen to try and prepare the ground for when it would once again become possible to get involved in active politics. He believed that the Popular Front leaders and activists must be ready to enter active politics the minute it becomes possible, and he went on repeating that such an opportunity would arise in the not too distant future. For Maleki readiness meant having a plan and a programme for running the country and carrying out major social reforms. It also meant a well-organised movement with a strong and effective leadership. Putting aside oil nationalisation and Mosaddeq, there never was and never became a time when such a programme and leadership were created. At any rate, almost all Popular Movement leaders believed that such an opportunity would not arise.

Nonetheless, Maleki drafted and published a proposal for the formation of the Socialist League of Iran in the tenth and final issue of *Nabard-e Zendegi*:

> In the ninth issue [of this journal] we promised to put forward our specific suggestions about what is to be done in the present circumstances. Perhaps for some reasons the time is not quite right for putting forward this proposal. But because the publication of this journal may be postponed for some time we decided to spell out a part of what must be said, and present to our readers a practical proposal at the end of a thousand pages of general material which we have published in these ten issues.[42]

There was need for a doctrine and an organisation, wrote Maleki, but there was a subjective and an objective barrier against them. The subjective obstacle for those who should potentially take part in this venture was that they were 'tired of party-mongering'. The objective obstacle was that, for reasons that need not be spelled out, the regime was frightened of parties and gatherings. But they could both be overcome once it was understood that politics was not just shouting slogans and arousing people without bearing their interests in mind, but was the art of organising and running society.

The League would have a merciless struggle against the corrupt wing of the regime but would tolerate the uncorrupt members of the establishment and cooperate with them in their fight against corruption. However, the opposition of the League against specific administrations would not be extra-constitutional. The League would want to achieve revolutionary ends by peaceful means. The League would not enter a coalition with communists since history has shown that such coalitions would lead to hegemony and takeover by communists. The League would regard as essential a scientific struggle against the ideology of communism so that young people would be attracted to democratic socialism instead.

Although opposed to communism, the League would try to establish friendly relations with the Soviet Union and the Eastern bloc, especially in view of Khrushchev's recent speech against Stalin and Stalinism in the twentieth congress of CPSU. The League would maintain independence from both blocs and would struggle against imperialism by peaceful means as was done in India and Egypt, though in the case of Iran it did not end well.

The League's ultimate aim was to arrive at democratic socialism, but this did not mean that all its members and associates need be socialist. The League's priority would be to carry out fundamental reforms such as a land reform – for which a fairly detailed draft outline was offered – women's rights and the fight against corruption. The country lacked sufficient capital for industrial development. Therefore, foreign aid and capital had to be attracted for industrial investment while care was taken that it would not compromise the country's independence. Other objectives such as a planned economy, redistributive tax reform, constitutional and democratic government and a welfare state were also which are detailed in the manifesto.⁴³

It is necessary to emphasise that up to 1963, when absolute and arbitrary rule was established, the Iranian regime resembled a European dictatorship based on a large political establishment which did include uncorrupt and reform-minded members such as Ali Amini and Abolhasan Ebtehaj. And the time would come when Maleki would advise the Popular Movement forces to tolerate Amini's government, though to no avail (see Chapter 7).

At any rate, following the publication of the proposal, Maleki and a group of like-minded people contacted Allahyar Saleh (de facto leader of the Iran party), Abdollah Mo'azzami (former Majlis speaker under Mosaddeq) and Shams al-Din Amir-Ala'i (former minister under Mosaddeq) to discuss the proposal, and managed to attract them to the idea. However, after a few meetings Saleh told Maleki that his 'Iran party friends' were opposed to it. In the end, Maleki suggested 'the minimum' to Saleh, namely that some kind of preparation be made for when the opportunity arises:

I suggested the minimum to Mr Saleh, saying that there would definitely be an opportunity [for political activity] in the future and that – during the then period of enforced inactivity – it was the duty of the [Popular Movement] leaders to study the various issues and problems so as to be ready to seize the opportunity when it comes. I then asked Mr Saleh whether he knew what to do [i.e. had a clear programme in mind] if the opportunity arose. He said he definitely did not, and that if he was offered a task [i.e. the premiership] at the time he would have to turn it

188

down. At any rate, even those small discussion meetings gradually disappeared until the heat of 'free elections' suddenly brought many out of their nests.[44]

'FREE ELECTIONS'

Three interrelated factors led to the shah's false promise of 'free elections' in the spring of 1960. First, the economic bust which had followed the continued waste of oil revenues and foreign aid on militarisation and a consumer boom for the modern middle class, based on an 'open-door' international trade policy, not to mention widespread corruption in higher places. Second, Senator John F. Kennedy, who had been outspoken about the corrupt governments in receipt of American aid, including Iran, had become president of the United States. Hence there was no American rush to pull the shah's chestnuts out of the fire. Third, following the shah's double-crossing of the Soviets which had ended with the Iran–American mutual defence pact, they had become his sworn enemies and were conducting vehement radio propaganda against him, his family and his regime.[45]

Meanwhile, there had been growing discontent within the establishment from those who were against corruption and believed in some fundamental social reform. In 1958 Major General Qarani, the army intelligence chief, was arrested, tried secretly on unknown charges and sentenced to three years' imprisonment. In fact he had been plotting a white coup to trim some of the shah's powers and establish a reformist regime. To this end he had contacted a wide range of political leaders, including Maleki, who had responded to his criticisms of the status quo cautiously, given his position as an intelligence chief.[46]

Hasan Arsanjani – close to Ali Amini and minister of agriculture in his future cabinet – had been deeply involved in the affair
and was put under arrest for a period, while Amini was dismissed
from his post as ambassador to Washington. According to Richard
Cottam, then a young diplomat working for the CIA in Tehran,
the American embassy was aware of Qarani's activities but did
not betray him to the shah. He believed that this was done by
the British embassy that had discovered the plot from other
sources.[47] Whether or not the US had been involved in this, the
fate of the plotters would have been very different without its
direct or indirect protection.[48]

The shah's promise of free elections came against the background of these developments, both long and short. The establishment reformers led by Ali Amini quickly took to the field.
Amini himself declared his candidacy, but he also published a
manifesto including a land reform programme, which showed
that ultimately he was seeking the premiership. Allahyar Saleh
nominated himself for Kashan, his home town and natural constituency, though not as an Iran party candidate. As the economic
situation further deteriorated such that the central bank could
not meet its weekly foreign exchange obligations, it was difficult
to maintain the façade of free elections while election rigging was
proceeding from town to town. The shah saw the need for major
scapegoats: he dismissed premier Eqbal and 'advised' those deputies who already had been elected to resign; and he appointed
Ja'far Shari-Emami, the minister of industry, to the premiership.

Had the Popular Movement leaders and parties been ready
for this opportunity under a strong leadership, they could well
have carried out a repeat performance of the sixteenth Majlis
elections and sent a few deputies to the Majlis with the backing of the people outside. Then the formation of a government

would have been in their grasp. Alas, all Maleki's efforts of those six years had gone to waste.

THE SECOND NATIONAL FRONT AND THE SOCIALIST LEAGUE

A few Popular Front leaders plus a number of others they had asked to join them held a couple of private meetings in the summer of 1960 at the end of which they issued a statement and declared the formation of the second NF. They included a few lacklustre men but they had not invited Maleki to their meetings and their high council which was thus established. Sanjabi regretted this in his memoirs, saying:

> At this point I should say that in the composition of this council a mistake was made for which a few of our friends and comrades were responsible ... Khalil Maleki was a highly patriotic and freedom loving, clean, enlightened and correct analyst of socialist ideas ... I and a few other people believed that he should be a member of the National Front council, but there were some who were seriously opposed to it. At the time, in the opinion of our friends and comrades there should be unanimity in decision taking [and] although his opponents were in the minority ... because of their opposition no decision was taken.[49]

Predictably, there was no programme, no policy, no manifesto; all they wanted was free elections and non-aligned foreign policy which by definition would have been achieved the moment they came to power. Although they were highly heterogeneous in terms of education, political experience, social background and civic culture, they could not agree on any major policy objectives. The members of the twenty-man council which, after further co-options had risen to thirty-six, each possessed a veto so that there had to be a consensus, even on relatively small issues.

However, with the elections already under way, they had no candidate, save for Saleh who had not signed their statement. But the shah came to their rescue, so to speak, by effectively annulling the elections midway, so new elections could be held. They had a lot of support from the bazaar, university students, the middle classes and ordinary people, almost all owing to their past association with Mosaddeq who by then had risen to the status of the most popular 'unperson' in the country. But, as Maleki put it then and time and time again, the NF was an amorphous mass, there being no real organisation and no able leadership to turn it into an effective force. If, as Maleki went on writing and saying for a couple of years, they had turned themselves into a modern political organisation, when elections restarted they could have put up a number of candidates in Tehran and some big and small cities and would have become a force to be reckoned with in the twentieth Majlis.

In fact, after long deliberations when the elections were once again starting, they could not even agree on fifteen candidates for Tehran, their strongest constituency, and as a result decided to boycott the elections. However, the campaign for the freedom of elections continued, largely led by students who broke their seven-year silence on the seventh anniversary of the killing of the three students in 1953. All the Popular Movement parties were more or less represented in separate committees which cooperated among themselves in organising campus meetings and demonstrations. The campaign included the student committee of the Socialist League of the Popular Movement of Iran, the new organisation led by Maleki.

The earlier proposal for the formation of an all-embracing Socialist League of Iran had got nowhere, but now that the second NF had been declared, Maleki and his group re-formed themselves into a socialist league with the lesser claim of being just one of the Popular Movement parties. The League published a forty-four-page manifesto, drafted by Maleki and finalised by the founding members, most of whom were old Third Force members. It began by pointing out that the failure of the Popular Movement had not been inevitable, and that if law and order had been established while accepting the International Bank's intervention or Henderson's proposal, failure would have been avoided.[50]

Regarding the type of activity, the League would be a legal organisation and would avoid any secret and illegal activity: 'in our view, in today's world, it is possible to achieve revolutionary aims by peaceful means ... We therefore respect the constitution.' The political establishment has two wings, it said, one of which is corrupt to the core and must be fought tooth and nail, while the other would agree with the anti-corruption struggle and responsible government: 'In a constitutional state, premiers, ministers and statesmen must be responsible to the Majlis, not "lackey" and "slave" [of the shah]; in a constitutional state power comes from the people, not from this or that individual.'[51]

The League would respect unblemished Islam but would not accept it as a reactionary instrument for the justification of the rich and reactionary, 'and depriving of their rights, the half of the society who bring up the other half on their laps [i.e. women]'. It believed in planning for development in a mixed economy which rejected *étatisme*, but included a welfare state. It included a fairly detailed land reform programme and declared non-alignment together with friendly relations with all powers as its foreign policy. It was a comprehensive party programme the like of which is difficult to find in the history of modern Iranian politics.

A little while later, the shah invited Maleki through Asadollah Alam to see him. The date of this meeting is sometimes put as 1962, whereas, in his letter to Mosaddeq, Maleki clearly says that it was 'after the shah annulled the first election', which was 1960.[52] Maleki asked Alam why they would not invite some other leaders of the Popular Movement as well, and was told that they had made plain their attitude towards the constitution and the Tudeh party in their manifesto, whereas the NF's position was unclear on these two subjects.

Maleki had once met the shah before the coup, again at the shah's invitation and with the support both of the Third Force executive committee and Mosaddeq. This time, apart from the consent of his executive committee, he sought the advice of Sadiqi and Sanjabi – two of the four most eminent NF leaders – who encouraged him to accept the invitation. According to his lengthy report to Mosaddeq, he spoke openly to the shah and even contradicted him when the latter claimed that Mosaddeq was no longer popular. The shah then sent a message to the NF leaders saying that he would be willing to bring them to power if they made their position vis-à-vis the constitution and the Tudeh party clear:

> I gave them this message but at the time absolute nega-
> tivity ruled the day, and the Popular Front leaders, just
> like the past, were not even populists but followers of the
> populous ... They showed that their aim is mere popular-
> ity, not social action and service which would make them
> popular in history ... At the time when the establishment
> was in a very precarious position it was possible to get all
> sorts of concessions for the Movement; issuing two words
> about the constitution and the Tudeh party could clarify
> the Movement's position internally as well as externally.

But the leaders maintained silence over these two matters until they themselves became defenders of the constitution and constitutional monarchy and, in response to SAVAK's finger of accusation, many times issued statement against the Tudeh and the Soviet Persian broadcasts ... At any rate, if they had acted wisely NF could have formed a government instead of Dr Amini.[53]

Had Maleki's meeting the shah been known at the time, he would have been accused of collaborationism, although Saleh's well-known visit to the shah at about the same time did not carry such charges. However, Maleki's visit became widely known when he circulated his letter of 1962 to Mosaddeq, by which time he was enjoying a certain amount of sympathy among NF supporters, and particularly students.

7

POWER STRUGGLES, 1960–1963

TEHRAN ELECTIONS AND THE STUDENTS' SIT-IN

The campaign against election rigging in Tehran continued even though the NF had boycotted the election. Late in January, the NF leaders decided to stage a protest sit-in in the senate against election rigging, given that the Majlis was in recess. But they excluded Karim Sanjabi as their general spokesman and Shapour Bakhtiar, who was their contact with the University of Tehran.[1] After an initial effort to make them leave the senate failed, the senate was put under siege so that no one could leave it.

The university students were then told by Bakhtiar to continue their habitual campus demonstrations but this time to try to break out into the street. Now, whenever there were such demonstrations the police would block the two entrance gates of the university to prevent the students leaving the campus in force. On the day, probably 25 January 1961, members of the Socialist League's student committee told the others that they should try to leave the campus if it was permitted by the police, but they were not instructed to attack the police. The police did not relent and the League students suggested that they stage a sit-in at the university – the first of its kind in history – in sympathy with NF leaders who had been besieged in the senate.

This was agreed and the students managed to obtain the keys to the Faculty of Letters at sunset. Meanwhile, efforts had been made throughout the day to bring food into the university, but at dusk the police cadets surrounded the whole of the university. At 11 p.m., when most of the lights had been put out, Shapour Bakhtiar suddenly arrived in the company of a younger luminary and was given a noisy reception. After congratulating the students on their efforts he then told them to go home. This came as a shock and was greeted with cries of 'No'. Some even shouted that their homes were in Shemiran and there was no way they could get home at that time. Suggesting that they should then leave the next morning, Bakhtiar left in a huff.

There followed discussion and debate among the students on what to do. The Socialist League committee were certain that if, in the weak situation which the regime generally found itself, the students could hold out for a couple of days the NF could extract important concessions from the regime. They then decided to send a delegation to Sanjabi, the other NF leader not in the senate, who was senior to Bakhtiar in rank to ask him to come to the university the next day and reverse Bakhtiar's order. Hushang Sayyahpur, Hossein Sarpulaki and Hossein Meftah (all members of the League itself), Amir Mas'ud Katouzian and Parviz Sanjabi (Karim Sanjabi's son) – who did not belong to any party – were secretly smuggled out of the campus to report to Sanjabi. He told them that at 9 p.m. the acting head of SAVAK – since General Bakhtiar was in America – had telephoned and asked him to go and tell the students to end their sit-in, and he had replied that the NF leader responsible for student affairs was Shapour Bakhtiar not him.

Next morning the argument over what to do led the Front's student activists to negotiate with the police outside to let the students leave and march in the street *silently* and without interference. Predictably, this was agreed, the students were led out and the minute they were all in the street they faced water cannon, baton charges and – if caught – arrest. The protest strike which had begun so well and had so alarmed the regime thus ended ingloriously, followed by bitterness and recriminations. It was yet another missed opportunity.

Today, Hushang Sayyahpur lives in Austria, Parviz Sanjabi lives in America, Hossein Meftah lives in Amol, Iran, and the other two members of the delegation have passed away. This author was witness to it all.

THE SECOND NATIONAL FRONT AND THE POPULAR MOVEMENT PARTIES

Not long after the second NF was formed, Khonji, who, together with Hejazi had been made a member of their council, put out a leaflet in October 1961 arguing that, for the NF to be an effective political force, all the Popular Movement parties and organisations should join it so their members would become individual members of the NF. Therefore, he wrote, 'the socialist party' dissolves itself into the NF. This was remarkable since such a party had never been declared and Khonji and Hejazi only had a handful of followers.

However, being experienced cadres – a rare commodity in the NF council – they could then try to dominate it in practice with the help of the Iran party, most of whose leaders were also council members, so that in effect the second NF would become, as it eventually did, the Iran party plus those two and their few supporters. And they were especially conscious of keeping Maleki and the Socialist League out of the Front, something with which a number of the Iran party leaders concurred. In addition, though the leaders of the old NRM such as Mehdi Bazargan were members of the NF council, there was no love lost between them and Iran party, so that by May 1961 they had formed their own separate organisation, the Freedom Movement of Iran (*Nehzat-e Azadi-ye Iran*).[2]

This was contrary to the first NF's tradition which had been created by organised parties and groups in addition to individual members, and it was destined to end up in direct conflict with Mosaddeq and the second NF (see below). Nevertheless, the Socialist League wrote a formal letter to the NF council and applied for membership. The NF never replied to this, and later remarkably explained to Mosaddeq that because some members of their executive had disagreed with the application they had decided 'to pass over it in silence'.

Many of the Iran party leaders disliked Maleki and the Third Force, which, according to Gholamhossein Sadiqi, was simply due to jealousy,[3] a trait that Maleki himself used to refer to as 'intellectual afflictions'. They had been unhappy that, in terms of membership, organisation and publications, the Third Force party had superseded them. But there were other factors. They feared that Maleki would dominate the council and executive committee by virtue of his intellectual superiority and full-time political activity; and they were afraid that it would offend the Tudeh party. Some of them explained their opposition to Maleki by calling him a 'split-monger'. But this was just a feeble excuse: Maleki had been asked by others to lead the Tudeh split; and it was Baqa'i who had left Zahmatkeshan, not Maleki (see Chapters 2 and 4).[4]

Meanwhile, the unrest in the bazaar and at the university continued, and a number of people were arrested. Hushang Sayyahpur had been arrested earlier, whipped and his head shaved, and released after a few weeks. When Maleki saw him in that state, he got so angry that, in his long open letter of 20 February 1960, he vehemently attacked the regime. He wrote towards the end of the letter:

> Now that you have incarcerated the National Front leaders in the Senate and left no reputation for the chamber and its old chairman ... Now that you shaved the head of the supporters of *Elm o Zendegi* and thrashed them, while you put university students in chains like criminals, why do you threaten to make trouble for me. I wrote this open letter so that if you like you would also come after me. I do not welcome it but neither am I frightened of it. When young, I was thrashed and my head was also shaved. Although hardly any hair is left on my head for your agents to shave, I am used to prison and torture and in the prison environment feel as if I am in my own home.

And he continued:

> I accuse you of having stolen the most sacred right of Iranian people, the right of electing and being elected; I accuse you of having plundered the wealth and property of Iranian people; I accuse you of playing with the destiny of the young generation, i.e. with the hopes of Iran's future, at one of the most sensitive moments of Iranian history. I bring these charges so that you will invite me to an open court. I shall ask the Iranian people for evidence and I am sure that your court and judges would suffocate under the weight of the people's evidence.

He concluded:

> The revolt of the universities and faculties of Tehran and provincial cities is the prelude to the explosion which we

have predicated many times. You thought that by spilling the blood of three student of the faculty of technology [in 1953, see Chapter 6] you had robbed every one of hope and faith. Today you have begun with whipping and shaving heads so you can repeat the scene of the technology faculty. But what the contemporary history of neighbouring countries reveals is that the order to shoot students will turn around the aim about a hundred and eighty degrees. This is the lesson of history and what you and we have seen in these days is no more a prelude since this is just the beginning.[5]

Next day Maleki was arrested but this time not for long. A month later at the Persian New Year all the recent Popular Movement prisoners including the NF leaders in the senate were released by General Teymur Bakhtiar, the SAVAK chief, who had just returned from America with great aspirations of his own. He had interviewed their leaders – apart from those in the senate, who were not in jail – including Maleki, one by one, and told them they were right to demand freedom!

AMINI'S PREMIERSHIP

The twentieth Majlis had barely begun its work when, in April 1961, the teachers' strike led by Mohammad Derakhshesh erupted in the streets of Tehran and a young teacher was shot dead by the police in Baharistan, the parliament square. This was the final straw, and if the NF had been an organised force with a strong leadership and a clear programme, the shah might well have invited them to form a government. This indeed was the second opportunity they lost within nine months. Instead, the shah asked

Amini, whom he both disliked and feared on account of his ability and independence, and sense of self-respect: he was after all a maternal grandson of Mozaffar al-Din Shah, Vosuq al-Dowleh's son-in-law, and had been close to Qavam, his wife's uncle.

Whatever the Amini lobby may have been in America, it is virtually certain that the US government did not – tacitly or explicitly – tell the shah to make him prime minister, although it is equally certain that the shah believed this is what the Americans expected of him. Amini agreed to act on the condition that the shah used his power under the constitutional amendment of 1949 to dismiss the parliament. Given his well-publicised intention of carrying out a land reform, he was concerned that the shah and the landlords would block his every move in the Majlis and force him out of office – as Mosaddeq would have put it – in a seemingly constitutional manner.

Once again there was dual sovereignty in Iran, with Amini's share of power declining after the first few months. He soon had to face the combined opposition of the shah, the landlords, the conservative religious leaders as well as the massive confrontation of the second NF and the campaign of Soviet and Tudeh Propaganda against him. At first he tried to woo the Front. The news of its activities suddenly appeared in the regular daily press and (in June 1961) the NF was allowed to hold the Popular Movement's first authorised open-air meeting since the coup at Tehran's racecourse. Inevitably there was a massive turnout, not least because false rumours had been spread that Mosaddeq himself would attend it.

Maleki devoted an entire extra issue of *Elm o Zendegi* to an analysis of Amini's government and the appropriate response of the Popular Movement's forces to it. He argued that Amini belonged to the uncorrupt and responsible wing of the establishment and intended to promote land reform, fight rampant corruption, open up society and politics to some extent and trim some of the shah's powers. That, in sum, was Amini's mission which, if fulfilled, would provide the grounds for the NF to succeed him. Therefore the NF should form itself into a critical shadow government and offer better alternative programmes but avoid entering a life-and-death struggle against Amini along with the reactionaries. He issued dire warnings – which he was to repeat regularly later – that if Amini failed because of the combined opposition of the shah, the reactionaries and the NF, he would be replaced by an absolute and arbitrary regime.[6]

Not only did this fall on deaf ears but Maleki became the target of fresh attacks as an agent of the regime. The NF led a confrontation with Amini describing him as a big landlord, as a liar, as an agent of America, as the signatory of the Consortium Oil Agreement, and as more of the same. Their only slogan was free elections which they knew could not be held for the reasons mentioned, and, even if they were, they could at most send a few deputies to the Majlis. After all, they had not managed to agree to a list of fifteen candidates for Tehran in the previous election (see Chapter 6).

Not only was Maleki castigated by the NF, the Tudeh, the reactionaries and the confederation of Iranian students abroad, but he was even subjected to criticism by some members of the League of Iranian Socialists in Europe, a sister organisation which was independent from Tehran and whose membership was largely made up of Iranian students in Europe. Replying to a letter of Amir Pichdad, the European League's secretary, he wrote on 16 August 1961:

> You have quoted some comrades as saying that they do not regard the journal *Elm o Zendegi* and its writers as socialist. It looks as if ... he is not socialist who, while

being in opposition to Amini's government, would tem-
porarily tolerate it so that in the meantime he would try
to mobilise the popular and progressive forces. He is a
socialist who would beat down Dr Amini in favour of
the shah and the court ... Derakhshesh [the minister of
education] has done so much more positive work in the
department of education within a month than the Popular
Movement ministers of education managed in the whole
of that period ... Although Amini unlike Eqbal is not a
lackey, power is not entirely in his hands. He regards the
pressures brought on university students as the work of
the reactionaries against his government ...[7]

A month or so earlier, in commemoration of the 21 July uprising,
the NF decided to call a mass meeting at the city's racecourse.
Amini told them that he would personally not have any objection
but it was not possible to sell the idea to the shah. He told them
that if they decided not to hold the meeting he would also stop
the shah from holding a similar meeting in commemoration of the
1953 coup, as he habitually did. However, they not only insisted
on holding the meeting but took no measures for organising and
running it, and stayed at home the evening before so they would
be put under protective detention for twenty-hours, as indeed
they were. They had not even published tracts and made banners
and placards for the occasion.

Maleki and the League were opposed to this decision, but felt
that if a show were not made, the Popular Movement would lose
much credit, not least among foreign observers. The city racecourse had been occupied by the army on the day and the streets
around it were packed with police and soldiers. Nevertheless a few
thousand people showed up, including the League's members who
led the demonstrations. Maleki himself also showed up despite

army and police baton charges, beatings and arrests.[8] He survived that, but his eighteen-year-old son Piruz was detained and savagely beaten. Yet this was not a glorious day for the Popular Movement.

MALEKI AND THE SOCIALIST INTERNATIONAL

On 7 July 1961, Albert Carthy, general secretary of the Socialist International, addressed a long letter to 'dear comrade Khalil Maleki', inviting a delegation to attend a conference on 'socialism and democracy' in Baden, Austria, followed by their biennial congress in Rome as observers, since the League was not affiliated to the Socialist International.[9] Maleki and the League accepted the invitation. He flew to Paris in October to see the leaders of the Socialist League in Europe, especially Amir Pichdad and his own brother Hossein Malek, and it was decided that Malek and another member of the European League would accompany him to Baden and, afterwards, Rome. He had insisted in his earlier letter to Malek that he would book a room in a cheap Paris hotel.[10] Carthy had written that he would be the guest of the Socialist International in Baden but all other expenses had to be borne by themselves. The Tudeh party's organ *Mardom*, now published in Eastern Europe, ran the headline: 'Khalil Maleki in the international opportunism front'.[11]

Maleki and the other two spoke in Baden in due course, mainly about problems of economic development in Iran, while in Rome they were just observers. However, they were also invited to a third conference in Salzburg on the relationship between developed and developing countries in which Maleki clashed with an American delegate. In his speech, Maleki had argued that foreign aid and investment were not helpful to economic development and as part of it he had mentioned the case of Iran's oil nationalisation and the ensuing Consortium Oil Agreement.

The American delegate speaking after him, while acknowledging the right of developing countries to nationalise their industries, had said that, nevertheless, international agreements must be respected. Maleki's reaction was fairly long but, briefly, he retorted: 'Yesterday I summarised my report [in German] in the interest of brevity. Now I have its English version at hand and although my English accent is bad, I shall read the missing part. My English accent is bad because I have learned it in prison, the same prisons that ruling regimes fill so as to enter the American delegate's "respectable international agreements" ...'[12]

While in Europe, Maleki was invited to visit Israel by Moshe Sharett, an Israeli socialist leader, ex-prime minister and ex-foreign minister who, 'after stepping down as Minister of Foreign Affairs on 18 June 1956 in protest at the new [Ben-Gurion]government's bellicose policy that he thought was dangerously precipitate', had decided to retire.[13] Maleki, like all European socialists in the 1950s, regarded Israel as a model socialist country and a viable alternative to the Soviet model, and *Elm o Zendegi* and *Nabard-e Zendegi* wrote favourable comments on its kibbutz farms while discussing possible programmes for an Iranian land reform. Regarding the Palestine issue, Maleki believed that the conflict should be settled through negotiation. This was long before the Six Day War of 1967, there was no Palestine Liberation Organization at the time and Israel was not yet a political issue in Iran. Jalal Al-e Ahmad and his wife Simin Daneshvar also visited Israel as guests shortly afterwards. He wrote a favourable travelogue – a genre he liked – but after the Six Day War added a highly critical chapter to it.[14]

Back in Iran, Maleki and the Socialist League continued their policy of criticising the second NF without confronting it

or adopting a hostile attitude towards it. Yet the NF were find-
ing their constructive criticisms more and more irritating, and
so stepped up their verbal campaigns of vilification, especially
against Maleki. In principle, the NF did not have any desire to
publish journals, not even a single daily or weekly for the large
crowds that were still sympathetic to them, unorganised as they
were, because they were afraid of offending specific individuals or social groups, including the landlords. That is why they
remained totally silent about land reform, any land reform, except
once when they published a pamphlet in which they practi-
cally argued that a land reform was meaningless because Iran
was not a feudal society.[15] It was just the perennial short leaflet
(*e'lamiyeh*) demanding freedom and denouncing corruption.
Still, the University of Tehran, a couple of other institutions of
higher education, the bazaar and one or two high schools were
the only semi-organised bodies on which it could rely.

21 JANUARY 1962 AND THE FALL OF AMINI

Maleki had barely returned to Tehran than the second NF committed one of the biggest blunders of its short life. In January 1962
Amini and Arsanjani announced the formulation of 'the land
reform law' (which later became known as the first stage of land
reform). In mid-January the rumour was suddenly spread that a
student of Dar al-Fonun high school had been expelled for political
reasons. On this slender pretext, orders went out from the Front to
the university activists to plan a massive demonstration in protest,
and 21 January (*Avval-e Bahman*) was set as the day of action. The
day before, rumours about a plot to force the government out of
office began to circulate widely both inside the government and
in Popular Movement circles. By then, the Socialist League, the

Freedom Movement and even some forces – such as Foruhar's People of Iran party – inside the NF were convinced that the students were being used as pawns in a plot of which the Front as a whole was unaware.

The most radical and vocal student activists – including Marxist-Leninists such a Bizhan Jazani, later to become mentor of the guerrilla group Fada'iyan-e Khalq (Devotees of the People) – began to counsel caution, and tried to prevent catastrophe. Various forces within and outside the Front tried hard to persuade it to postpone the demonstrations and conduct an enquiry into the plot allegations. Instead, some of those who were trying to stop the demonstrations were arrested the night before.

The plot was hatched by Teymur Bakhtiar, now the former SAVAK chief, some big landlords, some reactionary mullahs such as Ayatollah Behbahani and a number of leading racketeers. It was believed that the shah had also known about it. The idea was to send a detachment of regular soldiers to attack the crowd of demonstrators believing that it would force the government to resign. Having failed to dissuade the Front from its action, Amini managed to talk to the army leaders at the eleventh hour and order the troops to remain in barracks for twenty-four hours. They switched tactics and sent in an irregular and autonomous commando unit (comparable to the British SAS), something highly unlikely to have occurred without the shah's knowledge.

They attacked the university with bayonets and used rifle butts against everyone in sight – students, professors, administrators, library and laboratory assistants, etc. – with a savagery never experienced before. Students who took refuge in the faculty buildings were indiscriminately beaten, offices and scientific equipment were smashed, books burned and men, women and machines thrown out of the windows.

Far from resigning, the government blamed the whole event on a conspiracy. An army investigation committee hastily concluded that the NF as a whole had not been involved in the plot, although four of its leaders – Khonji, Hejazi, Sanjabi and Bakhtiar – had been put under arrest as probable accessories. The real plotters would have been brought to book if the shah had backed Amini over it, but all Amini could do was to ask the shah to order General Bakhtiar to leave the country. However, there was extreme anger and frustration among Popular Front supporters and this was specifically directed against Khonji and Hejazi. This was the origin of Mosaddeq's later charge against the NF council that it included some of 'our betters' (i.e. outside agents).[16]

In his letter of February 1961 to Hossein Malek (from Tehran to Paris), Maleki wrote:

The investigative committee has reported to the prime minister. The committee is respected by the NF as well. They also interviewed me respectfully as someone familiar with the situation at the university. Apparently the committee has not officially blamed the NF for the event, but has said that they had been set up, and that three people, i.e. Khonji, Hejazi and Bakhtiar had known about the right wingers' plot and had used the NF [to carry it out].[17]

Amini's government fell abruptly in July 1962 and, within a couple of months, the former prime minster was confined to Tehran by court order. In his earlier visit to the US the shah had told the American government that they should rid him of Amini or he would abdicate. Puzzled, they had told him that he was free to make his own decisions.[18] On the eve of his unexpected fall, the Socialist League published in a leaflet an analysis of the political situation and a frank evaluation of the NF's balance sheet which must be ranked as one of the most intelligent documents produced in the period. In its preamble it pointed out that the country was going through a transitional period 'which will leave its mark on the future history of Iran'.

It argued that for political victory the Popular Movement needed a firm social base among workers, peasants, artisans, the national bourgeoisie and progressive educated people, and that the Front had done nothing to ensure such a base. A detailed critique of the Front's tactics and strategies followed, criticising the Front for directing its campaign exclusively against the government's decision to postpone elections, whereas – because of the land reform issue and the government's fear of a landlord majority in the Majlis – this was the one issue on which no concessions could be obtained.

To declare a general strike without adequate preparation was a grave mistake. To do it again and again (when not a single bus ceased running and not even the bazaar closed down) was downright folly:

[On] the day that landlords and reactionary elements had designated their own day of victory, and had already appointed their cabinet, we entered a blind adventure, and this led to the catastrophe of 21 January (Avval-e Bahman). The amazing fact is that the leaders of the National Front had been warned by some well-informed people who knew about behind-the-scenes conspiracies ... And yet, the Front's leadership astonishingly insisted on throwing thousands of students over to whips, bayonets and batons, and (in return) gained several hundred injuries, the long-term closure of the university, and greater repression ... During this phase [of Amini's government] we could have turned ourselves into a great force ... But the balance sheet of our actions reveals a force which is on the verge of bankruptcy.

The analysis concluded with the following accurate prediction about the fate of the second NF:

> If things go on the same way, the National Front will disappear as a political force, and – instead of it being the centrepiece of the Popular Movement of Iran – would become a disused temple for its most faithful believers to attend only for each other's funeral and nod their heads to each other to renew their acquaintance and show their regret.[19]

Meanwhile, in February, Maleki had received an invitation from 'the Theodore Kuz fund' in Austria for a week-long conference on economic cooperation, and had chosen to speak on the causes of the success and failure of foreign aid. His expenses were paid, but he explained to his brother that he could not visit Paris following it, for lack of money.[20]

THE WHITE REVOLUTION AND THE NF CONGRESS

In August 1962, a month after the fall of Amini, Maleki wrote to Malek (from Tehran to Paris) that the NF had decided to hold a congress and that he had been told from inside the NF central council that they [the League] should write to the Front and apply to attend their congress. Maleki had replied that they had written to them before and would not do so again, and that they should initiate it themselves: 'a few days have passed now and there has been no news'. He went on to add: 'In any case, in the present situation there is no opportunity and future for the Front. And even assuming there was a chance, they are not capable enough to use it successfully.'[21]

That was August 1962, but the NF's first and last congress was held in January 1963, two weeks before the shah's referendum of 26 January for his White Revolution, while, for a few months, he had been drumming up his intention to continue the land reform, give the vote to women and carry out some other reform projects. As yet, the NF did not have any plan or programme at all. Maleki and the Socialist League were lucky not to have received an invitation, if only because the meeting started off on the wrong foot, with allegations of rigging in the election of sectional delegates.

When one delegate tried to raise questions about the 21 January fiasco he was physically thrown out of the room, and Foruhar's protest was shouted down. They had elected Mosaddeq congress president *in absentia*, and had asked him for a taped message which they played in the meeting. In it he had emphasised the need 'for the Front's gates to be opened to all individuals, groups and parties ... and every effort be made so that those who seek the freedom and independence of Iran are brought into the circle of activists'.[22] But this fell on deaf ears, and the Freedom Movement withdrew their delegation.

At last the NF declared a programme, but there was nothing concrete or specific in it. For example, it talked about 'women's progress and the affirmation of their rights' while the shah was proposing to give them the right to vote and be elected.[23] Their agricultural policy reflected the conflict of opinion among them:

> The National Front of Iran believes that the reform of the agricultural system should take place in such a way that farmers (*keshavarzan*) would be freed from bondage and

benefit from the fruits of their labour ... In order to fulfil these objectives, it would be necessary to *remove the owner-ship of those individuals who have obtained their ownership of land by illegal means.* The landlord–peasant system and *all kinds of landownership which involve the exploitation of farmers* must be abolished.[24]

Apart from the contradictory nature of these statements, it is clear that the Front still had no land reform 'programme'.

The supreme vagueness occurred in their foreign policy. They dropped their age-old policy of non-alignment in favour of what they called 'independent national policy'. The shah was soon to adopt this meaningless phrase as the description of his own foreign policy.

Maleki had responded to Amini's land reform programme by offering the alternative of 'nationalisation of land and water', by which he meant the transfer of land ownership in every village collectively to the peasantry by a single law, and extend credit and technical services to the cultivators. This would (a) allow the *nasaq* (traditional rights) holders to retain the landlord's share for themselves; (b) prevent the breaking up of estates into very small farms either then or later through inheritance; (c) leave the village as the historical unit of production, and useful traditional techniques and institutions such as *qanat* (irrigation channels) and the *boneh* (cooperative production unit) undisturbed; (d) maintain the position of the *khoshneshin* (landless peasantry) as before, rather than subjecting them to social and legal disposses-sion; (e) discourage rapid migration to the towns; (f) cut all the legal and bureaucratic problems of dividing up the land.[25]

The origins of this proposed policy were in *Niru-ye Sevvom*, but they were further developed as a serious programme in *Nabard-e Zendegi* and *Elm o Zendegi*. Studious and logical though it looks, it was nevertheless not a realistic programme for its type, if only because it went totally beyond the understanding of the peasantry who by reform only recognised the division of land.

The shah's six-point programme was put to the public vote on 26 January 1953 and, inevitably according to official reports, won a landslide victory. This completely disarmed the Front, who, before the referendum, issued a leaflet ending with 'land reform, yes I agree; dictatorship, no I disagree'.[26]

The people's grievances against the regime's corruption had not dissipated, however, but been enhanced. Amini and his circle were in opposition and under surveillance, but the landlords and conservative politicians were also angry with the shah, and their leaders – individuals such as Hossein Ala, the court minister, Qaem Maqam al-Molk, hitherto very close to the shah, Ayatollah Behbahani, the Hekmat cousins, etc. – were dismissed and received harsh replies in their private representations to him.

The religious community were also agitated for a combination of different reasons. Some opposed land reform and the women's franchise, while others not necessarily opposed to land reform were concerned about the rising tide of dictatorship. Many were also concerned about the fate of the *Vaqf* (religious endowments) property which they normally administered. Beyond reactionary social attitudes, and above all, was the fear of the imminent rise of absolute and arbitrary rule which by definition would abolish the role and influence of the political and the religious establishment.

Qom was restless and for the first time troops attacked the seminary students and beat and arrested some of them. The students of the University of Tehran were also agitated, and this time busloads of hirelings – described as workers and peasants, angry with the opposition of students to their liberation – were sent by the regime to beat them up with sticks and clubs. Ayatollah Khomeini's daring sermons and public speeches against the regime quickly turned him into the most distinguished leader of a popular revolt which finally erupted in June 1963, and led to the famous riots which were savagely put down by the army.

It was in many ways a dress rehearsal for the revolution of 1979, not least because almost every social class and every ideology was represented in it. The fact that the NF did not openly back the demonstrations was partly because some of its leaders had been in jail, and partly because of its usual inertia and fear of making serious decisions. But this did not discourage its sections and grassroots from getting fully involved.

Maleki described the riots as a response to the regime's total insensitivity towards the public, whose leadership had fallen into the non-Popular Movement hands because of the second NF's longstanding inability to organise and lead. He wrote:

> Unfortunately a comparison of the intensity of the people's resistance ... during the recent events with the more-or-less similar events of the past two years reveals that the self-styled leaders of the people [i.e. NF leaders] were incapable of providing effective leadership to mobilise the people ... behind progressive aims, and that landlords, reactionaries and their allies were technically better equipped ...[27]

He was writing from Vienna.

MALEKI IN EUROPE

In February 1963, shortly after the shah's referendum, Maleki went to Vienna with his eldest son Piruz who was twenty at the time. As he wrote to Mosaddeq, he had decided to go to Europe five months earlier but it had taken him that long to get a passport.[28] There were three reasons for his decision: treatment of his ailing heart (from which he was to die six years later); enrolling Piruz as a student in a university, especially as he was feeling guilty for not having devoted enough time to his children; and wishing to be away from Tehran politics, since his enemies had identified the Socialist League with him personally, and identified him with the devil.

It was then that he wrote his very long letter to Mosaddeq, which has been cited several times in previous chapters. In it, he both discussed the recent and current Iranian politics, and showed how the second NF had missed a few opportunities and that it was not ready to govern even if it got the chance, and gave a detailed report of his and his parties' activities since the 1953 coup. He ended the letter by introducing some of his prominent comrades in Iran and Europe, and, above all, mentioning his debt to his wife, partially quoted in Chapter 1.

He made a stop in Rome en route to Vienna, from where he wrote his first letter to the League of Iranian Socialists in Europe. He expressed hope that the League in Iran would be better off without him, and said that he did not intend to be active in Europe other than giving counsel if necessary. He also made some critical observations on the state of Iranian agriculture and land reform.[29]

Vienna brought a certain amount of relief to Maleki. He was no longer a full-time (not even a part-time) political activist and had been relieved from the daily effort of reforming the NF into a serious political force and being castigated for it. Members of the Vienna unit and Graz unit of the European Socialist League had received him with much respect and appreciated his company. Piruz was preparing to go to university and Maleki himself was preparing to start treatment for his heart disease. This was March 1963 and he had agreed to attend the European Socialist League's congress, if it was held in Germany, but not if in Geneva.[30]

However, hardly had a month passed since Maleki's arrival in Europe than two events exploded over his head: two letters, one after the other, from the League of Iranian Socialists in Europe, one to the Soviet government, the other to the Iranian National Front in Europe. The tone of both letters was polite, not to say friendly. In the letter to the Soviets, the European League had criticised the recent friendly turn in Soviet policy towards the Iranian regime – which the Tudeh party, willy-nilly, had greeted with the slogan 'long live the friendship of Iran and the Soviets' – and expressed hope that they would reconsider this change of policy.

The letter to the European NF was simply an application from the League to join it as such, i.e. as an organised body, and not as individual members, however, emphasising that it was an independent body. The letters were tactical. The League neither expected the Soviets to change their policy nor the NF to admit them as an organised body, since, as noted, their policy in Iran, and even more so in Europe, was that organised parties as such could not join them. They were intended as exposures of policies with which the League disagreed.

Maleki was badly hurt and felt that he had been abandoned to the Soviet Union and NF. More than anything else, perhaps, it was the letters' more or less friendly tone that conveyed this feeling to him. He lost his cool and wrote a very long, upbraiding and censorious, but highly logical and well-argued, letter to the League in Europe, not just complaining about being person-ally abandoned to his enemies but criticising the actions from a purely political viewpoint. He did consider the possibility of the letters being tactical but he dismissed it by saying that they were more likely to deceive their own members than enlighten their opponents. He declared in the end that he would not go to the congress in Bonn in April.[31]

It took some time for Amir Pichdad, the European League's secretary (in Paris) to write a detailed letter in response and – most important of all – reassure Maleki of the esteem in which he was held by the Iranian socialists in Europe, although many of them had already done so in various ways.[32] Meanwhile, Maleki had spent time in hospital and, after leaving, his doctor had advised him to rest completely for six months and had put him on medication. He replied in a short letter: 'Your letter which I was waiting to receive for a long time … made me very happy so that I managed to get over my laziness, sense of uselessness and psychological disaffection.' And in a following long letter he explained that the reason why in the meantime he had not written to Pichdad, apart from illness, was a kind of mental fatigue which was probably more due to family problems than heart disease: 'My eldest son Piruz who had accompanied me to Austria is especially talented in social and general matters but is not too keen to study … In the end he did not like Austria and Europe and with his own particular logic, and despite the wishes of me and his mother, returned to Iran.'[33]

Meanwhile, remarkable events were taking place in Iran. While the top leaders of the NF had been in jail since February 1963, the regime announced that the twenty-first Majlis elections would be held in September. As noted above, while Amini was prime minister the Front had spent almost all of its energies demanding that he should hold the Majlis elections without delay. Students and other activists sent word to the jailed leaders, urging the Front to fight the elections with full force. They replied that 'prisoners should not express any views' and referred the students to leaders who were free.

The latter were of the opinion that the executive committee should give them the lead, but declined to commit themselves and implied that the students were free to make their own decisions.[34]

This they did and planned a public demonstration in Baharistan, the parliament square. Two days before, the top leaders were released from prison and immediately issued a written order to the students not to hold the event. The demonstration was held, nevertheless, and was attacked by the police. In the event, the NF did not take part in the elections (it did not even boycott it) and issued a directive to the students to go on vacation (*morrakhasi*) for some time.

Needless to say, the resulting Majlis was packed with whoever the regime would pick and choose. Even the political establishment had been consigned to the dustbin of history. The Front's executive committee resigned and the central council gave full executive powers to Allahyar Saleh, who suggested they adopt 'the policy of patience and forbearance (*sabr o metanat*) and refrain from any action that would lead to a reaction from the regime'. There were some disagreements but in the end both decisions were confirmed.[35]

There is no comment in any of Maleki's letters to the European League concerning these developments, as he could hardly be surprised by what he had accurately predicted. Meanwhile, his wife, Sabiheh Khanom, and Noruz, his youngest son, joined him in Vienna, Sabiheh Khanom returning fairly soon but Noruz continuing to study for some time. Maleki was not directly involved in politics and, apart from regular correspondence, often in long letters, with Iranian socialists in Europe, he was active in writing papers, translating material, and even writing unsigned articles in the monthly organ of the League of Iranian Socialists in Europe, although he excused himself from writing lead articles because of his differences of opinion with the European League over current issues.

He wrote to his brother Hossein Malek (from Vienna to Delhi, where the latter was a UN consultant) that he was studying the conflict between China and the Soviet Union. He wrote that he was neither pro-Khrushchev nor pro-Chinese but from the viewpoint of world peace, etc., he found Khrushchev's attitude more realistic: 'However, it looks as if the situation is such that in the Soviet Union the rule of "the new class" is still in place':

> Regarding Iran, I am more-or-less regularly in touch with Tehran friends … Nothing has happened since [the revolt of] 6 June [15 Khordad]. My analysis of 6 June is the same as before. The comrades in Tehran are slowly coming round to the same conclusion. There was no difference from the viewpoint of practical tactics, but we had differences in interpretation. [36]

Maleki had expressed a wish to pay a short visit to Paris and see Pichdad and others, many of whom were members of the European League's central committee. Once it was all but organised but due to some problems it fell through. Once again in February 1964, when he was thinking of going, his illness discouraged it. He had gone on a trip by bus in Austria and had found it difficult and tiring. Therefore he had consulted his doctor and had been warned not to go on a long-distance trip even by train. Obviously he could not afford to fly to Paris. He wrote to Pichdad: 'This is the second time that I went back on my promise but I am sure you would agree that the fault is my illness, not mine.' In the same letter he wrote that the cataract in one of his eyes from which he had suffered in Tehran had returned and was making reading difficult.[37]

A few days later he wrote to the Iranian socialists in Graz that he wished to visit them for a couple of days now that he had been forbidden to travel the long distance to Paris. He explained that he would soon return to Tehran, and was warmly welcomed by the socialists in Graz. Returning to Vienna he wrote to Pichdad that that could be the last letter by him from Europe, this time specifically complaining that the trouble with his eye had made it impossible for him to finish his study of the Sino-Soviet dispute. But it was not his last letter. He wrote a couple of other short letters, the last one from Rome en route to Tehran. It was dated 21 March 1964. He returned to Tehran via Istanbul.[38]

8

MALEKI: THE LAST PHASE

THE DEMISE OF THE SECOND NATIONAL FRONT

While Maleki was on his way back to Iran, on 20 March 1964 the Tehran Students' Committee sent Mosaddeq a letter of greetings for the oil nationalisation day and the Persian New Year, which included an account of their activities. He wrote a short letter in reply saying that he was 'extremely pleased that the worthy Committee are still concerned about the problems which face the people of Iran, and have not closed down [their activities]'.[1] This was a jibe at the second NF who, a few months earlier, had told their members to go on vacation. By then he had made up his mind to intervene directly in the Movement's troubled affairs.

Two days later he addressed a lengthy letter to the executive committee of the National Front Organisations in Europe which was to explode like a bombshell throughout the whole movement. In their letter of 5 March, the committee had sent Mosaddeq a report on their activities, emphasising that they had disbanded the European outposts of the Popular Movement parties within the European organisations of the NF. Mosaddeq wrote in reply:

I should be very grateful that that worthy committee have informed me about the activities of the Front's European organisations ... and that despite the fact that you have been aware of my message of 24 December 1962 to the first congress of the National Front via a recorded tape, you have decided to disband the [Popular Movement] parties ... In my view the action has not been right ... The National Front should be regarded as the central organisation of all the parties which believe in a common principle, namely the freedom and independence of the country. If parties and groups do not join the Front, the Front will become exactly what it now is ... incapable of taking a step in defending [the rights of the people] ... They [i. e. the congress] asked me to send them a message, but paid no attention to it, and brought the Front into such a state that it is unable to do anything ...[2]

The recipients decided to suppress the letter, thereby proving Mosaddeq's point when – in reply to their request to name a leader – he had written with some sarcasm that even if he did so 'no one would pay any attention to it'.[3] But he had sent copies to other Popular Movement parties and organs, and it was reproduced and circulated in Iran and published by the League of Iranian Socialists in Europe.

Maleki had just returned from Europe and it is not difficult to imagine the joy with which he had received the good news. Almost two weeks later the Front's central council and new executive committee in Tehran addressed a letter to 'the exalted leader' explicitly in response to his letter to the NF in Europe. This was a long letter and contained much unnecessary detail.[4] It claimed that parties had not been excluded from the Front, and the Freedom Movement had been told that it could remain a member on condition that it would purge its 'undesirable elements' and send a report on this to the Front's council. The Tudeh party was the only party that had several times applied and had been turned down due to its unsuitability.[5] The letter contained a long argument that the 1953 coup would have been avoided had the first NF been organised along the lines of the second. They then accused their Popular Front critics of a plot to destroy the Front from within:

> Since the beginning of the [Front's] activities, these elements have analysed every decision of the Front ... under the magnifying glass in the hope of finding a point for attacking, provoking and falsifying [its activities] thus creating confusion and preventing the right course of action. Right now such elements [i.e. the Socialist League, the Freedom Movement, Foruhar's People of Iran, and the Students' Committee] are using your letter [to the Front's European organisation] for a propaganda drive against the organisation of the National Front of Iran, so as to present us with an organisational and political crisis, and disappoint and disperse the activists.[6]

The letter concluded by saying that now the Front's leadership faced an even bigger dilemma because, on the one hand, to oppose Mosaddeq's views 'is not in the interest of the country, the people or the Movement', and, on the other hand, 'it could not act against its own beliefs, and the decision of the congress which has created its council':

> If despite the above explanations, his Excellency still retains the views he has expressed in the letter [to the European organisations], it may result in the destruction

of the National Front organisations. And, given the great wave of opposition [to the regime] which has swept all classes [of the people] there can be no doubt that the ruling establishment would be much happier to see the destruction of the only organisation which can maintain its position in the interest of the people.

But the old man was neither impressed by the threat nor by the empty boast. His reply was harder than before. Alluding with sarcasm to the long lecture he had been given about parties and organisations, he said that they obviously had more experience of such matters and that what little he had known about them he had forgotten during his eleven years of imprisonment and banishment:

Yet when you were about to hold the congress you asked me to send a message which I obeyed, and I mentioned that the Front's gates should be opened to parties and groups ... And I certainly did not have the Tudeh party in mind, which you have mentioned in your letter and used as a red herring [with which to put down my argument]. The Tudeh party is the same party which in the first year of oil nationalisation vehemently opposed it – but since the society did not buy or approve of their views – it gave up its opposition to the oil nationalisation policy, but in any case remained in opposition. [My reference was] to those parties and groups which were ready to sacrifice everything they had on the path to freedom.[7]

Why had the Socialist League not been invited to attend the NF's congress, he enquired? They had written that they had asked the parties affiliated to the Front to supply the full list of their members and a brief description of their past activities to the Front's secretariat; and here he dealt a mortal blow to the leaders:

> I am bound to say that, given the presence of a few of our betters (*as ma behtaran*, i.e. agents of the regime) in the [Front's central] council, these people would be very naïve to give their dossiers to the National Front ... and end up with the same fate as the poor his Excellency.[8]

Immediately after receiving this letter the central council called an emergency meeting. They wrote back on 2 April 1964 that they had no intention of 'arguing with the esteemed leader', but had tried to show that the information which others had sent him was 'not in accord with the truth'. However, they explained that since the Socialist League's application (of May 1961) for membership of the Front had been 'opposed by some gentlemen in the then executive committee of the Front', it had been decided not to take a decision on it, and their application 'has not been discussed in the central council to this day'. They concluded by saying that since he was 'the leader of the Popular Movement' they did not wish to confront him. On the other hand, they were not prepared to change their rules. Therefore, unless he accepted the content of this and their previous letter 'this council would be unable to continue its work'.[9]

> Mosaddeq sent a copy of their letter to the Students' Committee, who wrote back answering it point by point. They wrote that the Freedom movement had not been admitted to the congress as a political party, only as individuals. The Socialist League's membership had not been considered (by the NF's own admission) for four [in fact, three] years. The opposition within the Front itself

consisted not of a few individuals and groups, but all of the affiliated parties save for Iran party but including its youth and activists as well as the bazaar and the university.[10] Mosaddeq wrote a short reply congratulating them and adding 'now that I am unable to do anything, and I am living in jail, I pray God for your ever increasing success with a heavy heart and tearful eyes'.[11]

Still he refused to give up. He wrote again to the NF council on 19 May, enclosing the replies and reactions of the Students' Committee, the Freedom Movement, the Socialist League and the other dissident parties. He once again told them to put aside their opposition to the full representation of all the Popular Movement parties, and ended by saying that if they did not accept his suggestion, that would be his last letter to them.[12] They did not even bother to reply. Six weeks later (on 12 June) he wrote an extremely polite and friendly (even humble) letter to Saleh, pleading with him to do something. Saleh wrote back saying he himself was unwell, and that regarding the question of 'the Front's constitution to which – once again – you have referred, the answer is the same as has been given to you in the formal letters of the Front's council and executive committee'.[13]

The regime was getting stronger by day, the Freedom Movement's top leaders had already been put on military trial, and the Front had been unable to do anything at the best of times in the four years that had passed since its foundation. It was just the right time to quit the stage, blame everything on Mosaddeq's 'interference' and resume their own normal business activities. Having dealt so contemptuously with the man to whose immense prestige and popularity they owed almost all their public support, and whom they had otherwise turned into an idol who was beyond criticism (except by themselves), the second National

Front withered away, and most of its members in Europe and America (and some in Iran) soon turned to Maoism and other brands of Marxism-Leninism.

THE THIRD NATIONAL FRONT

Maleki, who had returned to Iran a couple of days after the Persian New Year (21 March), was informed of these events from the very beginning. On 25 March he wrote to Pichdad that Mosaddeq was very unhappy with the Front's leaders but encouraged the students (who were no longer committed to the leaders) not to stop their activities, and hated the 'wait and see policy' which Saleh and the others had adopted. He had heard about Mosaddeq's critical letter to the European NF but had not seen it yet.[14]

A few days later he wrote a letter to an Iranian socialist in Graz and profusely thanked their unit for their kindness to him while he was there. He alluded to the situation of two leaders of the Socialist League who were in jail and the fact that they had now been banished to a jail in the south of Iran:

> There is not much news. Those two travellers, the account of whose problems you have read, have now gone on another journey, and there is not much hope [for them]. The oppression has reached its peak. The third National Front has not yet been declared. From every viewpoint the situation has turned in our favour but due to the difficult conditions it is not taken advantage of.[15]

Three weeks later, on 23 April 1964, he informed Pichdad, and through him the League in Europe, of Mosaddeq's letter to the NF and pointed out that its leadership was virtually finished as they hardly had any remaining supporters, saying that there was division even within the Iran party which was all that was left of the second NF. He explained that the prestige of and support for the Freedom Movement has considerably increased and that they had good relations with the League:

> A few days ago I visited [Mehdi] Bazargan, [Ayatollah] Taleqani and [Ezzatollah] Sahabi [Freedom Movement leaders in jail] and we had a chat. Taleqani, in particular, spoke about [the need for] unity in the [Popular] Movement. It was agreed that I would see them again on other special days when there is more time.[16]

Meantime, there was regular exchange on writing articles for *Sosialism*, both quarterly and monthly, raising funds from Tehran comrades and friends in support of their publication, and receiving copies of them in Tehran by every means other than regular post, due to censorship. For example, Pichdad would buy a copy of the popular Paris magazine *Paris Match*, cut through most of its pages and place a number of copies of the monthly *Sosialism* inside it and post it as a copy of *Paris Match*! *Elm o Zendegi*, both quarterly and weekly, had been banned since 1961, and remained so forever.

In his letter of 24 May to Pichdad, Maleki wrote about these events and reported that Hamid Mahamedi had been arrested. Mahamedi had been a leading member of the European Socialist League as well as a prominent student leader in London. On his return, he had joined the League in Iran. Another activist of the League in Iran had also been arrested: 'they kidnap people from their homes while their families have no idea about where they are and what are the charges against them.'[17]

At the time, though very active in writing, translating, corresponding and exchanging news and views with the socialists in Europe, nevertheless, he kept repeating that he was no longer in the leadership of the League in Iran, but he did see its members and gave them counsel when asked. In his next letter to Pichdad, Maleki wrote that the League had issued a short leaflet commemorating the revolt of June 1963, and as a result a few of its leaders had been arrested. However, by previous agreement, Manuchehr Safa and Abbas Aqelizadeh had accepted responsibility for it, so they were detained and the others released. SAVAK had said 'for now it is not necessary for Maleki to come [for interrogation]'.[18] 'Although I am personally not thinking of participating in any party and leadership, nevertheless I try to persuade various Iranian socialists to organise themselves.'[19]

September 1864 had seen the formation for the International Workingmen's Association, usually known as the First International. It was dissolved in 1876 and the Second International, the organisation of which Albert Carthy was general secretary, was formed in 1889. Nevertheless, they had decided to hold the centenary conference of the First International in September 1964 in Brussels, and Carthy had written to Maleki inviting him to it. Maleki wrote to Pichdad that he would not go, but would try to see if someone else could go in his place. He also expressed the wish that Carthy would send the League in Europe an invitation as well. He had indeed, and the League in Europe sent a delegation to the conference in September. Al-e Ahmad was in Brussels at the time, and returning from Europe he told Maleki that Pichdad's speech was one of the best.[20]

However, Maleki criticised the decision of the League in Europe for keeping their participation in the conference secret so they would not be branded as social democrats. He wrote that they should not be afraid of accusations by cowardly people who, because they do nothing themselves, are good at verbal radicalism and labelling the activists. When he had been released from Falk al-Aflak, he wrote, and had begun open and peaceful activity again, a famous poet who was totally inactive and kept company with powerful servants of the regime had criticised him for not using harsh language against 'the great idol' (i. e. the shah). Typically, he pointed out that the aim and the strategy should not be sacrificed to tactical expediency. Indeed, he was to write to the League in Europe time and again that they should not follow the others in their unrealistic radicalism and that they should not do anything which would make it impossible for them to return to Iran. Occasionally they nodded, but never changed their tactics.

Regarding the question itself, he wrote that they should not have a brand of socialism in their pockets and compare it to every other brand, and, if they did not match, totally reject the other brands.

> I should briefly remind you first that it is possible to doubt the scientificity of Marx's own Marxism without committing a great sin and becoming a political renegade ... Doubtless sociology will become a science one day, but that day is far away and, in particular, Marx's socialism. To put it briefly and generally: the extreme pauperisation of the majority of people and proletarisation of not only all the workers but also the petit and middle bourgeoisie; the polarisation of the society; socialist revolution in the industrial societies before the agricultural societies; the necessity of the development of capitalism in backward societies, and the inevitability of socialist revolution in advanced industrial societies; ... and other predictions,

theories and scientific laws have in practice proven to be unscientific and the process of history has denied their veracity. Given all this, how can Marx's socialism be called scientific?[21]

In his long letter of 29 September to Pichdad, Maleki reported on the situation in Tehran. He wrote of the matchless oppression which existed 'in the era of the royal revolution, or as the *Ettela'at* daily has put it, the revolution of revolutions'. Aqelizadeh and Safa had been sentenced to three years' imprisonment in a closed military court because of the leaflet about the anniversary of the revolt of June 1963, as well as being accused of 'insulting the shah' and belonging to an organisation, i.e. the League, which was opposed to constitutional monarchy, for neither of which latter charges they offered any evidence. A couple of prominent military defence lawyers were being prosecuted simply because they had defended Mehdi Bazargan and Ayatollah Taleqani. In some cases, the charges related to their defence, in others they had used other pretexts; for example, they arrested General Baharmast for whoring whereas he was a homosexual.

Apparently, the regime had got anxious and angry at the demise of the former NF's central council and the rise of the third NF's council which was emerging with the League's participation ... Safa and Aqekizadeh were in the same prison ward as Ayatollah Zanjani and Ayatollah Taleqni. Members of the Freedom Movement of which these were two of the most prominent had expressed the wish that their situation in the Qasr prison be reported in the monthly *Sosialism*.

Apart from other pressures, prison officers pressed the political prisoners to partake in state festivals and anniversaries in jail, which were initiated by non-political prisoners, or the political ones who had sold their souls. And when they refused they made

233

up new charges against them. The Freedom Movement prisoners were kept in the same ward as smugglers, heroin dealers and embezzlers who enjoyed all sorts of privileges and ceaselessly caused trouble for political prisoners. For example, they had hurled insults at Bazargan and Taleqani for refusing to participate in the anniversary celebrations of the 1953 coup.

Not having been in Iran at the time, Baqer Kazemi, finance minister and foreign minister under Mosaddeq, had saved himself from the fate of the second NF leaders and said that he was in perfect agreement with Mosaddeq. He headed the three-man committee charged with setting up the founding convention of the third NF. The convention would then invite three members of the parties, groups, etc., to make up the third NF's council. So far they had asked seven parties, groups, etc., which would make up a twenty-one-man council. But since the presence of so many would attract attention, they were thinking of reducing it to seven. Kazemi had told a leader of the Socialist League that he would like to see Maleki, but he had been told that Maleki was not well and rarely left home.[22]

Maleki kept in constant touch with every aspect of the situation in Iran, and with the Socialist League in Europe. In all of his (mainly long) letters to the European League via Pichdad, he reported on the Iranian political and economic situation, commented on activities in Europe, and especially on the monthly *Sosialism* which he said they impatiently waited to receive since they had no outlet at all of their own.[23] He also wrote intermittently on the books on the third world development, etc. – e.g. Tibor Mende's *Un Monde Possible* (1963) – which he had translated from French but was not allowed to publish under his own name.

He wrote on 18 October 1964 that the Office of Propaganda, now named the Department of Information, is spending most of its budget on articles that were published in second- and third-rate foreign journals. They had surpassed Goebbels and his like in exaggeration 'and according to the Shah who claims he has carried out a revolution, it is years that Iran has put the socialist countries behind it'. He added that there is a shortage of wheat since the peasants have been 'freed' (in the sense of having lost all they had), and they have imported $100 million worth of wheat from America, claiming that it is a free grant. Also there is a near famine situation in Azerbaijan and its governor says he is under pressure to run vanloads of flour in town but he is worried that they would be looted. The governor of Isfahan says they have shut down some bakeries and now they are told to reopen them but this is not possible without more flour.

Furthermore, Nur al-Din Alamuti, Amini's justice minister, is about to be put on trial and will apparently be sentenced to three years' imprisonment. Under him, the justice ministry was as good as it was during Mosaddeq's premiership and in some ways even better since more official thieves were prosecuted while he was minister. Now, instead, a number of ultra-thieves who had embezzled a great deal of money from the state fishing company have been acquitted and freed.[24]

In the next letter, Maleki mentioned his financial difficulties 'as a private matter'. He also reported on the passage of the capitulation law for Americans in Iran in the parliament, and Ayatollah Khomeini's damning of it which had led to his exile in Turkey. He wrote that the bill had been first passed by the senate so quietly that 'the great idol' [the shah] himself had been surprised. So they encouraged the Majlis deputies to make some noise when the bill went there, and they made such a racket that they were expurgated. Another scandal was the government's borrowing of $200 million from American banks to spend on the army.[25] They had made up a joke for

Hasan'ali Mansur, the prime minister, that Dr Ludwig Erhard, known for his 'economic miracle' in Germany, has written and asked him to go and solve Germany's financial problems.[26]

Regular correspondence continued and Maleki kept members of the League in Europe informed of the happenings in Iran. On one occasion he wrote that 150 members of the Corps of Knowledge (young conscripts who were sent to villages to teach) were recommended to become regular civilian teachers after the end of their service, and it had turned out that 110 of them had backgrounds of theft and rape.[27] Recently the regime had made a lot of noise about Abd al-Nasser's putting an agent in a box to send him off somewhere. The truth of the matter is that the regime in Iran had shut the hands, feet, mouths and pens of everyone: 'the whole of Iran today is like a box in which the entire Iranian people are imprisoned.'[28]

Maleki was following the developments in China, and the Maoist movement in general. He subscribed to *Pékin Information* (the French version of *Peking Review*) which he received via Germany or France and regularly read and talked about.[29] In his letter of 21 April 1965 he wrote to Pichdad:

> In the Stalinist era we suffered a lot until the whole world admitted that there are different roads to revolutionary objectives. Very unfortunately, a China has now emerged and anyone who would want to be an acute freedom-lover must confirm its view and divide the world into two camps ... Both in socialism and in communism pluralism is undeniable.

In the same letter Maleki briefly referred to the recent assassination attempt on the shah (see page 237) and passed some positive as well as negative comments on the third NF which had taken a long time to be formed but had not yet been publicly declared.[30]

On 11 April, a number of young men, some of them educated in Britain, were arrested on the bogus charge of conspiracy to assassinate the shah. The shah had indeed survived an attack by Reza Shamsabadi, an imperial soldier at his office, but only one member of the group, Ahmad Manusri Tehrani, had known the soldier. However, during the arrests they discovered a discussion paper written by Parviz Nikkhah, the group's leader, studying possible guerrilla warfare in rural areas. The young men were put on military trial and sentenced to various prison terms, including life. But of the group only Mansuri, along with his friend Kamrani, were convicted of having known Shamsabadi's general wish to assassinate the shah.[31] However, the fact that none of them was executed was largely due to the intervention of forty-nine British Labour party MPs and one peer with the shah. Hamid Mahamedi was also arrested, though he had been representing the Socialist League in the preparatory meetings of the third NF. He did not belong to the above-mentioned group but had been arrested by mistake by the army intelligence who were initially handling the case.

This was a blessing in disguise since, when the files were handed over to SAVAK, Mahamedi was told that he was lucky because they had been about to arrest him for the right reasons and put him in jail for a long time. So his case was dismissed after six months in jail. Later he went to Harvard University where he got his Ph.D. He was still in prison when Maleki was arrested and saw him. Maleki mentioned him in his last letter, of 29 July, before imprisonment, to Pichdad. In that letter Maleki enthusiastically reported the public announcement of the formation of the third NF, saying that though the regime had threatened ('our friends, especially') to take severe measures against it, nevertheless they had done nothing. He was speaking too soon.[32]

MALEKI IN PRISON AGAIN

On 18 August 1965 SAVAK broke into Maleki's home at dawn, ransacked his house and arrested him. At the same time three leaders of the Socialist League, Alijan Shansi, Reza Shayan and Hossein Sarshar, were arrested at their homes. Maleki could not have been arrested without the shah's prior approval. Within days, the news reached the Secretariat of the Socialist International in London. They immediately sent telegrams and wrote letters to European socialist parties and asked them to protest to the Iranian government and demand Maleki's release. They advised those parties, such as the Labour party, who were in government, to protest through their foreign ministries as well. Albert Carthy was in Australia at the time after he had made a stop in Tehran and seen Maleki. Hence the Secretariat was convinced that that was the reason for Maleki's arrest, because the Iranian embassy had taken a long time and asked many questions before they issued a visa for him.

There was another British connection. A few months before, Princess Ashraf, the shah's interfering twin sister, had called an international women's conference in Tehran to which Margaret McKay,[33] the ex-communist Labour MP for the Clapham constituency in London had been invited. Jock and Millie Haston,[34] who were leading members of that constituency and quite influential in the trade unions and Labour party, had suggested to her that she see Maleki on her visit to Tehran. Having been looked after well in Iran, and having heard Maleki's complaints about lack of freedom and democracy in her room in the Hilton hotel, she had defended the regime vehemently and had asked Maleki (and Hamid Mahamedi, who was accompanying him) to leave.

When the news of Maleki's arrest reached the British press, her meeting with Maleki was mentioned as a possible cause of his arrest. She responded angrily and said that 'two men of deplorable views' had visited her in Tehran and she did not wish her name to be associated with them. The Hastons called a meeting of the constituency party in Clapham and asked her for an explanation, to which she had responded by saying that Maleki had been a Stalinist who had later turned fascist. The matter came up again in 1970 when she was asked to answer for other doubtful activities; she was the first member of the British parliament to be deselected by her constituency which meant that she lost her seat in the House of Commons.

A matter that came up prominently in interrogations was the text of a lecture by T. Cuyler Young[35] – the well-known archaeologist of Iran and the Middle East at the University of Toronto – apparently delivered at Harvard University. It had been a long and severe criticism of the Iranian regime, ending by saying that if the shah's days are not numbered, his years are.[36] Maleki had written about this to Pichdad. He wrote that he had a copy of the lecture which was just like a report that they themselves would have written about Iran. They had produced a summary of it in Persian and were hoping to produce copies of the English text and circulate it in Tehran.[37] SAVAK knew about this and much more through the agents they had planted in the Socialist League.[38] They were indeed aware that they were being watched closely, but Maleki kept reassuring himself that it did not matter because they were not involved in illegal activities, as if law mattered any more.

There were many other pretexts for which Maleki and his colleagues had been arrested, but the chief cause was the public announcement of the formation of the third NF, which SAVAK wanted to kill in its infancy, as it in fact did.

At any rate, the following is an excerpt of how SAVAK reported the news of Maleki's arrest in a article planted in the newspaper daily *Keyhan* even before there was any interrogation, let alone a trial:

> It has been announced that, during the last few days, Khalil Maleki and some of his colleagues have been arrested by the security authorities on the charge of spreading Marxist and communist (*eshteraki*) ideas, poisoning [the people's] minds and acting against the country's security ...
>
> According to the background, Khalil Maleki has been one of the promoters of the *eshteraki* ideology in Iran, and along with fifty-two other leaders of the Tudeh party has launched that party [sic] ... and afterwards, when, because of his ambitiousness, he has run into conflict with that party's leaders over party positions, has managed to persuade a group [of party members] to split with the party under his leadership.
>
> The above-mentioned person, while sticking to his [old] ideology, had been looking for an opportunity to implement his malicious ideas ... and, following the national uprising of 19 August, he was imprisoned and banished for that reason.
>
> After a while, according to the [Arabic] expression 'Public amnesia is my shield' (*nisyan al-nasu hisni*) he took sinister advantage of the forgetfulness of some people, especially the young, and in the name of sympathy for the labouring classes, securing public welfare and extending social justice, he injected dreams and mirage-like ideas in the minds of a small number of people who were prepared to work with him, so that he would thus acquire power, and in the end manage to satisfy his passion for, and his cult of, great power. At this juncture, Iranian society was led towards an opulent standard of living as a result of the 6 Bahman [January

1963] White Revolution and [other] progressive projects, and consequently [Khalil Maleki's group] lost its deceitful propagandist weapon.

Khalil Maliki who had one day promised the reform of the workers' and peasants' living standards as a dream, and believed that it would only be possible through a series of revolutionary actions involving devastation and massacre, realised that [even better reforms have been carried out without any bloodshed and] the Iranian people look forward to a hopeful and brilliant future, and henceforth they would not pay any attention to the balderdash put out by Khalil Maleki and his friends, in the hope of achieving his perverse and power-seeking wishes. So he looked for a new instrument, and following that, he declared the subversive riots of 6 June [1963] – which caused much financial and spiritual damage to the motherland – a national [or, popular] revolt.[*][39]

The above diatribe leaves little room for discussing the prolonged process of interrogation and the sham military trial that followed it. They tortured Shansi so savagely to make false confessions against Maleki, especially that he tried to create an underground organisation, that he tried to commit suicide.[40] Sarshar told them that Maleki had been involved in raising funds to send to Europe in support of the publication of *Sosialism*, and had been involved in distributing Cuyler Young's lecture. When he was confronted with Maleki, he not only did not retract his claims but made completely false accusations against him as well.[41]

As may be expected, the trial looked more like anything but a judicial process. First, General Farsiu, the military prosecutor, delivered a speech against Maleki virtually to prove that

* This, of course, was not true; see Chapter 7.

he had been a traitor from birth. He even said that he had been Maleki's pupil at school and remembered from then that he was a trouble-maker. He repeated all the charges of the Tudeh party against Maleki especially that he had led the Tudeh split because he had not been elected to its central committee (four years before the event!). The upshot was that he had rebelled against the constitution and conspired to endanger the country's security.

Maleki defended himself logically and on points of law but did not turn the tables on the court and make it into a sensational confrontation, something that he came to regret afterwards.[42]

He said in the court that he had been kept in solitary confinement in a 2 x 2 metre cell with a platform made of stones and bricks on which it was not possible to stretch out normally. There was a little barred window near the ceiling so, given his heart disease, he often had to stand on the platform to breathe through the window. The prison doctor had examined him, confirmed his heart disease, and suggested that the door of his cell be kept open, but after twenty-four hours the SAVAK interrogator – a man called Reza Attarpur, whose professional cover name was Hosseinzadeh – had shown up and ordered it to be shut. 'It is very clear that they behave like this in order to break the prisoner's spirit.' He was not physically tortured, but was subjected to long interrogations well into the night, and one night the interrogation had been accompanied by threats, while a thug was standing behind him ... 'They tortured Shansi so badly that he had to be stopped from committing suicide.'[43] Maleki was convicted and sentenced to three years' solitary confinement. The other three received shorter terms.

But he was released sooner, in late October 1966. The most important reason behind this was the constant pressure brought on the Iranian government by European socialists, including the Socialist International, to the extent that he had a letter (dated

May 1966) smuggled out of jail (through Jalal Al-e Ahmad, who was regularly visiting him in prison) addressed to Albert Carthy, thanking him for his efforts on his behalf.[44] When in the winter of 1966 the socialist President Franz Jonas of Austria visited Tehran, prompted by his party, he intervened with the shah on Maleki's behalf, but the shah told him that 'Maleki is not a European-type socialist; he is a pro-Chinese communist'.[45] At any rate, they wrote in the official Iranian press that Maleki was not being tried for being a socialist but for having rebelled against constitutional monarchy.

When they were deciding to recommend 'pardon' for Maleki before finishing his sentence, the SAVAK emphasised that up till then 'Shahanshah Aryamehr and other Iranian authorities have received countless letters from different official and unofficial international bodies, mainly Western socialists, requesting that he be pardoned'. And they continued: given that Maleki is suffering from heart and eye disease, he would better be released so he would not die in jail, resulting in the creation of another 'saint' (*Imamzadeh*).[46]

MALEKI'S LAST YEARS

Maleki was greeted by his family and a small number of close friends, including Jalal Al-e Ahmad and Simin Daneshvar, at home. Despite all that he had endured his spirits were high and he was ready to resume activities as much as possible though he wrote his first letter to Pichdad on 15 December. This was a reply to Pichdad's welcoming letter on behalf of the socialists in Europe. He had been much impressed, and very grateful. He expressed his hope in their activities since 'as you know, there is absolute silence here'. He had also received a letter from Albert

Carthy and would write a reply to him soon. He suggested that the League in Europe also write and thank the Committee for the Defence of Political Prisoners in Iran (led by Jean-Paul Sartre), or tell Maleki to write to them from Iran. He said that many had tried to have him released from jail, but it all was due to action from outside the country.

He had had an eye operation and was not allowed to write much until a new pair of glasses for reading and writing was made for him. In a postscript addressed to his brother Hossein he wrote that 'the situation in Iran is not encouraging' and after what he had been through he added: 'in their fear and cautiousness the people are ahead of SAVAK, that is, they are more afraid than SAVAK expects them to be.'[47]

On 26 January 1967 he addressed a letter to Pichdad and Malek. 'Today is the anniversary of the revolution of the shah and the people. They have all stopped working and schools are closed as well. Everyone is willingly and enthusiastically celebrating this auspicious festival,' he wrote with sarcasm. Mosaddeq was in Tehran at his son's house for treatment. His health had improved 'but I heard that he has returned to hospital'. Maleki had translated a few books which had remained unpublished. There was a lot of thirst for good books, he wrote. The people in the know were saying that if *Elm o Zendegi* was now published it would sell ten times more copies than in the past. 'This is due to total political silence and inactivity.'[48]

Both before and after imprisonment, Maleki frequently wrote about his sons Piruz and Noruz, but especially the former who was studying in Rome – his second son Behruz's intelligence was below average; his parents had accepted the fact and found him a suitable job. However, Maleki mentions Piruz in his letters to Pichdad and Malek usually in relation to two particular things: what he calls his 'social activities', by which he means student and political activities; and the question of sending him his allowance through Malek.[49]

On 5 March 1967 Mosaddeq died in a Tehran hospital which had been endowed by his mother and was run by his son.[50] The news upset Maleki terribly, as it did many Iranians. In his letter of 29 March he wrote to Pichdad that, 'after the passing of the exalted father [i.e. Mosaddeq]' he had sent two letters to the new address which he had been given for correspondence and wondered if they had received it.[51] In the following letter, he once again enquired if they had received the two letters 'regarding the death of the exalted father'.[52] These letters have not been found but there is one written after the anniversary of Mosaddeq's death, reporting that he had accompanied Mosaddeq's son to visit his estate where he had been buried.[53] The authorities had not let them bury Mosaddeq in the cemetery of his own choosing or any other public cemetery.

Another fairly frequent theme was Maleki's reference to books he was receiving from Europe as well as the many books he had translated, both before imprisonment and while in prison, which they did not allow to be published. Thus he wrote to a friend in England:

Both in and out of prison I have written or translated many books and articles none of which at present can be published, not because of their subjects but only because I am the author or translator ... For some time I have been writing on the Sino-Soviet conflict, some of which have been published under a pen name.[54]

He later wrote to Pichdad: 'I wrote three articles on the Sino-Soviet dispute under a pen name for the *Ferdowsi* magazine but they stopped their publication, not because of their content but because of their sensitivity towards me.'[55]And still later he wrote to his brother Hossein that whatever he wrote and translated would not be published when the authorities realised he was the author. He had recently translated Isaac Deutscher's *The Unfinished Revolution*. At first they welcomed it with open arms, but when they realised it was his they refused publication.[56]

Twice he commented on the situation in Iran from the viewpoint of the regime's plans and activities. In both cases he included both 'positive' and 'negative' points. He wrote that although the landlord system has not been entirely abolished, progress had been made to a large extent. Regarding the so-called revolutionary corps and formal rights for women, the measures were positive at least from a legal, but not practical point of view. The technocracy has the better of the bourgeoisie. The industrial plants, built with the help of the Soviets and Eastern European countries, are palpably helpful towards industrialisation, and so on.

On the other hand, the regime had stabilised imperialism's oil interests, and the arms they bought from them and the Soviet Union were intended solely for maintaining their own security. There was a lot of unnecessary expenditure in addition to the army and arms purchases in all the high organs of the state. They spent a great deal on propaganda both inside and outside the country which placed a heavy burden on the people, but had worked well for them. Although a certain amount of economic progress had been made, corruption tended to nullify its effects, but then the high oil revenues 'filled up all the holes'. In foreign policy there were good relations with the Soviet bloc but their regional politics favoured reactionary states such as Jordan and Saudi Arabia.[57]

The Malekis had a modest income which included Sabiheh Maleki's salary as the principal of a girls' school. But they were now in dire financial difficulty because the ministry of education

would not pay Maleki's pension as he had been a 'criminal con-
vict', and they had to finance Piruz in Rome as well as Noruz who
was at Pahlavi University in Shiraz. Maleki spoke to Asadollah
Alam, minister of the royal court, who had been instrumental in
Maleki's visit to the shah several years before and who had sometimes helped with the release of socialist prisoners on Maleki's
request. Alam arranged for him to work with the Department of
Publication and Translation at Melli University.[58]

However, in July 1968 he wrote to his brother Hossein:

> The situation here is silent and stable as before. For me
> and others like me there is perfect oppression as concerns
> politics and publication. They do not pay my pension
> despite the fact that I have earned it. Even the small amount
> of money which I was receiving from Melli University's
> Department of Publication and Translation was cut off
> by Dr (Mohammad Ali) Mojtahedi – who had become
> president of the University.[59]

He had held the job only for five months.

There has been a rumour since Maleki's death that after leaving
jail his spirit was broken. His correspondence shows the opposite.
He did face financial difficulties and was unable to see people
regularly and publish his books and articles, but he was constantly
reading and writing, nevertheless. His letters show that he was not
only concerned about the situation in Iran and the world, but was
studying the main social and political issues in regard to them. In a
letter Pichdad had asked him if there was any 'news' in Iran, meaning political activities, etc. His reply was that 'there is no news that
there is not', alluding to a verse by Hafiz. 'If occasionally there is
some news it is killed in infancy.'[60] And he later wrote to another
friend: 'I have a lot of subjects for reading and writing, both about

the past and my memoirs and about the present and the future. I cannot just live in the past like some old people.'[61] And still later: 'Regarding genealogy! I have no interest in the past, especially of an aristocratic family. Although I have got old, I look to the future.'[62]

Maleki had for some time been optimistic that de-Stalinisation in Russia and the rise of relatively moderate Eurocommunism might result in more progress in the communist world. Then came the Soviet invasion of Czechoslovakia. He wrote:

> Mr Brezhnev and his colleagues have really surpassed Stalin because Stalin did not attack Yugoslavia. They have even surpassed American imperialism, since at least America is in Vietnam at the invitation of the [South Vietnamese] government and is fighting its ideological enemies. Whereas the Warsaw Pact comrades have militarily attacked a fraternal party, and violated a fraternal country ... of course not forgetting the amount of bloodshed in Vietnam.[63] ... I gratefully received the two volumes about Czechoslovakia (and the Prague spring).[64]

Maleki's last letter to Pichdad, and probably the last letter he ever wrote, was dated 25 June 1969. In it he made a typically remarkable comment on the Iranian Freemasonry. A book on Iranian Freemason societies and their membership had virtually exploded in Tehran. SAVAK documents published in the 1980s have revealed that they had secretly aided and financed that project in accordance with the shah's wishes, in all probability in order to discredit those named, and often also pictured in the three volumes, most of whom belonged to the social and political establishment. Freemasonry in Iran was at the time universally regarded as a den of the most hardened and corrupt 'British spies'. Maleki wrote:

In the last two months, the publication of *Faramushkhaneh ya Framasonary dar Iran* (in three volumes) ... has been the topic of conversation in the social and political circles of Tehran. In Iran they attach more importance to this organisation than it in fact is worth, and show its members in a worse light than they deserve.[65]

Two weeks later Maleki died of a heart attack while undergoing an operation for bleeding of the stomach. According to his will, no public memorial meeting was held for him. His wife, Sabiheh Khanom, wrote to a friend: 'Khalil did not at all wish to leave this world. He always had long and wide plans for himself ... At any rate, death suddenly claimed him.'[66]

EPILOGUE

Maleki's Success and Failure

K halil Maleki was a unique phenomenon in the politics of twentieth-century Iran. Born in 1901, his life spanned the Constitutional Revolution, the First World War and the rise of Reza Shah, the Second World War, the emergence of the Tudeh party, the nationalisation of Iranian oil, the 1953 coup, the dictatorship of the 1950s, the power struggles of the early sixties, the shah's White Revolution and the restoration of one-man arbitrary rule until his death in 1969. Had he lived longer, he could have seen the revolution of February1979, but he is unlikely to have played any significant role in it because he was an advocate of reform, not revolution.

He is, of course, unlikely to have remained silent even at that age and in those circumstances, and would have tried to revive the old Socialist League, but to little effect, since many if not most of its members had already converted to Marxism or even Marxism-Leninism, although they did not join any of the existing parties. Indeed, immediately after the revolution they reorganised themselves into 'The Socialist League of Iran' with a virtually Marxist-Leninist manifesto, but when the revolutionary power struggles began in earnest they simply withered away. Very few of the new generations had even heard of Maleki's name, let alone his political career, and the older generation remembered him at best as a compromising social democrat with the entire negative connotations with which they held such a position. The other non-Islamist and non-Marxist-Leninist parties and groupings did not fare much better: the real contest was between revolutionary Leftists and Islamists in which the latter, who had a much wider social base and were led by the revolution's supreme leader, emerged as victors.

The irony is that it was some time after the revolution that many subscribing to Marxist-Leninist ideologies changed their minds and many younger Islamists turned to reformist politics. The legacy of Maleki and his ideas has indirectly provided alternative paradigms and filled some of the vacuum. Even those who would like to change the Islamic regime now advocate the application of peaceful means to that end.

What shall one make of Maleki's record in view of the evidence before us in this volume? He was a selfless intellectual who spent almost the whole of his active life working for the improvement of his country and the lot of its people: he firmly believed in freedom, democracy and social justice. He was a theorist, analyst, writer, translator and journalist. He read and wrote a vast amount. He wanted power, not for himself, but for the movements which he sincerely served, and that is why he shunned all opportunities for becoming a parliamentary deputy. He worked full-time for his political projects and programmes ever since his forced retirement from his teaching post after the 1953 coup.

He was not a charismatic personality vis-à-vis large masses of the people, but he was a most effective speaker and writer for the educated classes, especially the young among them. A major reason for his personal failures was the fact that he rejected populism while expecting elites that enjoyed a wide following to take his advice. He believed so much in the correct long-term strategies that he ignored the tactics for realising them. He relied on reason and evidence without establishing the right public relations for attracting a large following. He kept saying that you should not follow the crowd but make the crowd follow you; but how could this be done when he would write at the top of the cover of *Elm o Zendegi*: 'For the writers of *Elm o Zendegi* the right criterion is the truth, not deceiving the public, or wishing to please them, or being afraid of their disapproval'? How then could he draw the public to his ideas? He relied on the mass support of the Tudeh party and following it the Popular Movement, before the second NF took it away from him. He saw his best role as an organiser of elite groups and adviser to mass leaders, not as a mass leader himself. Although not quarrelsome, he was frank, even blunt, in expressing his views and ideas, making a lot of enemies and hurting a lot of feelings. To give but one example, he wrote in the Socialist League's manifesto (1960) that, 'For the long run, the non-oil economics policy was and is stupid'. Ignoring 'the long run' qualification, his detractors would say that he means Mosaddeq was stupid. If Maleki made any major mistakes, then these were indeed the mistakes he made.

At every major turning point he presented the right analysis and put forward the correct prediction which, however, was ignored or denounced by mass leaders. He was an 'outsider' and 'radical' in the old sense of the term. An outsider is one who does not quite fit in with the prevailing social and intellectual framework, watching or judging it from outside. In politics this goes far beyond simply being in opposition to the existing government or even the established regime. Oppositions, too, have their own framework, their own rules of 'proper' conduct, their own internal censorship. 'Radicals' in the old sense are those who speak their minds regardless of the sensitivities of the existing power centres: they do not recognise such boundaries, even if they are formally affiliated to them; and sooner or later they leave, are ignored or expelled.

Therefore, in both science and society, radicals and outsiders are original in the traditional meaning of the term in the history of art, science and socio-political thought. They tend to be critical of almost all the contemporary norms and prejudices but offer unpopular ideas and methods, and have no large power centres of their own to which they can attract converts, clients and fellow travellers. Most do not succeed in their lifetime and only receive recognition from future generations.

Maleki did not achieve his long-term goals, it is true. But nor did the mass movements which he unsuccessfully tried to direct to the path of success.

SELECT BIBLIOGRAPHY

ENGLISH BOOKS AND ARTICLES

Abrahamian, Ervand. *THE COUP: 1953, The CIA, and the Roots of Modern U.S.-Iranian Relations*. New York and London, The New Press, 2013

Acheson, Dean. *Present at the Creation: My Years in the State Department*. London, Hamish Hamilton, 1970

Afary, Janet, *The Iranian Constitutional Revolution, 1906–1911*. New York: Columbia University, 1996

Alvandi, Roham. *Nixon, Kissinger and the Shah*. New York, Oxford University Press, 2014

Atabaki, Touraj. *Azerbaijan: Ethnicity and the Struggle for Power in Iran*. London and New York, I. B. Tauris, 2000

Azimi, Fakhreddin. *The Quest for Democracy in Iran: A Century of Struggle against Authoritarian Rule*. Cambridge, MA, and London, Harvard University Press, 2008

———. *Iran: The Crisis of Democracy, 1941–1953*. London, I. B. Tauris, 1989

Bakhash, Sahul. '"Dear Anthony, Dear Leo", Britain's Quixotic Flirtation with Dynamic Change in Iran during World War II', *Iran Nameh, A Quarterly of Iranian Studies*, Special Issue Dedicated to Homa Katouzian for his Lifetime Service to Iranian Studies, 30, 4, winter 2016

Bharier, Julian. *Economic Development in Iran, 1900–1970*. London, Oxford University Press, 1971

Bill, James, and Roger Louis, eds, *Musaddiq, Iranian Nationalism and Oil*. London, I. B. Tauris and Austin: University of Texas Press, 1988

Chaqueri, Cosroe. 'Did the Soviets Play a Role in the Foundation of the Tudeh party in Iran?' *Cahier de le monde Russe*, 3, 1999, pp. 497–528; also *https://monderusse.revues.org/pdf/22*

Chehabi, H. E. 'The banning of the veil and its consequences', in Stephanie Cronin, *The Making of Modern Iran: State and Society under Riza Shah, 1921–1941*. London and New York, Routledge, 2003

Eden, Anthony. *Full Circle: The Memoirs of Sir Anthony Eden*. London, Cassell, 1960

Enayat, Hamid. *British Public Opinion and the Persian Oil Crisis*, MSc. (Econ) thesis. University of London, 1958

Evans, Richard J. *The Third Reich at War, 1939–1945*. London, Allen Lane, 2008

Fawcett, Louise. 'Revisiting the Iranian Crisis of 1946: How Much More Do We Know?', in Roham Alvandi, guest editor, *Iranian Studies*, 47, 3, May 2014; *Iran and the Cold War: The Azerbaijan Crisis of 1946*. Cambridge, Cambridge University Press, 1992

Gasiorowski, Mark J., and Malcolm Byrne. *Mohammad Mosaddeq and the 1953 Coup in Iran*, eds. Syracuse, Syracuse University Press, 2004

Gasiorowski, Mark J. 'The Qarani Affair and Iranian Politics', *International Journal of Middle East Studies*, 25, 4 November 1993

Hasanli, Jamil. *At the Dawn of the Cold War, the Soviet-American Crisis over Iranian Azerbaijan, 1941–1946*. Oxford, Rowman & Littlefield, 2006

Jafari, Reza. *Centre-Periphery Relations in Iran: The Case of the Southern Rebellion in 1946*. D.Phil. thesis, University of Oxford, 2000

Kasravi, Ahmad. *History of the Iranian Constitutional Revolution*, trans. Evan Siegel. Costa Mesa, CA, Mazda Publishers, 2006

Katouzian, Homa. 'Mosaddeq and the Intervention of the International Bank', *The Middle East in London*, 10, 1, December 2013–January 2014

_____. 'The Revolution for Law: A Chronographic Analysis of the Constitutional Revolution of Iran', in *Middle Eastern Studies*, 47, 5, 2011, reprinted in *IRAN: Politics, History and Literature*. London and New York, Routledge 2013

_____. *The Persians: Ancient, Mediaeval and Modern Iran*. New Haven and London, Yale University Press, paperback edition, 2010

_____. *State and Society in Iran: The Eclipse of the Qajars and the Emergence of the Pahlavis*. London and New York: I. B. Tauris, paperback edition, 2006

_____. 'The Revolt of Shaikh Mohammad Khiyabani'. *IRAN, Journal of the British Institute of Persian Studies*, 1999, reprinted in *Iranian History and Politics*. London and New York, Routledge, 2003

———. *Sadeq Hedayat: The Life and Legend of an Iranian Writer*. London and New York, I. B. Tauris, paperback edition, 2002

———. *Musaddiq and the Struggle for Power in Iran*. London and New York, I. B. Tauris revised paperback edition, 1999

———. *The Political Economy of Modern Iran*. London and New York, Macmillan and New York University Press, 1981

Khozhanov, Nicolay A. 'The Pretexts and Reasons for the Allied Invasion of Iran in 1941', *Iranian Studies*, 45, 4, July 2012

Kuzichkin, Vladimir, *Inside the KGB: Myth and Reality*, trans. Thomas B. Beattie, intro. Frederick Forsyth. London, Andre Deutsch, 1990

Ladjevardi Habib. *Labor Unions and Autocracy in Iran*. Syracuse, NY, Syracuse University Press, 1985

Lapping, Brian. *End of Empire*. London, Granada, 1985

Martin Vanessa. *Islam and Modernism, the Iranian Constitutional Revolution of 1906*. London and New York, I. B. Tauris, 1989

Mosaddeq, Mohammad. *Musaddiq's Memoirs*. London, Jebhe, 1988 (the English translation of the memoirs translated, with S. H. Amin, and edited and annotated, together with an eighty-one-page introduction by Homa Katouzian).

Pahlavi, Mohammadreza Shah. *Answer to History*. New York, Stein and Day, 1980

———. *Mission for My Country*. London: Hutchinson, 1961

Rahnema, Ali. *Behind the 1953 Coup in Iran: Thugs, Turncoats, Soldiers and Spooks*. Cambridge, Cambridge University Press, 2015

Randjbar-Daemi, Siavush. 'Down with the Monarchy: Iran's Republican Moment of August 1953', *Iranian Studies*, 46, 4, July 2016

Roosevelt, Kermit. *Countercoup: The Struggle for the Control of Iran*. New York, McGraw-Hill, 1979

Shuster, William Morgan. *The Strangling of Persia, A Record of European Diplomacy and Intrigue*. London, T. Fisher Unwin, 1912

Van Hook, ed. *Foreign Relations of the United States, 1952–54, Iran, 1951–54*, Washington, DC, United States Government Publishing Office, 2017, https://history.state.gov/historicaldocuments/frus1951-54Iran

Wilber, Donald. http://headquarters.opinionware.net/donald-n-wilbers-1954-report

Woodhouse, C. M. *Something Ventured*. London and New York, Granada, 1982

Wright, Denis. *The Persians Amongst the English: Episodes in Anglo-Persian Relations*. London, I. B. Tauris, 1985

BOOKS AND ARTICLES IN PERSIAN

Abdoh, Jalal (public prosecutor in the cases brought against Reza Shah's police chief, etc.), *Chehel Sal dar Sahneh* (Forty Years in the Scene), ed. Majid Tafreshi. Tehran, Rasa, 1989

Afshar, Iraj, ed. *Nameh-ha-ye Tehran* (Letters from Tehran). Tehran, Farzan, 2006

Alavi, Bozorg. *Khaterat-e Bozorg-e Alavi* (The Memoirs of …), ed. Hamid Ahmadi. Sweden, Nashr-e Baran, 1997

_____. *Panjah o Seh Nafar* (The Fifty-Three). Tehran, Amir Kabir, 1978

Al-e Ahmad, Jalal. 'Piremard Cheshm-e Ma Bud' (The Old Man Was Our Eye), in *Majmu'eh-ye Maqalat*, ed. Mostafa Zamani-Nia, vol. 1, Tehran: Mitra, 1994

_____. *Dar Khedmat va Khiyanat-e Roshanfekran* (On the Services and Betrayals of the Intellectuals). Tehran, Entesharat-e Ferdows, 1993

Amir Khosravi, Babak. *Nazar az Darun beh Naqsh-e Hezb-e Tudeh-ye Iran* (A Look from the Inside at the Role of the Tudeh Party of Iran). Tehran, Ettela'at, 1996

Anon., *Ruhaniyat va Asrar-e Fash Nashodeh* (The Clergy and the Undisclosed Secrets). Qom, Dar al-Fekr, n.d. (preface signed 1979)

Aqeli, Baqer, ed. *Khaterat-e Mohammad Sa'ed-e Maragheh'i* (Memoirs of …). Tehran, Nashr-e Namak, 1994

Avanesian, Ardeshir, *Khaterat-e Ardeshir Avanesian* (Memoirs of …), ed. Babak Amir Khosravi, Germany, Entesharat-e Hezb-e Demokratik-e Mardom Iran, 1980

Baqa'i, Mozaffar, interview with Habib Ladjevardi. *The Harvard Oral History Project*. http://www.fas.harvard.edu/~iohp/BAGHAI09.PDF

_____. *Cheh Kasi Monharef Shod* (Who Deviated?). Tehran: Senobar, 1984

_____. *Dar Pishgah-e Tarikh* (Before History). Kerman, Parma, n. d. (preface signed in June 1979)

Bayat, Kaveh. '*Ankeh Yek Nafas Asudegi Nadideh Manam*' (The One Who Has Not Rested for a Moment is Me). *Andisheh-ye Puya*, no. 36, August 2016

Bozorgmehr, Jalil, ed. *Mohammad Mosaddeq dar Mahkameh-ye Nezami* (Mosaddeq in the Military Court), vol. 1. Tehran, Entesharat-e Dustan, 2000

Dashti, Ali. *Avamel-e Soqut-e Mohammad Reza Pahlavi* (The Causes of the Fall of …), ed. Mehdi Mahuzi. Tehran, Zavvar, 2004

Eskandari, Iraj. *Khaterat-e Iraj Eskandari* (Memoirs of Iraj Eskandari, interview by Babak Amir Khosravi and Fereydun Azarnur). Tehran, Mo'asseseh-ye Motale'at va Pazhuhesh-ha-ye Siyasi, 1993

Fateh, Mostafa. *Panjah Sal Naft-e Iran* (Fifty Years of Iranian Oil). Tehran, Entesharat-e Payam, 1979

Hedayat, Mediqoli (Mokhber al-Saltaneh). *Khaterat o Khatarat* (Memoirs and Hazards). Tehran, Zavvar, 1984

Ghani, Qasem. *Yaddasht-ha-ye Doktor Qasem Ghani* (The Diary Notes of ...), ed. Cyrus Ghani (original London edition, vols 1–12), vols 1–8. Tehran, Zavvar, 1978

Kambakhsh, Abdossamad. *Nazari beh Jonbesh-e Kargari va Komonisti dar Iran* (A Look at the Proletarian and Communist Movement in Iran). Entesharart-e Hezb-e Tudeh-ye Iran, 1972 (published in East Germany)

Kasravi, Ahmad. *Tarikh-e Mahsruteh-ye Iran* (History of the Constitutional Revolution of Iran). Tehran, Amir Kabir, 1994

Katouzian, Homa, and Amir Pichdad, eds. *Yadnameh-ye Khalil Maleki* (Essays in Memory of Khalil Maleki). Tehran: Enteshar, 2015

Katouzian, Homa. 'Mosaddeq va Pishnahad-e Bank-e Jahani' (Mosaddeq and the World Bank Proposal), in *Estebdad, Demokrasi va Nehzat-e Melli* (Arbitrary Rule, Democracy and the Popular Movement). Tehran, Nash-re Markaz, sixth impression, 2013

Keshavarz, Fereydun. *Man Mottaham Mikonam* (I Accuse). Tehran, Ravaq, 1979

Khajeh Nuri, Ebrahim. *Bazigaran-e Asr-re Tala'i* (Actors of the Golden Era). Tehran, Jibi, 1978

Khameh'i, Anvar. *Az Enshe'ab ta Kudeta* (From the Split to the Coup). Tehran, Entesharat-e Hafteh, 1984

———. *Forsat-e Bozorg-e az Dast Rafteh*. Tehran, Entesharat-e Hafteh, 1983

———. *Panjah Nafar va Seh Nafar* (The Fifty and the Three). Tehran, Entesharat-e Hafteh, n.d. but published in the early 1980s

Kiyanuri, Nureddin. *Khaterat-e Nureddin Kiyanuri* (The Memoirs of ...). Tehran, Moassesseh-ye Tahqiqati va Entesharati-ye Didgah, 1992

———. *Drabareh-ye Bist o Hasht-e Mordad*. Tehran, 1979

Kuhi Kermani, Hossein. *Az Shahrivar-e 1320 ta Faje'eh-ye Azerbaijan* (From September 1941 to the Catastrophe of ...), vol. 1. Tehran: Kuhi, n. d.

Makki, Hossein *Tarikh-e Bistsaleh-ye Iran* (The Twenty-Year History of Iran), vol. 7. Tehran, Elmi, 1985

_____, ed. *Doktor Mosaddeq va Notq-ha-ye Tarikhi-ye U* (—and his historical speeches). Tehran, Javidan, 1985

_____. *Ketab-e Siyah* (The Black Book, first edition 1951). Tehran, Entesharat-e Naw, 1978

Malek, Hossein. '*Baradaram Khalil Maleki*' (My Brother Khalil Maleki). *Cheshmandaz*, 24, autumn 2005

Maleki, Khalil. *Nameh-ha-ye Kahlil Maleki* (Khalil Maleki's Letters), eds Homa Katouzian and Amir Pichdad. Tehran, Nashr-e Markaz, 2002, second edition, 2016.

_____. *Khaterat-e Siyasi*, ed. and with a long introduction by Homa Katouzian. Tehran, Enteshar, second edition, 2013

_____. *Barkhord-e Aqayed o Ara* (The Conflict of Ideas), eds Homa Katouzian and Amir Pichdad. Tehran, Nashr-e Markaz, 1987

_____. '*Trazhedy-ye Qarn-e Ma*' (The Tragedy of Our Century). *Elm o Zendegi* (weekly), November–January 1960

_____. *Bayanieh-ye Jame'eh-ye Sosialist-ha-ye Nehzat-e Melli-ye Iran* (The Manifesto of the Socialist League of the Popular Movement of Iran). Tehran, September 1960

_____. '*Mobarezeh ba Bozorgtarin Khatari keh Nehzat-e Melli ra Tahdid Mikond*' (The Struggle Against the Greatest Danger that Threatens the Popular Movement). *Elm o Zendegi*, June 1953

_____. *Sosilism va Kapitalism-e Dowlati* (Socialism and State Capitalism). Tehran, Niru-ye Sevvom Publications, 1952, reprinted by Adabiyat va Enqelab, Germany, July 1989

_____. *Niru-ye Sevvom dar Moqabel-e do Paygah-e Ejtema'i-ye Amperialism* (The Third Force Facing the Two Social Bases of Imperialism). Tehran, Niru-ye Sevvom publications, 1952

_____. *Niru-ye Moharrekeh-ye Tarikh* (The Motivating Force of History). Tehran, Zahmatkeshan party publications, 1952

_____. '*Dar Pishgah-e Sarnevesht va dar Moqabl-e Tarikh*' (Before Destiny and Facing History). *Elm o Zendegi*, March 1952

_____. '*Siyasatmadar-e Novin*' (The Modern Politician). *Elm o Zendegi*, January–February 1952

_____. '*Nehzat-ha-ye Melli-ye Iran va Asia*' (The Popular Movements of Iran and Asia). *Elm o Zendegi*, 1, December 1951–January 1952

_____. *Niruy-e Sevvom Piruz Mishavad* (The Third Force Will Triumph). Tehran, Zahmatkeshan party publications, 1951

_____. *Niruy-e Sevvom Chist* (?) (What Is the Third Force?). Zahmatkeshan party publications, 1951

_____. *Dar Barabar-e Bozrgtarin Azmayesh-e Tarikh*. Tehran, Zahmatkeshan publications, 1951

Meftah, Abdolhossein. *Rasti Birang Ast* (Truth Is Colourless). Paris, Parang, 1983

Mosaddeq, Mohammad. *Notq-ha va Maktubat* (Speeches and Letters). Paris, Entesharat-e Mosaddeq, 1970s, various volumes

Mosavvar Rahmani, Colonel G. *Khaterate- Siyasi: Bist-o-panj Sal dar Niruy-e Hava'i-ye Iran* (Political Memoirs: Twenty-Five Years in the Iranian Air Force). Tehran, Ravaq, 1984

Nechehri, Arman. '*Khalil Maleki va Emtiyaz-e Naft-e Shomal*' (Khalil Maleki and the Concession of North Iranian Oil), *Negah-e Nou*, 101, Spring 2014

Nejati, Gholamreza. *Tarikh-e Bist o Panj Saleh-ye Iran: az Kudtea ta Enqelab* (The Twenty-Five Year History of Iran: From the Coup to the Revolution). Tehran, Rasa, 2008

Qashqa'i, Naser. *Salha-ye Bohran* (The Critical Years), ed. Nasrollah Haddadi. Tehran, Rasa, 1987

Ra'in, Isma'il. *Asrar-e Khaneh-ye Seddon* (The Secrets of Seddon's House). Tehran, Amir Kabir, 1979

Rassa, Manuchehr. '*Roshanfekr-e Tashkilat Saz*' (The Organising Intellectual). *Andisheh-ye Puya*, 36, August 2016

Ruhani, Foad. *Tarikh-e Melli Shodan-e San'at-e Naft-e Iran* (History of the Nationalisation of Iranian Oil). Tehran, Jibi, 1974

Sadiqi, Gholamhossein. http://gate2home.com/Farsi-Persian-Keyboard/ Google-Search#q=نامه غلامحسین صدیقی به همایون کاتوزیان

Sanjabi, Karim. *Omid-ha va Naomidi-ha* (Hopes and Despairs). London, Jebhe, 1995

Shokat, Hamid. *Dar Tir-res-e Hadeseh: Zendegi-ye Siyasi-ye Qavam al-Saltaneh* (The Political Life of …). Tehran, Nashr-e Akhtaran, 2006

Tabari, Ehsan. *Kazhraheh, Khaterati az Tarikh-e Hezb-e Tudeh* (The Wrong Way, Some Memoirs from the History of the Tudeh Party). Tehran, Amir Kabir, 1988

Torbati-ye Sanjabi, Mahmud. *3 Mard dar Barabar-e Tarikh* (Three Men Facing History). Tehran, Nashr-e Alborz, 2011

Torkaman, Mohammad. *Asrar-e Qatl-e Razmara* (The Secrets of Razmara's Assassination). Tehran, Rasa, 1991

_____. *Tote'eh-ye Robudan va Qatl-e Sarlashkar Afshartus* (The Conspiracy to Kidnap and Murder General Afshartus). Tehran, Torkaman, 1984

Vezarat-e Ettela'at. *Khalil Maleki beh Ravayat-e Asnad-e SAVAK* (Khalil Maleki According to SAVAK Documents). Tehran, Markaz-e Barresi-ye Asand-e Tarikhi-ye Vezarat-e Ettela'at, 1990

Vosuq, Ali. *Chahar Fasl.* Tehran, Vosuq, 1982

Zebardast, Bahman. '*Charlie and Reza: az Sazman-e Afsaran-e Hezb-e Tudeh-ye Iran ta Sazman-e Amniyat-e Alman-e Sharqi*' (Charlie and Reza: From the Tudeh Party Army Organisation to the East German Secret Service). *Negah-e Nou*, 26, 113, Spring 2017

JOURNALS

Andisheh-ye Puya (Dynamic Thought)
Bakhtar-e Emruz (Daily West)
Beh Su-ye Ayandeh (Towards the Future)
Elm o Zendegi (Science and Life; quarterly)
Elm o Zendegi (weekly)
Ettela'at (Information; news)
Keyhan (The World)
Mardom bara-ye Roshanfekran (People, for Intellectuals)
Mardom (People)
Nabard-e Zendegi (Battle of Life)
Naqd o Bar-resi-ye Ketab-e Tehran (Tehran Review of Books)
Niru-ye Sevvom (Third Force; daily)
Niru-ye Sevvom (weekly)
Rahbar (Leader)
Shahbaz (Condor)
Shahed (Witness)
Sosialism (Socialism; quarterly)
Sosialism (monthly)

NOTES

1. KHALIL MALEKI AND THE FIFTY-THREE

1   Hossein Malek, 'Baradaram Khalil Maleki' (My Brother Khalil Maleki),
     Cheshmandaz, 24, Autumn 2005, pp. 110–18. See also Hushmand
     Saedloo, 'Gotogu ba Hossein Malek darbreh-ye Khanevadeh-ash'
     (Conversation with Hossein Malek About His Family) in Naqd o Barresi-
     ye Ketab-e Tehran, February 2007, pp. 55–7.
2   Sources on the Constitutional Revolution are innumerable. See, for
     example, Ahmad Kasravi, Tarikh-e Mahsruteh-ye Iran (A History of the
     Constitutional Revolution of Iran), Tehran: Amir Kabir, 1994; Janet
     Afary, The Iranian Constitutional Revolution, 1906–1911, New York:
     Columbia University Press, 1996; Vanessa Martin, Islam and Modernism,
     the Iranian Constitutional Revolution of 1906, London and New York,
     I. B. Tauris, 1989; Homa Katouzian, State and Society in Iran, The Eclipse
     of the Qajars and the Emergence of the Pahlavis, London and New York:
     I. B. Tauris, paperback edition, 2006, and 'The Revolution for Law: A
     Chronographic Analysis of the Constitutional Revolution of Iran', in
     Katouzian, IRAN, Politics, History and Literature, London and New York:
     Routledge 2013.
3   For the Shuster episode see Katouzian, State and Society, Chapter 3;
     Morgan Shuster, The Strangling of Persia, A Record of European Diplomacy
     and Intrigue, London: T. Fisher Unwin, 1912.
4   Malek, 'Baradarm', p. 111; Interview with Houshang Tale' (Maleki's
     nephew), August 2016.

5 Taqi Makkinezhad, 'Khalil Maleki, Taqi Arani and Hezb-e Tudeh' in Homa Katouzian and Amir Pichdad, eds., *Yadnameh-ye Khalil Maleki* (Essays in Memory of Khalil Maleki), Tehran: Enteshar, 2015, pp. 273–6.

6 '*Trazhedy-ye Qarn-e Ma*' (Tragedy of Our Century), *Elm o Zendegi* (weekly), 5 November 1960.

7 See, for example, Homa Katouzian, *State and Society in Iran; The Persians: Ancient, Mediaeval and Modern Iran*, New Haven and London: Yale University Press, paperback edition, 2010.

8 Ibid., *Elm o Zendegi* (weekly), 25 December 1960.

9 Ibid.

10 Ibid.; *Elm o Zendegi* (weekly), 8 January 1961.

11 Ibid.

12 *Khaterat-e Iraj Eskandari* (Memoirs of Iraj Eskandari, interview by Babak Amir Khosravi and Fereydun Azarnur), Tehran: Mo'asseseh-ye Motale'at va Pazhuhesh-ha-ye Siyasi, 1993, pp. 49–51.

13 *Elm o Zendegi* (weekly) 26 January 1961.

14 Interview with Houshang Tale, Maleki's nephew.

15 Maleki's long letter to Mosaddeq, in *Nameh-ha-ye Kahlil Maleki* (Khalil Maleki's Letters), Katouzian and Pichdad, eds, Tehran: Nashr-e Markaz, 2002, second edition, 2016.

16 See Homa Katouzian, *Musaddiq and the Struggle for Power in Iran*, London and New York: I. B. Tauris revised paperback edition, 1999, p. 30.

17 Mokhber al-Saltaneh (Mediqoli Hedayat), then prime minster, quotes the shah in a cabinet meeting to this effect. See his *Khaterat o Khatarat* (Memoirs and Hazards), Tehran: Zavvar, 1984, p. 386.

18 *Khaterat-e Bozorg-e Alavi* (The Memoirs of …), ed. Hamid Ahmadi, Sweden: Nashr-e Baran, 1997, p. 147.

19 He belonged to the 'Rab'eh' or Group of Four, which also included Mas'ud Farzad and Mojtaba Minovi. See Homa Katouzian, *Sadeq Hedayat: The Life and Legend of an Iranian Writer*, London and New York: I. B. Tauris, paperback edition, 2002.

20 *Khaterat-e Bozorg Alavi*, pp. 151–2.

21 Ibid., p. 153.

22 *Khaterat-e Iraj Eskandari*, p. 50.

23 *Khaterat-e Bozorg Alavi*, pp. 152–3.

24 Anvar Khameh'i, *Panjah Nafar va Seh Nafar* (The Fifty and the Three), Tehran: Entesharat-e Hafteh, n.d. but published in early 1980s, p. 70.

25   Ibid., p. 75.

26   *Khaterat-e Bozorg Alavi*, p. 153.

27   Ibid., p. 154; *Khaterat-e Iraj Eskandari*, p. 62; Khameh'i, *Panjah Nafar va Seh Nafar*, p. 75.

28   *Khaterat-e Iraj Eskandari*, pp. 57–8 and 74.

29   Ibid., p. 80.

30   Ibid., p. 83.

31   Ibid., p. 86.

32   Khalil Maleki, *Niru-ye Sevvom dar Moqabel-e do Paygah-e Ejtema'i-e Amperialism* (The Third Force Facing the Two Social Bases of Imperialism), Tehran: Niru-ye Sevvom publications, 1952.

33   Khameh'i, *Panjah Nafar va Seh Nafar*, p. 87.

34   *Khaterat-e Iraj Eskandari*, pp. 70–71.

35   Ibid., p. 90; Khameh'i, *Panjah Nafar va Seh Nafar*, pp. 101–2.

36   *Khaterat-e Bozorg Alavi*, p.161.

37   Maleki, *Niru-ye Sevvom dar Moqabel*, p. 20. Eskandari even says that Kambakhsh had written 'a book' full of details and submitted to the police, *Khaterat-e Iraj Eskandari*, p. 89.

38   Khameh'i, *Panjah Nafar va Seh Nafar*, p. 106.

39   *Khaterat-e Bozorg Alavi*, p. 205.

40   Khameh'i, *Panjah Nafar va Seh Nafar*, pp. 107–8.

41   Bozorg Alavi, *Panjah o Seh Nafar* (The Fifty-Three), Tehran: Amir Kabir, 1978, pp. 71–2.

42   Khameh'i, *Panjah Nafar va Seh Nafar*, p. 111.

43   Bozorg Alavi, *Panjah o Seh Nafar*, p. 72.

44   Khameh'i, *Panjah Nafar va Seh Nafar*, pp. 134–9.

45   Khalil Maleki, *Khaterat-e Siyasi* (Political Memoirs), ed. Homa Katouzian, Tehran: Enteshar, second edition, 2013, p. 238.

46   Babak Amir Khosravi, *Nazar az Darun beh Naqsh Hezb-e Tudeh-ye Iran* (A Look from the Inside at the Role of the Tudeh Party of Iran), Tehran: Ettela'at, p. 60. See also Khameh'i, *Panjah Nafar va Seh Nafar*, especially pp. 113–16.

47   *Khaterat-e Bozorg Alavi*, p. 161; *Khaterat-e Iraj Eskandari*, p. 93. Amir Khosrovi, *Nazar az Darun*, p. 63.

48   *Khaterat-e Bozorg Alavi*, p. 161.

49   Amir Khosrovi, *Nazar az Darun*, pp. 61–4.

50   *Khaterat-e Bozorg Alavi*, pp. 254–5.

51 Khameh'i, *Panjah Nafar va Seh Nafar*, pp. 46–7.

52 Ibid., p. 146.

53 Khalil Maleki, *Khaterat-e Siyasi*, pp. 218–19.

54 Bozorg Alavi, *Panjah o Seh Nafar*, p. 65.

55 *Maleki, Khaterat-e Siyasi*, p. 219.

56 Khameh'i, *Panjah Nafar va Seh Nafar*, pp. 146–8; Bozorg Alavi, *Panjah o Seh Nafar*, p.65; Maleki, *Niru-ye Sevvom dar Moqabel*, p. 22.

57 Ibid.

58 Bozorg Alavi, *Panjah o Seh Nafar*, p. 65.

59 See for details, Maleki, *Khaterat-e Siyasi*, pp. 216–24; Maleki, *Niru-ye Sevvom dar Moqabel*, pp. 20–24.

60 Khameh'i, *Panjah Nafar va Seh Nafar*, p. 149.

61 For the attitude of the old communists towards Pishevari see Ehsan Tabari, *Kazhraheh, Khaterari az Tarikh-e Hezb-e Tudeh* (The Wrong Way, Some Memoirs from the History of the Tudeh Party), Tehran: Amir Kabir, 1988.

62 Ibid., and Maleki, *Khaterat-e Siyasi*.

63 *Khaterat-e Bozorg Alavi*, p. 226.

64 Maleki, *Khaterat-e Siyasi*, pp. 223–6.

65 *Khaterat-e Bozorg Alavi*, p. 227.

66 Maleki, *Khaterat-e Siyasi*, p. 228.

67 Ibid., pp. 229–33; Maleki, *Niru-ye Sevvom dar Moqabel*, pp. 25–9.

68 Khameh'i, *Panjah Nafar va Seh Nafar*, p. 153.

69 *Alavi, Panjah o Seh Nafar*, p. 111.

70 Ibid., pp. 102–11; *Khaterat-e Bozorg Alavi*, pp. 226–31; Khameh'i, *Panjah Nafar va Seh Nafar*, pp. 152–62; *Khaterat-e Iraj Eskandari*, pp. 97–8.

71 Maleki, *Khaterat-e Siyasi*, pp. 256–7.

72 *Nameh-ha-ye Kahlil Maleki*, p. 89; Khameh'i, *Panjah Nafar va Seh Nafar*, p. 152.

73 Maleki, *Khaterat-e Siyasi*, pp. 258–63.

74 Ibid., p. 263.

2. THE TUDEH PARTY

1 See further, Richard J. Evans, *The Third Reich at War 1939–1945*, London: Allen Lane, 2008.

2 See further, Nicolay A. Khozhanov, 'The Pretexts and Reasons for the Allied Invasion of Iran in 1941', *Iranian Studies*, 45, 4, July 2012.

3   Ahmad Faramarzi to Taqizadeh, *Nameh-ha-ye Tehran* (Letters from Tehran), ed., Iraj Afshar, Tehran: Farzan, 2006, p. 352.

4   See for example, Houchang Chehabi, 'The banning of the veil and its consequences' in Stephanie Cronin, *The Making of Modern Iran: State and Society under Riza Shah, 1921–1941*, London and New York: Routledge, 2003, p. 204.

5   See Abbasqoli Golsha'iyan, '*Yahddasht-ha-ye Abbasqoli Golsha'iyan*' (Golsha'iyan'd Diary notes') in *Yaddasht-ha-ye Doktor Qasem Ghani* (The Diary notes of …) ed. Cyrus Ghani, vol. 4, Tehran: Zavvar, 1978, p. 557.

6   Reader Bullard, *The Camels Must Go: An Autobiography*, London: Faber and Faber, 1961, and the author's conversations with Sir Reader, Oxford, 1973.

7   Golsha'iyan, '*Yahddasht-ha*', pp. 560–63.

8   Ibid., pp. 562–4.

9   For a more elaborate discussion of this point see Homa Katouzian, 'Reza Shah's Political Legitimacy and Social Base' in Stephanie Cronin, ed., *The Making of Modern Iran*, pp. 32–3.

10   See Hossein Makki, *Tarikh-e Bistsaleh-ye Iran* (The Twenty-Year History of Iran), vol. 7, Tehran: Elmi, 1985, pp. 214–16; Golsha'iyan, '*Yaddasht-ha*', p. 560.

11   For example by Ali Dashti quoted in Ebrahim Khajeh Nuri, *Bazigaran-e Asr-re Tala'i* (The Actors of the Golden Era), Tehran: Jibi, 1978, pp. 188–91; Soltan Ali Soltani, quoted in Hossein Kuhi Kermani, *Az Shahrivar-e 1320 ta Faje'eh-ye Azerbaijan* (From September 1941 to the Catastrophe of …), vol. 1, Tehran: Kuhi, n.d., pp. 222–9.

12   See Jalal Abdoh (public prosecutor in the cases brought against Reza Shah's police chief, etc.,), *Chehel Sal dar Sahneh* (Forty Years in the Scene), ed., Majid Tafreshi, Tehran: Rasa, 1989.

13   Golsha'iyan, '*Yaddasht-ha*', p. 568.

14   See further, Shaul Bakhash, '"Dear Anthony, "Dear Leo", Britain's Quixotic Flirtation with Dynamic Change in Iran during World War II', *Iran Nameh, A Quarterly of Iranian Studies*, 30, 4, Winter 2016; Denis Wright, *The Persians Amongst the English, Episodes in Anglo-Persian Relations*, London: I. B. Tauris, 1985.

15   FO 371 35117.

16   Abdossamad Kambakhsh, *Nazari beh Jonbesh-e Kargari va Komonisti dar Iran* (A Look at the Proletarian and Communist Movement in Iran), Entesharart-e Hezb-e Tudeh-ye Iran, 1972, p. 52.

17   *Khaterat-e Iraj Eskandari*, pp. 122 and 125.

18   Ehsan Tabari, *Kazhraheh*, p. 43; Nureddin Kiyanuri, *Khaterat-e Nureddin Kiyanuri* (The Memoirs of …), Tehran: Moassesseh-ye Tahqiqati va Entesharati-ye Didgah, 1992, p. 77.

19   Cosroe Chaqueri, 'Did the Soviets play a role in the foundation of the Tudeh party in Iran?' *Cahier de le monde Russe*, 3, 1999, pp. 497–528, also file:///C:/Users/Homa/Downloads/monderusse-22.pdf.

20   Tabari, *Kazhraheh*, p. 44.

21   *Khaterat-e Iraj Eskandari*, pp. 114–29. See further *Khaterat-e Ardeshir Avanesian* (Memoirs of …), ed. Babak Amir Khosravi, Germany: Entesharat-e Hezb-e Demokratik-e Mardom Iran, 1980.

22   Kambakhsh, *Nazari beh Jonbesh-e Kargari*, pp. 55–6.

23   Anvar Khameh'i, *Forsat-e Bozorg-e az Dast Rafteh* (The Lost Great Opportunity), Tehran: Entesharat-e Hafteh, p. 45.

24   *Barkhord-e Aqayed o Ara*, eds Homa Katouzian and Amir Pichdad, Tehran: Nashr-e Markaz, 1987, p. 82.

25   *Khaterat-e Iraj Eskandari*, p. 116.

26   Khameh'i, *Forsat-e Bozorg*, p. 45.

27 · Khalil Maleki, *Khaterat-e Siyasi*, pp. 277–8.

28   Khameh'i, *Forsat-e Bozorg*, pp. 71–2.

29   Maleki, *Khaterat-e Siyasi*, p. 278.

30   See Julian Bharier, *Economic Development in Iran, 1900–1970*, London, etc.: Oxford University Press, 1971, Table 7, p. 82.

31   See Homa Katouzian, *The Political Economy of Modern Iran*, London and New York: Macmillan and New York University Press, 1981, Chapter 8.

32   Quoted in Fakhreddin Azimi, *Iran, the Crisis of Democracy, 1941–1953*, London: I. B. Tauris, 1989, p. 82.

33   *Khaterat-e Iraj Eskandari*, p. 137.

34   *Khaterat-e Ardeshir Avanesian*, p. 9.

35   *Khaterat-e Bozorg Alavi*, pp. 160, 248, 258, 260.

36   Maleki, *Khaterat-e Siyasi*, p. 279.

37   Khameh'i, *Forsat-e Bozorg*, p. 104.

38   See Maleki's letter to Nushin, in *Niruyeh Sevvom dar Moqabl*, pp. 40–42.

39   Khameh'i, *Forsat-e Bozorg*, p. 105.

40   *Khaterat-e Iraj Eskandari*, pp. 147 and 482.

41   Hossein Key-Ostovan, *Siyasat-e Movazenehye Manfi* (The Politics of Passive Balance), Tehran: Key-Ostovan, vol. 1, 1950; *Khaterat-e Iraj Eskandari*;

Homa Katouzian, *Mosaddeq and the Struggle for Power in Iran*, London and New York: I. B. Tauris, revised paperback edition, 1999, Chapter 5.

42   Maleki, *Khaterat-e Siyasi*, p. 254.

43   *Khaterat-e Iraj Eskandari*, p. 146.

44   Avanesian says that Keshavarz had tied with another delegate but that Soleyman Mirza arbitrarily chose him. *Khaterat-e Ardeshir Avanesian*, pp. 108–9.

45   *Rahbar* (the party organ), 2 August 1944 et. seq. Khameh'i, *Forsat-e Bozorg*, pp. 196–217; Maleki, *Khaterat-e Siyasi*, pp. 281–2.

46   Kambakhsh, *Nazari beh Jonbesh-e Kargari* p. 74.

47   Ibid.; Khameh'i, *Forsat-e Bozorg*, pp. 121–3.

48   Ibid., pp. 121–122; Maleki, *Khaterat-e Siyasi*, 287–8.

49   *Rahbar*, 14, 10, 1944.

50   Key-Ostovan, *Siaysat-e Movazeneh*.

51   Jalal Al-e Ahmad, *Dar Khedmat va Khiyanat-e Roshanfekran* (On the Services and Betrayals of the Intellectuals), Tehran: Entesharat-e Ferdows, 1993, p. 416.

52   Khameh'i, *Forsat-e Bozorg*, pp. 134–5.

53   *Khaterat-e Iraj Eskandari*, pp. 169–70.

54   Conversations of Abedi, Eprime Eshag and the author in Oxford, 1994.

55   *Mardom bara-ye Roshanfekran* (People, for Intellectuals), a Tudeh newspaper, 11. 11. 1944.

56   Baqer Aqeli, ed., *Khaterat-e Mohammad Sa'ed-e Maragheh'i* (Memoirs of ...) Nashr-e Namak: Tehran, 1994.

57   See Rahimiyan's recollections in *Omid-e Iran* (Iran's Hope), new series, no. 11, 16 April 1979.

58   *Rahbar*, nos 436–448, December 1944.

59   The Tudeh responses, including Maleki's, to the Soviet demand are extensively covered in Arman Nechehri's fairly well documented, though polemical, 'Khalil Maleki va Emtiyaz-e Naft-e Shomal' (Khalil Maleki and the Concession of North Iranian Oil), *Negah-e Nou*, 101, Spring 2014.

60   See further, Habib Ladjevardi, *Labor Unions and Autocracy in Iran*, Syracuse, NY: Syracuse University Press, 1985.

61   *Khaterat-e Iraj Eskandari*, pp. 478–9.

62   Tabari, *Kazhraheh*, p. 53.

63   Khaterat-e Avanesian, pp. 236–9.

64 Maleki, *Khaterat-e Siyasi*, pp. 294–302.

65 Ibid.

66 *Khaterat-e Iraj Eskandari*, pp. 177–9.

67 Ibid., p. 178.

68 Maleki, *Khaterat-e Siyasi*, p. 290.

69 Homa Katouzian, 'The Revolt of Shaikh Mohammad Khiyabani', *Iranian History and Politics*, London and New York: Routledge, 2003.

70 Khameh'i, *Forsat-e Bozorg*, pp. 188–200; Maleki, *Khaterat-e Siyasi*, pp. 302–18

71 Homa Katouzian, *Political Economy*, p. 151.

72 For a long and severe critique of Pishevari and his Ferqeh see *Khaterat-e Avanesian*, especially pp. 218–19.

73 Ibid., p. 310.

74 *Khaterat-e Iraj Eskandari*, p. 174.

75 Kambakhsh, *Nazari beh Jonbesh-e Kargari*.

76 Ibid., p. 197.

77 *Ragbar* (Shower), 13 November 1945.

78 Maleki, *Khaterat-e Siyasi*, pp. 342–3.

79 Tabari, *Kazhraheh*, pp. 79–81.

80 Khameh'i, *Forsat-e Bozorg*, pp. 277–80.

81 For example, Louise L'Estrange Fawcett, *Iran and the Cold War: The Azerbaijan Crisis of 1946*, Cambridge: Cambridge University Press, 1992; Jamil Hasanli, *At the Dawn of the Cold War, the Soviet-American Crisis over Iranian Azerbaijan, 1941–1946*, Oxford: Rowman & Littlefield, 2006; Touraj Atabaki, *Azerbaijan: Ethnicity and the Struggle for Power in Iran*, London and New York: I. B. Tauris, 2000.

82 Maleki, *Khaterat-e Siyasi*, pp. 320–5; Khameh'i, *Forsat-e Bozorg*, pp. 300–6.

83 *Khaterat-e Avanesian*, pp. 76–8.

84 *Rahbar*, 11 June 1946.

85 *Nakhostin Kongreh-ye Nevisandegan-e Iran* (The Iranian Writers' First Congress), Tehran, 1947, reprinted, 1978.

86 Mostafa Fateh, *Panjah Sal Naft-e Iran* (Fifty Years of Iranian Oil), Tehran: Entesharart-e Payam, 1979, pp. 435–47; Katouzian, *Musaddiq*, pp. 55–6; Khameh'i, *Forsat-e Bozorg*, pp. 314–18.

87 *Khaterat-e Iraj Eskandari*, pp. 205–6.

88 Maleki, *Khaterat-e Siyasi*, pp. 326–31; Khameh'i, *Forsat-e Bozorg*, pp. 322–4.

89   Tabari, *Kazhraheh*, p. 75.

90   For a detailed study of the revolt of southern tribes, see Reza Jafari, *Centre-Periphery Relations in Iran: The Case of the Southern Rebellion in 1946*, D.Phil. thesis, University of Oxford, 2000. See also *Khaterat-e Iraj Eskandari*, pp. 208–10.

91   Khameh'i, *Forsat-e Bozorg*, p. 372.

92   *Khaterat-e Iraj Eskandari*, p. 237.

93   Tabari, *Kazhraheh*, pp. 76–7.

94   Maleki, *Khaterat-e Siyasi*, pp. 340–1.

95   See for the full text of the letter, Hasan Qae'miyan, Darbareh-ye *Zohur va Ala'em-e Zohur* (On the Advent and its Signs), Tehran: Amir Kabir, 1962.

96   *Khaterat-e Iraj Eskandari*, p. 239.

97   Khameh'i, *Forsat-e Bozorg*, pp. 414–15

98   *Khaterat-e Iraj Eskandari*, pp. 239–41.

99   Ibid., pp. 248–51; Khameh'i, *Forsat-e Bozorg*, pp. 373–4.

100   Maleki, *Khaterat-e Siyasi*, pp. 46–7.

101   Tabari, *Kazhraheh*, p. 82.

102   Kiyanuri, *Khaterat-e Nureddin Kiyanuri*, p. 167.

103   Kambakhsh, *Nazari beh Jonbesh-e Kargari*, p. 122.

104   I was reassured on this point also by Eprime himself with whom I was in regular contact between 1986 and 1998, the year of his death. See Sepehr Zabih, *The Communist Movement of Iran*, Berkley: University of California Press, 1966.

105   Kambakhsh, *Nazari beh Jonbesh-e Kargari*, pp. 107–10.

106   Khameh'i, *Forsat-e Bozorg*, p. 434.

107   Al-e Ahmad, *Dar Khedmat va Khiyanat*, pp. 422–3.

108   Ibid., 423–4.

109   Anvar Khameh'i, *Az Enshe'ab ta Kudeta* (From the Split to the Coup), Tehran: Entesharat-e Hafteh, 1984, pp. 15–19.

110   Ibid., pp. 20–1.

111   Maleki, *Khaterat-e Siyasi*, pp. 53–65.

3. POWER STRUGGLES AND OIL NATIONALISATION

1   See however Qavam's later defence (though not complete denial) of this practice in his long and important 'open letter' aimed at the shah (which

was widely, but privately circulated) in Ghani, *Yaddashha*, vol. 9, 1982. See further Ali Vosuq, *Chahar Fasl* (Four Seasons), Tehran: Vosuq, 1982.

2   For example, the shah won the support of Reza Hekmat, chairman of the central committee of the Democrat party, against Qavam, by paying off his gambling debts. See Azimi, *Crisis of Democracy*, pp. 175–6.

3   See 'Seyyed Hasan Taqizadeh: There Lives in a Lifetime' in Homa Katouzian, *IRAN, Politics, History and Literature*, London and New York; Routledge, 2013, p. 68.

4   See Fateh, *Panjah Sal Naft*.

5   Tabari, *Kazhraheh*, p. 83.

6   Ibid.

7   For full details of all these cases see Fereydun Keshavarz, *Man Mottaham Mikonam* (I Accuse), Tehran: Ravaq, 1979; Khameh'i, *Az Ensh'ab ta Kudeta*; Tabari, *Kazhraheh*. Kiyanuri denies his involvement in Mas'ud's assassination, attributing it only to Khosrow Ruzbeh and Captain Abbasi of Tudeh's secret military organisation for which Kiyanuri himself was the official contact. See Kiyanuri, *Khaterat*.

8   Ali Akbar Siyasi, *Gozaresh-e Yek Zendegi* (Report on a Life), London: Siyasi, 1988, pp. 214–15; Aqeli, ed., *Khaterat-e Mohammad Sa'ed* (The Memoirs of...), Nashr-e Namak: Tehran, 1994.

9   Khameh'i, *Az Ensh'ab ta Kudeta*, pp. 144–5.

10   Kiyanuri, *Khaterat*, pp. 201and 162.

11   For the full text of Qavam's letter to the shah, objecting to the constitutional amendments, see Ali Vosuq, *Chahar Fasl*, pp. 33–43.

12   Katouzian, *Musaddiq*, Chapter 6; Azimi, *Crisis of Democracy*, Chapter 14, and *Quest for Democracy in Iran: A Century of Struggle against Authoritarian Rule* (Repossession), Cambridge, MA, and London: Harvard University Press, 2008.

13   See Mozaffar Baqa'i's interview with Habib Ladjevardi, *The Harvard Oral History Project*, http://www.fas.harvard.edu/~iohp/BAGHAI09.PDF; Hossein Makki, *Khal'-e Yad* (Repossession), Tehran: Bongah-e Trajomeh va Nashr-e Ketab, 1981; Khameh'i, *Az Ensh'ab*.

14   *Mardom*, 23 October 1949.

15   Amir Khosravi, *Nazar Az Darun*, p. 252.

16   Homa Katouzian, 'Fadīyyan-i Isām', *The Encyclopaedia of Islam*, third edition, September 2013; Katouzian, *The Persians*; Katouzian, *Musaddiq*.

17   Amir Khosravi, *Nazar as Darun*, p. 159.

18   For a lengthy account of their activities, see Khameh'i, *Az Ensh'ab*.
19   Al-e Ahmad, *Dar Khedmat va Khiyanat*, pp. 435–6. For a more detailed account of Maleki's first meetings with Baqa'i, see Khalil Maleki, 'Ebda' Konandeh-ye Tez-e Melli Shodan-e Naft Kist?' (Who Initiated the Oil Nationalisation Thesis?), *Niru-ye Sevvom*, 180, 28 May 1953.
20   Khalil Maleki, *Barkhord-e Aqayed o Ara*, ed., Homa Katouzian and Amir Pichdad various articles.
21   Ibid., p. 205.
22   Ibid., p. 206.
23   Ibid., p. 207.
24   Examples abound. For four famous historical sources, all of them showing visible symptoms of the conspiracy theory, domestic and – especially – foreign, see Hossein Makki, *Tarikh-e Bistsaleh-ye Iran* (The Twenty-Year History of Iran), various editions, Mahmud Mahmud, *Tairkh-e Ravabet-e Siyasi-ye Iran va Inglis*, various editions, Mehdi Bamdad, *Sharh-e Hal-e Rejal-e Iran*, vols 1–6, various editions, and Khan-Malek-e Sasani, *Siyasatgaran-e Dowreh-ye Qajar*, Tehran, n p., n.d. (date of preface, 1959).
25   See, Khalil Maleki, '*Kabus-e Badbini: Ancheh mured darad va ancheh bimured ast*' (The Nightmare of Pessimism: What Is Appropriate and What Is Inappropriate) in Katouzian and Pichdad, eds, *Barkhord-e Aqayed o Ara*, p. 41.
26   'Maraz-e Esti'mar-zadeg' (The Disease of Imperial-Struckness), *Bakhord-e Aqayed*, p. 43.
27   Ibid., p. 44.
28   Katouzian, *Musaddiq*.
29   R. W. Ferrier, 'The British Government, the Anglo-Iranian Oil Company, and Iranian Oil' in James Bill and Roger Louis, eds, *Musaddiq, Iranian Nationalism and Oil*, London: I. B. Tauris and Austin: University of Texas Press, 1988.
30   Katouzian, *Musaddiq*, pp. 67–8.
31   *Bakhtar-e Emruz*, 13 October 1950.
32   Ibid., 14 October 1950.
33   Khalil Maleki, 'Ebda' Konandeh', *Niru-ye Sevvom*, 180, 28 May 1953.
34   *Niru-ye Sevvom*, 14 October 1952.
35   *Shahed*, 14 November 1950.
36   Mohammadreza Shah Pahlavi, *Answer to History*, New York: Stein and Day, 1980; British embassy in Washington to Sir Robert Matkins,

21 May 1953. For a photocopy of this document see Doktor Karim Sanjabi, *Omid-ha va Naomidi-ha* (Hopes and Despairs), London: Jebhe, 1995, p. 449. Ali Dashti, *Avamel-e Soqut-e Mohammad Reza Pahlavi* (The Causes of the Fall of ...), ed., Mehdi Mahuzi, Tehran: Zavvar, 2004, pp. 44–5; Katouzian, *The Persians*, p. 252.

37   *Nashriyeh Ta'limati* (educational pamphlet) No. 12, Tudeh publication, 1951.

38   Vladimir Kuzichkin, *Inside the KGB: Myth and Reality*, trans, Thomas B. Beattie, intro., Frederick Forsyth, London: Andre Deutsch, 1990; *Siyast va Sazman-e Hezb-e Tudeh az Aghaz ta Forupashi* (The Tudeh Party Organisation and Politics from the Beginning to Downfall) vol. 1, Tehran: Mo'asseseh-ye Motal'eat va Pazhuhesh-ha-ye Siyasi, Tehran: 1991; Tabari, *Kazhraheh*; Kiyanuri, *Khaterat-e Nureddin Kiyanuri*. 'Parvandeh-ye Vizheh-ye Hezb-e Tudeh' (special reportage on the Tudeh party after the revolution of February 1979), *Andisheh-ye Puya*, 38, October 2016, pp. 59–95.

39   For details of the Majlis proceedings on that day (27 June 1950), see *Notqha va Maktubat* (Speeches and Letters), Paris: Entesharat-e Mosaddeq, 1970s various volumes. vol. 1.

40   For a full account of the incident, see Baqa'i's defiant speech in the Majlis in *Dar Pishgah-e Tarikh* (Before History), Kerman: Parma, n.d. (preface signed in June 1979).

41   For some graphic description of Razmara as an army leader see Colonel G. Mosavvar Rahmani, *Khaterate- Siyasi: Bist-o-panj Sal dar Niruy-e Hava'i-ye Iran* (Political Memoirs: Twenty-Five Years in the Iranian Air Force), Tehran: Ravaq, 1984.

42   See, for example, *Shahed*, 9 October 1950: 'What is the source of Iran-Soviet rapprochement?' See also below for Imami's reference to this.

43   *Shahed*: 'The coordination of the London, Moscow and Washington press in defending Razmara's policies', 24 March 1951, a couple of weeks after Razmara's assassination.

44   See for full documentation, Khameh'i, *Az Ensh'ab ta Kudeta*, pp. 283–6.

45   Ghani, *Yaddasht-ha*, 1984, vol. 11.

46   *Shahed*, 22 June 1950.

47   Quoted in *Keyhan* (The World), 19 March 1951. See also George McGhee, *Envoy to the Middle World: Adventures in Diplomacy*, New York: Harper and Row, 1983.

48 *Besu-ye Ayandeh*, 21 April 1951.
49 Khameh'i, *Az Ensh'ab*; Keshavarz. *Man Mottham Mikonam*.
50 *Shahed*, May–June 1950, various issues.
51 *Bakhtar-e Emruz*, 17 December 1950.
52 See the full quotation from official records in Hossein Makki, *Ketab-e Siyah* (The Black Book, first edition 1951), Tehran: Entesharat-e Naw, 1978.
53 Amir Khosravi, *Nazar az Darun*, pp. 227–31.
54 Makki, *Ketab-e Siyah* p. 297, though here Imami was reacting to the recent Iran–Soviet trade agreement.
55 Naser Qashqa'i, *Salha-ye Bohran* (The Critical Years), ed. Nasrollah Haddadi, Tehran: Rasa, 1987, p. 146; Ghani, *Yaddasht-ha*, vol. 11.
56 Qasqa'i, *Salha-ye Bohran*.
57 This was the real reason for his dismissal by the shah after a short period of premiership, following the 1953 coup, despite his indispensable role in saving the shah's throne for him.
58 See Mosaddeq's and Razmara's public revelations about their meetings, etc., in Mosaddeq *Notqha va Maktubat*, various volumes. Naturally, Mosaddeq did not name the shah as such, but that was clear by virtue of the fact that Imami was an enemy of Razmara and close to the shah. See Mosaddeq *Notqha va Maktubat*, vol. 5, p. 1, and vol. 6, p.160.
59 Qashqa'i, *Salha-ye Bohran*, p. 146.
60 Mosavvar Rahmani, *Khaterat-e Siyasi*, pp. 272–3.
61 Ibid., p. 275. For a documentary study of Razmara's assassination see Mohammad Torkaman, *Asrar-e Qatl-e Razmara* (Secrets of Razmara's Assassination), Tehran: Rasa, 1991.
62 Shepherd to the Foreign Office, 19.1.1951: FO 371 / 91452.
63 See, for example, the arrogant and indignant letter of 23 February 1951 from the British ambassador Francis Shepherd to Razmara, asking why he had not made the offer public, Fateh, *Panjah Sal*.
64 Makki, *Ketab-e Siyah*, p. 297.
65 See for the report's full text, *Shahed*, 12 December,1950.
66 Fateh, *Panjah Sal*.
67 Makki, *Ketab-e Siyah*, p. 356.
68 Ibid., p. 225.
69 Ibid., p. 752.
70 Ibid., p. 737.

4. THE TOILERS PARTY

1   *Ettela'at* (Information), 21 April 1951.
2   *Bakhtar-e Emruz*, 2 April 1951.
3   Khameh'i, *Az Ensh'ab ta Kudeta*, pp. 368–71.
4   Amir Khosravi, *Nazar az Darun*, p. 175.
5   Katouzian, *Musaddiq*.
6   Anon., *Ruhaniyat va Asrar-e Fash Nashodeh*, (The Clergy and the Undisclosed Secrets) Qom: Dar al-Fekr, n.d., (preface signed: 1979), p. 132.
7   Katouzian, ed., *Mossadiq's Memoirs*, Book II.
8   Shepherd to the Foreign Office, 15 March 1951: FO 248 1518.
9   Shepherd to the Foreign Office, 22 June 1951: ibid.
10 *Mosaddeq's Memoirs*, Book II, and *Notqha va Maktubat*, various volumes.
11 Isma'il Ra'in, *Asrar-e Khaneh-ye Seddon* (The Secrets of Seddon's House), Tehran: Amir Kabir, 1979.
12 FO 371 / 91459 / EP105 / 201.
13 Foad Ruhani, *Tarikh-e Melli Shodan-e San'at-e Naft-e Iran* (History of the Nationalisation of Iranian Oil), Tehran: Jibi, 1974, Chapter 9.
14 *Mosaddeq's Memoirs*, Book II.
15 http://web.stanford.edu/group/tomzgroup/pmwiki/uploads/3195-1951-11-Keesings-a-OEP.pdf.
16 The *New Statesman* was the exception that proved the rule, although there were some variations in the views and tone of the others as well. The *Daily Express* concluded one of its articles on the subject by saying, 'The Persians are trying to grab something that does not belong to them at all.' See Hamid Enayat, 'British Public Opinion and the Persian Oil Crisis, M.Sc. (Econ.) thesis, University of London, 1958.
17 Sir Eric Drake's recollections of his report to the full meeting of the British cabinet at the time in Brian Lapping, *End of Empire*, London: Granada, 1985.
18 George McGhee, *Envoy to the Middle World*, and 'Recollections' in James Bill and Roger Louis, eds, *Musaddiq, Iranian Nationalism and Oil*.
19 Katouzian, *Mussadiq*.
20 Conversations with Maleki in Tehran, 1960.
21 McGhee, *Envoy to the Middle World*, and 'Recollections' in James Bill and Roger Louis, eds, *Musaddiq, Iranian Nationalism and Oil*, Dean

Acheson, *Present at the Creation: My Years in the State Department*, London: Hamish Hamilton, 1970; Lapping, *End of Empire*.

22 Anthony Eden, *Full Circle, The Memoirs of Sir Anthony Eden*, London: Cassell, 1960; Chapter IX, p. 201.

23 *Teaching Pamphlet*, No. 12, Tehran: the Tudeh party, 1952

24 Conversations with Mohammad Soruri, Tehran 1970.

25 Foad Ruhani, *Tarikh-e Melli Shodan*, p. 254; Homa Katouzian, 'Mosaddeq va Pishnahad Bank-e Jahani '(Mosaddeq and the World Bank Proposal), *Estebdad, Demokrasi va Nehzat-e Melli* (Arbitrary Rule, Democracy and the Popular Movement), Tehran: Nash-re Markaz, sixth impression, 2013; Homa Katouzian, 'Mosaddeq and the Intervention of the International Bank', *The Middle East in London*, 10, 1, December 2013–January 2014; 'Mosaddeq and the Intervention of the International Bank: Rejoinder to Mr Diba's Comment', *The Middle East in London*, 10, 2, February–March, 2014; Katouzian, *Musaddiq*; Fateh, *Panjah Sal*, p. 590.

26 Homa Katouzian, 'Oil Boycott and the Political Economy: Musaddiq and the Strategy of Non-Oil Economics' in J. A. Bill and William. R. Lewis, eds, *Musaddiq, Iranian Nationalism and Oil*, London and Austin: I. B. Tauris and University of Texas Press, 1988.

27 For a comprehensive analysis of the strategy of non-oil economics see Homa Katouzian, 'Oil Boycott and the Political Economy: Musaddiq and the Strategy of Non-Oil Economics, in Bill and Louis, eds, *Musaddiq, Iranian Nationalism and Oil*.

28 *Bayanieh-ye Jame'eh-ye Sosialist-ha-ye Nehzat-e Melli-ye Iran* (The Manifesto of the Socialist League of the Popular Movement of Iran): Tehran, September 1960, p. 13.

29 See, for example, Naser Qashqa'i, *Salha-ye Bohran*.

30 *Mosaddeq's Memoirs*, Book II.

31 Ibid. and *Notqh va Maktubat*.

32 *Mosaddeq's Memoirs*, Book II, Chapter 8 (Chapter 5 in the Persian edition).

33 Ibid.

34 *Niru-ye Sevvom*, 5 December 1952.

35 Mozaffar Baqa'i, *Cheh Kasi Monharef Shod* (Who Deviated?), Tehran: Senobar, 1984.

36 Katouzian *Political Economy*, Chapter 9.

37 *Rohaniyat va Asrar*.

38   Hamid Shokat, *Dar Tir-res-e Hadeseh, Zendegi-ye Siyasi-ye Qavam al-Saltaneh* (The Political Life of ...), Tehran: Nashr-e Akhtaran, 2006.

39   *Rohaniyyat va Asrar*, pp. 156–7.

40   Katouzian, *Musaddiq*.

41   Mozaffar Baqa'i, *Cheh Kasi Monharef Shod*.

42   See, for example, *Niru-ye Sevvom* (weekly) 3 October 1952.

43   '*Nameh-ye Sar-goshadeh-ye Khalil Maleki beh Ayatollah Kashani*' [Khalil Maleki's Open Letter to ...] *Niruy-e Sevvom* (daily, no. 1, 15 October 1952), reprinted in Katouzian and Pichdad, eds, *Nameh-ha-ye Khalil Maleki*, p. 518.

44   Al-e Ahmad, *Dar Khedmat va Khiyanat*, p. 437.

45   Conversations with Amir Pichdad, who was present in the meeting, various dates, in Paris; Khalil Maleki, *Khaterat-e Siyasi*, p. 86.

46   Conversation with Zia Sedqi, who was present in the meeting, in Boston, 1988.

47   *Nameh-ye Sar-goshadeh-ye Khalil Maleki*, pp. 518–19.

48   Ibid., p. 519. Four days later Al-e Ahmad wrote a sardonic open letter addressed to Baqa'i entitled 'Letter to My Leader'. See *Niruy-e Sevvom*, no. 4, 18 October 1952.

49   *Shahed*, 15 October 1952.

50   Ibid., 12 October 1952.

51   *Niru-ye Sevvom* (daily), no. 2, 16 October 1952.

52   *Khalil Maleki beh Ravayat-e Asnad-e SAVAK* (Khalil Maleki According to SAVAK Documents), Tehran: Markaz-e Barresi-ye Asand-e Tarikhi-ye Vezarat-e Ettela'at, 1990, pp. 24–5.

53   Quoted in *Niru-ye Sevvom* (daily), 2, 16 October 1952.

5. THE THIRD FORCE

1   Documented in Amir Khosravi, *Nazar az Darun*, Chapter 20.

2   *Foreign Relations of the United States, 1952–54, Iran, 1951–54*, ed. James C. Van Hook, Washington: United States Government Publishing Office, 2017, https://history.state.gov/historicaldocuments/frus1951-54Iran.

3   *Niruy-e Sevvom Piruz Mishavad* (The Third Force Will Triumph), Tehran: Zahmatkeshan party publications, 1951, p. 3.

4   Ibid., pp. 4–5.

5   Ibid., p. 21.

6   Ibid., p. 26.

7   Khalil Maleki, *Niruy-e Sevvom Chist* (?) (What Is the Third Force?), Zahmatkeshan party publications, 1951, p. 11.

8   Khalil Maleki, *Barkhord-e Aqayed o Ara*, p. 30.

9   Khalil Maleki, 'Nehzat-ha-ye Melli-ye Iran va Asia' (The Popular Movements of Iran and Asia), *Elm o Zendegi*, 1, December 1951–January 1952.

10   *Niruy-e Sevvom Chist* (?), pp. 11–12.

11   Ibid., pp. 2–4.

12   Ibid., p. 8.

13   Khali Maleki, *Niru-ye Moharrekeh-ye Tarikh* (The Motivating Force of History), Tehran: Zahmatkeshan party publications, 1952, pp. 28–9.

14   Ibid.

15   Khalil Maleki 'Siyasatmadar-e Novin' (The Modern Politician), *Elm o Zendegi*, January–February 1952.

16   Khalil Maleki, *Niru-ye Moharrekeh*, p. 5.

17   Ibid.

18   Ibid., pp. 6–7.

19   Khalil Maleki, 'Dar Pishgah-e Sarnevesht va dar Moqabl-e Tarikh' (Before Destiny and Facing History), *Elm o Zendegi*, March 1952.

20   Khalil Maleki, *Do Ravesh Bara-ye Yek Hadaf*, pp. 8 et seq.

21   *Niru-ye Moharrekeh*, pp. 33–4.

22   Khalil Maleki, *Dar Barabar-e Bozrgtarin Azmayesh-e Tarikh*, (Facing the Greatest Test of History), Tehran: Zahmatkeshan publications, 1951, p. 12.

23   Khalil Maleki, *Sosilism va Kapitalism-e Dowlati* (Socialism and State Capitalism), Tehran: Niru-ye Sevvom Publications, 1953, reprinted by Adabiyat va Enqelab, Germany, July 1989, p. 28.

24   Ibid., p. 32.

25   Ibid., pp. 32–4.

26   'Mobarezeh ba Bozorgtarin Khatari keh Nehzat-e Melli ra Tahdid Mikond' (Struggling Against the Biggest Danger that Threatens the Popular Movement), *Elm o Zendegi*, June 1953.

27   Correspondence with Kazem Hasibi, 1989; conversations with Mohammad Hossein Khan Qashqa'i (then a Popular Movement deputy), London, 1987.

28   Garner had told Abolhasan Ebtehaj in Paris on returning from Tehran, and Ebtehaj told this author in Tehran in 1977.

29   It was at this point that Richard Stokes – now out of office – followed up his moral dilemma of the year before and, in his long letter of 6 September to *The Times*, criticised the British government for refusing to negotiate directly with Iran.

30   Ruhani, *Tarikh-e Melli Shodan*, Chapter 20; Fateh, *Panjah Sal*, pp. 609–29.

31   Ruhani, *Tarikh-e Melli Shodan*, Chapter 23, emphasis added; Fateh, *Panjah Sal*, pp. 637–43.

32   Ibid.

33   199. Telegram from the embassy in Iran to the Department of State, Tehran, 4 May 1953, https://history.state.gov/historicaldocuments/frus1951-54Iran/d199.

34   Ibid.

35   Abrahamian, *THE COUP: 1953, the CIA, and the Roots of Modern U.S.-Iranian Relations*.

36   *Nameh-ye Sar Goshadeh beh Ayatollah Kashani*, p. 515.

37   *Niru-ye Sevvom*, 21, 9 November 1952, p. 2.

38   Ibid., 47, 12 December 1952, pp. 1 and 4.

39   Ibid., 54, 19 December 1952, pp. 1, 2 and 4.

40   Ibid., various issues until 5 January 1953.

41   Ibid., 84, 25 January 1953.

42   Conversations with Mohandes Ahmad Razavi, Tehran 1960.

43   *Niru-ye Sevvom*, April–July 1953, various issues.

44   Katouzian *Musaddiq*, Chapter 10.

45   Ibid., Chapter 12.

46   *Niru-ye Sevvom*, 81, 21 January 1953, p. 3.

47   See for the full text of his speech, Hossein Makki, ed., *Doktor Mosaddeq va Notq-ha-ye Tarikhi-ye U* (… and his Historic Speeches), Tehran: Javidan, 1985, and *Mosaddeq's Memoirs*, Book I.

48   Here *Beh Su-ye Ayandeh* is misleading: no such Middle East Treaty existed.

49   *Mosaddeq's Memoirs*, Book II.

50   *Niru-ye Sevvom*, 91, 2 February 1952.

51   See, for example, Ervand Abrahamian, *THE COUP, 1953, the CIA, and the Roots of Modern US-Iranian Relations*.

52   This is documented in the following article and its sources: Bahman Zebardast, '*Charlie and Reza: az Sazman-e Afsaran-e Hezb-e Tudeh-ye Iran ta Sazman-e Amniyat-e Alman-e Sharqi*' (Charlie and Reza: From

the Tudeh Party Army Organisation to the East German Secret Service), *Negah-e Nou*, 26, 113, pp. 207, 213, Spring 2017.

53 *Niru-ye Sevvom, dar Moqabl*, pp. 10–11.

54 *Mosaddeq's Memoirs*, Book II, and *Notqha va Maktubat*, various issues.

55 Mosaddeq's statement of 6 April 1953, reprinted in *Memoirs*, Book II; Baqa'i *Cheh Kasi Monharef Shod*.

56 *Mosaddeq's Memoirs*, Book II, Chapter 7.

57 See Mo'azzami's full account in the Majlis meeting of 26 May 1953, reprinted in Baqa'i, *Cheh Kasi Monharef Shod*.

58 Mosaddeq's statement of 6 April 1953.

59 Mohammad Reza Shah, *Mission for My Country*, London: Hutchinson, 1961.

60 Baqa'i, *Cheh Kasi Monharef Shod*.

61 *Niru-ye Sevvom* (daily), 26 February 1953.

62 For the full text see, Abdolhossein Meftah, *Rasti Birang Ast* (Truth Is Colourless), Paris: Parang, 1983; for one of his letters to the shah see Maleki, *Khaterat*; for the other public statement see *Keyhan*, 28 February 1953; the remaining letter has not been published although Kashani mentions it in the existing one.

63 *Niru-ye Sevvom*, 22–30 April.

64 Ibid., 161, 7 May 1953.

65 For example, ibid., 158, 3 May 1953.

66 Mohammad Torkaman, *Tote'eh-ye Robudan va Qatl-e Sarlashkar Afshartus* (The Conspiracy of Kidnapping and Murdering General Afshartus), Tehran: Torkaman, 1984; *Keyhan* and *Niru-ye Sevvom* (daily), 20–27 April 1953. See also Gholamhossein Sadiqi's detailed account of his discovery that Afshartus had been kidnapped at Khatibi's home and the arrest and questioning of the culprits in Mahmud Torbati-ye Sanjabi, *3 Mard dar barabar-e Tarikh* (3 Men Facing History), Tehran: Nashr-e Alborz, 2011, Chapter 13. Sadiqi was deputy prime minister as well as interior minister at the time.

67 Dispatch from the embassy in Iran to the Department of State, No. 982, Tehran, 20 May 1953 https://history.state.gov/historicaldocuments/frus1951-54Iran/d208.

68 *Mosaddeq's Memoirs*, Book II

69 For the late Gholamhossein Sadiqi's long letter to this author about the subject in hand, see http://gate2home.com/Farsi-Persian-Keyboard/Google-Search#q=نامه غلامحسین صدیقی به همایون کاتوزیان

70 The author's conversation with Sanjabi, Tehran, January 1961. In a video released posthumously, Foruhar has denied having attended that meeting.

71 For Sanajbi's recollections see his *Omid-ha va Naomidi-ha* (Hopes and Despairs), London: Jebhe, 1989, and Maleki, *Khaterat.*

72 *Niru-ye Sevvom*, 28 July–5 August, various issues.

73 See however Mosaddeq's own defence of this decision in his *Memoirs,* Book II.

6. THE 1953 COUP AND AFTER

1 The most recent evidence on the coup is to be found in the American government's recent release of documents entitled 'Planning and implementation of Operation TPAJAX' in *Foreign Relations of the United States, 1952–1954, Iran, 1951–1954*, ed. James C. Van Hook, Washington: United States Government Publishing Office, 2017 https://history.state.gov/historicaldocuments/frus1951-54Iran/ch3?start=1. For detailed secondary accounts see, for example, Abrahamian, *THE COUP*; Ali Rahnema, *Behind the 1953 Coup in Iran: Thugs, Turncoats, Soldiers and Spooks*, Cambridge: Cambridge University Press, 2015; *Mohammad Mosaddeq and the 1953 Coup in Iran*, eds, Mark J. Gasiorowski and Malcolm Byrne, Syracuse: Syracuse University Press, 2004; Amir Khosravi, *Nazar as Darun*; Brian Lapping, *End of Empire*, London: Granada, 1985; Katouzian, *Musaddiq.*

2 Gasiorowski and Byrne, *Mohammad Mosaddeq and the 1953 Coup.*

3 For the accounts of those who organised the coup see, for example, C. M. Woodhouse, *Something Ventured*, London and New York: Granada, 1982; Kermit Roosevelt, *Countercoup: The Struggle for the Control of Iran*, New York: McGraw-Hill, 1979; Donald Wilber's 1954 Report: http://headquarters.opinionware.net/donald-n-wilbers-1954-report.

4 *Foreign Relations of the United States, 1952–1954, Iran, 1951–1954*; https://history.state.gov/historicaldocuments/frus1951-54Iran.

5 Ruhani, *Tarikh-e Melli Shodan.*

6 Amir Khosravi, *Nazar az Darun*, Chapter 20.

7 Ibid.

8 Gasiorowski and Byrne, *Mohammad Mosaddeq and the 1953 Coup*, p. 254.

9 Richard Cottam's recollections in Brian Lapping, *End of Empire.*

10 See 'TPAJAX', document 307, 'Record of Meeting in the Central Intelligence Agency', 28 August 1953, in which, inter alia, Kermit Roosevelt reports that,

a few days after the coup, he had told the shah to execute General Riyahi, Mosaddeq's army chief of staff.

11   Manuchehr Rassa, 'Roshanfekr-e Tashkilat Saz' (The Organising Intellectual), *Andisheh-ye Puya*, 36, August 2016, p. 56.

12   'Shah farari shodeh / Savar-e gari shodeh'.

13   Gasiorowski and Byrne, *Mohammad Mosaddeq*; Richard Cottam in *End of Empire*.

14   *Musaddiq's memoirs*, Book II, and, Jalil Bozorgmehr, ed., *Mohammad Mosaddeq dar Mahkameh-ye Nezami* (Mosaddeq in the Military Court), Tehran: Entesharat-e Dustan, 2000, vol. 1.

15   Karim Sanjabi, *Omid-ha va Naomidi-ha* (Hopes and Despairs), London: Jebhe, 1989, p. 142.

16   See further, Siavush Randjbar-Daemi, 'Down with the Monarchy: Iran's Republican Moment of August 1953, *Iranian Studies*, 50, 2, March 2017 http://www.tandfonline.com/doi/full/10.1080/00210862.2016.1229120; Kaveh Bayat, 'Ankeh Yek Nafas Asudegi Nadideh Manam' (The One Who Did Not Rest for a Moment Is Me), *Andisheh-ye Puya*, no. 36, August 2016.

17   Maleki, *Khaterat*. However, this instruction to members appeared in a note without mentioning Mosaddeq's name in *Niru-ye Sevvom*, 247, 19 August 1953.

18   Rahnema, *Behind the 1953 Coup in Iran: Thugs, Turncoats, Soldiers and Spooks*; Katouzian, *Musaddiq*.

19   Katouzian, ibid.

20   https://www.youtube.com/watch?v=6RZRIyiUDE0&app=desktop and https://www.youtube.com/watch?v=S05q9tbuwEA.

21   Nur al-Din Kiyanuri, *Drabareh-ye Bist o Hasht-e Mordad*, Tehran, 1979.

22   Interview in Mahmud Torbati-e Sanjabi, *3 Mard da barabar-e Tarikh* (Three Men Facing History).

23   Ibid.

24   Amir Khosravi, *Nazar az Darun*, Chapter 26.

25   Maleki's open letter of late August 1953 in Katouzian and Pichdad, ed., *Nameh-ha-ye Khalil Maleki*, p. 496.

26   'Zhandi benegar gardesh-e charkh-e falaki ra / kavardeh beh nazd-e taw Khalil-e Maleki ra'.

27   Maleki's open letter of 20 February 1961 to the political establishment, *Nameh-ha-ye Khalil Maleki*, p. 509.

28   Maleki's letter to Mosaddeq in *Nameh-ha-ye Khalil Maleki*, pp. 68–9.

29 Ibid., p. 69.
30 Maleki's open letter of 20 February 1961, *Nameh-ha-ye Khalil Malek*, p. 508.
31 Jalal Al-e Ahmad, 'Piremard Cheshm-e Ma Bud' (The Old Man was our Eye) in *Majmu'eh-ye Maqalat*, ed., Mostafa Zamani-Nia, vol. 1, Tehran: Mitra, 1994, pp. 301–24; http://www.gahrom89.blogfa.com/post-76.aspx.
32 Maleki, *Khaterat*.
33 Maleki's letter to Mosaddeq in *Nameh-ha-ye Khalil Maleki*, pp. 67–71; conversations and correspondence with Sedqi, Malek and Borhan, various dates; Abdollah Borhan, 'Beh Bahaneh-ye Naql-e Chand Khatereh az Khalil Maleki' in Katouzian and Pichdad, eds, *Yadnameh-ye Khalil Maleki*.
34 Maleki's letter to Mosaddeq in *Nameh-ha-ye Khalil Maleki*.
35 Conversations with Hamid Enayat, Oxford, 1980.
36 *Asnad-e Nehzat-e Moqavemat-e Melli,-ye Iran* (Documents of . . .), Tehran: Nezat-e Azadi-ye Iran, vo. 2, pp. 201–2.
37 Khalil Maleki, *Dars-e 28 Mordad . . .* (The Lesson of 19th August . . .), ed. Kaveh Bayat, Tehran: Pardis-e Danesh, 2015.
38 Ibid., p. 310.
39 Maleki, *Dars-e 28 Mordad . . .*
40 Maleki's letter to Mosaddeq in *Nameh-ha-ye Khalil Maleki*, p. 72.
41 *Asnad-e Nehzat*, vol. 2, pp. 466 and 471.
42 *Nabard-e Zendegi*, vol. 1, 10 May 1956, p. 1.
43 Ibid., pp. 1–14.
44 Maleki's letter to Mosaddeq *Nameh-ha-ye Khalil Maleki*, pp. 74–5.
45 Katouzian *Political Economy* and *The Persians*; Roham Alvandi, *Nixon, Kissinger and the Shah*, New York: Oxford University Press, 2014.
46 Qarani's interview with *Omid-e Iran*, 30 April 1979. For a lengthy study of the subject, see Mark J. Gasiorowski, 'The Qarani Affair and Iranian Politics', *International Journal of Middle East Studies*, 25, 4, November 1993, pp. 625–44.
47 Conversations with Richard Cottam, London, 1980.
48 See further Katouzian, *Musaddiq*.
49 Sanjabi, *Omid-ha va Naomidi-ha*, p. 204.
50 *Bayniyeh-ye Jame'eh-ye Sosilaist-ha*, pp. 9–21.
51 Ibid., p. 23.
52 Maleki's letter to Mosaddeq in *Nameh-ha-ye Khalil Maleki*, p. 76.
53 Ibid., pp. 78–9.

7. POWER STRUGGLES, 1960–1963

1   Sanjabi, *Omid-ha va Naomidi-ha*, p. 207.
2   For a study of the history of the Freedom Movement see H. E. Chehabi, *Iranian Politics and Religious Modernism: The Liberation Movement of Iran under the Shah and Khomeini*, London: I. B. Tauris, 1990.
3   Daryush Ashuri's interview with *Andish-ye Puya*, 36, August 2016, pp. 62–3.
4   Homa Katouzian, 'Kahlil Maleki va Mas'aleh-ye Adam-e Gheir-e Adi' (Kahlil Maleki and the Problem of the Unusual Person), in Katouzian and Pichdad, eds, *Yadnameh*, p. 254.
5   Maleki's 'Open Letter', *Nameh-ha-ye Khalil Maleki*, pp. 502–10.
6   *Elm o Zendedgi*, extra issue, June 1961.
7   Maleki to Pichdad, *Nameh-ha-ye Khalil Maleki*, pp. 30–4.
8   Manouchehr Rassa, *Roshanfekr-e Tashkilat Saz* (The Organising Intellectual), *Andisheh-ye Puya*, pp. 56–7; Maleki, *Khaterat*, pp. 126–127.
9   Carthy to Maleki in *Nameh-ha-ye Khalil Maleki*, pp. 37–40.
10   Maleki to Malek, ibid., pp. 41–3.
11   *Kahlili Maleki dar jebheh-ye oportunism-e jahani*.
12   Maleki to Mosaddeq, ibid., p. 84.
13   https://en.wikipedia.org/wiki/Moshe_Sharett.
14   See http://www.pri.org/stories/2014-01-07/iran-s-hemingway-visited-israel-1963-and-wrote-about-it and http://www.tabletmag.com/jewish-arts-and-culture/books/234656/iranian-intellectual-admired-israel.
15   *Khatt-e Asli-ye Jebheh-ye Melli*, Tehran, 1963.
16   See further, Katouzian, *Musaddiq* and *Political Economy*.
17   Maleki to Malek in Katouzian and Pichdad, eds, *Khalil Maleki's Letters*, p. 51; also pp. 56–7.
18   Conversations with Richard Cottam, London 1980.
19   For the full text see *Sosialism* (published by the League of Iranian Socialists in Europe), November 1962. For extensive excerpts see Maleki, *Khaterat*, pp. 137–9.
20   Maleki to Malek in *Nameh-ha-ye Khalil Maleki*, p. 51.
21   Ibid. pp. 57–8.
22   Mosaddeq, *Maktubat*, vol. 10, pp. 1–3.
23   I am grateful to the late Hushang Keshavarz-e Sadr (himself a delegate) for putting a copy of the programme at my disposal.
24   Ibid. Emphasis added.

25 Homa Katouzian, 'The Agrarian Question in Iran' in A. K. Ghose, ed., *Agrarian Reform in Contemporary Developing Countries*, London: Croom Helm, 1983; *Political Economy*; *Musaddiq*.

26 See for details, Katouzian, *Political Economy*; *Musaddiq*; *The Persians*.

27 The article entitled 'Who Bears the Responsibility for the Bloodbath of June 1963' was written a few days after the riots and was circulated in Europe and Tehran.

28 Letter to Mosaddeq, *Maleki's Letters*, p. 46; Maleki, *Khaterat*, p. 365.

29 *Maleki's Letters*, pp. 92–7.

30 Ibid., pp. 99–110.

31 Ibid., pp. 110–26.

32 Ibid., pp. 129–30.

33 Ibid., pp. 130–5.

34 Mosaddeq, *Maktubat*, vol. 10.

35 See the report of these meetings to Ali Shaigan and the NF organisations abroad in ibid. pp. 128–9. In fact Saleh's words were '*sabr o entezar*' (wait and see).

36 Ibid., pp. 150–3.

37 Ibid., pp. 173–9.

38 Ibid., pp. 173–95.

8. MALEKI: THE LAST PHASE

1 Mosaddeq, *Maktubat*, vol. 10, p. 8.

2 Ibid., pp. 10–13.

3 Ibid., p. 12.

4 Ibid., pp. 20–35.

5 Ibid., p. 26.

6 Mosaddeq, *Maktubat*, vol. 10, pp. 34–5.

7 Ibid., pp. 37–8.

8 Ibid., p. 41. He was ridiculing the super-polite style of the council in addressing himself in their letters, not just as 'your Excellency' but as 'his Excellency'.

9 Ibid., pp. 43–9.

10 Ibid., pp. 43–63.

11 Ibid., p. 64.

12 *Maktubat*, vol. 10, pp. 69–73.

13   Ibid., p. 68.

14   *Nameh-ha-ye Khalil Maleki*, p. 198.

15   Ibid., p. 200.

16   Ibid., pp. 202–3.

17   *Nameh-ha-ye Khalil Maleki*, pp. 210–12.

18   Ibid., 5 June 1964, pp. 213–16.

19   Ibid., p. 20.

20   Ibid., pp. 220, 227–8 and 235.

21   Ibid., pp. 232–3.

22   Ibid., pp. 247–55.

23   Ibid., p. 259.

24   Ibid., pp. 258–62.

25   Ibid. pp. 263–9.

26   Ibid., p. 271.

27   Ibid., p. 273.

28   Ibid., pp. 272–5.

29   Ibid., various pages.

30   Ibid., pp. 304–13.

31   http://article.tebyan.net/359158/%D8%B1%D8%B6%D8%A7-
      %D8%B4%D9%85%D8%B3-%D8%A2%D8%
      A8%D8%A7%D8%AF%DB%8C-%D9%88-%D8%AF%D8%A7%D8%B
      3%D8%AA%D8%A7%D9%86-%D8%AA%D8%B1%D9%88%D8%B1-
      %D8%B4%D8%A7%D9%87; Gholamreza Nejati, *Tarikh-e Bist o Panj
      Saleh-ye Iran, az Enqelab ta Kudeta* (The Twenty-five-Year History of Iran,
      from the Coup to the Revolution), Tehran: Rasa, 2008.

32   Ibid., pp. 323–5.

33   https://en.wikipedia.org/wiki/Margaret_McKay.

34   https://en.wikipedia.org/wiki/Jock_Haston.

35   http://www.hippeis.com/young.

36   *Khalil Maleki beh Ravayat-e Asnad-e Savak*, pp. 405–7.

37   *Nameh-ha-ye Khalil Maleki*, p. 315.

38   *Khalil Maleki beh Ravayat-e Savak*.

39   *Kahaterat-e Siyasi Maleki*, second edition, introduction, pp. 403–5;
      Keyhan, 12 September 1965.

40   *Defa'iyat-e Alijan Shansi dar Dadgah-e Nezami* (Alijan Shansi Defence
      Speech in the Military Court), League of Iranian Socialists in Europe,
      1966.

41 *Khalil Maleki beh Ravayat*, pp. 393–407.

42 *Nameh-ha-ye Khalil Maleki*, pp. 435–6.

43 *Khaterat-e Maleki*, pp. 137–8; 'Defa'iyat-e Khalil Maleki dar Dadgah-e Nezami' (Khalil Maleki Defence Speech in Military Court), the quarterly *Sosialism*, April 1966, pp. 51–2.

44 *Nameh-ha-y Maleki*, pp. 342–3.

45 *Khalil Maleki beh Ravayat*, p. 451.

46 Ibid., pp. 492–3.

47 *Nameh-ha-ye Khalil Maleki*, pp. 376–9.

48 Ibid., pp. 381–3.

49 Ibid., various pages.

50 For details see Katouzian, *Musaddiq*.

51 *Nameh-ha-ye Khalil Maleki*, p. 365.

52 Ibid., p. 367.

53 Ibid., p. 398.

54 Ibid., p. 394.

55 Ibid., p. 406.

56 Ibid., p. 443.

57 Ibid., pp. 408–9 and 432–3.

58 Ibid., letter to Pichdad, p. 419.

59 Ibid., p. 443. See also, *Memoirs of M. A. Mojtaehdi*, ed. Habib Ladjevardi, Harvard University Iranian Oral History Project, 2000, pp. 166–8. He claims that the shah told him he would tell them to pay Maleki from another source, but this in fact did not happen. Mojtahedi had been made president of Melli University, in February 1968. Thus Maleki had held his job for five months.

60 *Nameh-ha-ye Khalil Maleki*, p. 446.

61 Ibid., p. 472.

62 Ibid. Letter to his brother Hossein Malek, p. 476.

63 Ibid., p. 453.

64 Ibid., letter to Pichdad, p. 469.

65 Ibid., p. 490.

66 Maleki, *Khaterat*, Introduction, p. 141.

INDEX

289

KHALIL MALEKI

and Maleki 234–7, 246
and political camps 128–9
and Third Force 134–6
Iran party 51–2, 98, 199–200
Iraq 184
Islam 66–7, 100–1, 184, 194, 215; *see also*
1979 Revolution
Israel 207

Jackson, Basil 105
Jazani, Bizhan 209
Jonas, Franz 243
Jordan 246
July uprising 117–18, 144, 167

Kaftaradze, Sergei 40, 41
Kamal, General 122
Kambakhsh, Abdossamad 13, 40, 46–7,
55, 56
and Fifty-Three 14, 15–17, 23–4
and Tudeh party 31, 36–7, 38–9
Kashani, Ayatollah Seyyed Abolqsem xv,
xvi, 64, 96, 117, 119
and Islam 100–1
and 1953 Coup 158, 160–1, 168, 184
Kashani, Seyyed Mostafa 171
Kasravi, Ahmad 67
Katouzian, Amir Mas'ud 198
Kazemi, Baqer 234
Kennedy, John F. xvii–xviii, 189
Keshavarz, Ferydun 37, 38, 40, 50, 52
Khameh'i, Anvar 12–13, 58, 68, 97
and Fifty-Three 17, 18–19, 23
and Tudeh party 34, 36–7
Khatibi, Hossein 162
Khazeni, Nosratollah 171
Khiyabani, Shaikh Mohammad 45
Khomeini, Ayatollah 215–16, 235
Khonji, Mohammad Ali 100, 170, 176–7,
199–200, 210
Khrushchev, Nikita 187, 221
Khuzistan 51, 62, 69, 95–6, 107
kiln workers 166
Kiyanuri, Nureddin 31, 38, 58, 63–4, 67
and 1953 Coup 171

and revolt 55, 56, 57
Koestler, Arthur 100
Korean War 128
Kurds 52

labour movement 32
Lahuti, Abolqasem xii
land reforms xviii, xix, 148, 151, 187
and Amini 203, 208
and Maleki 214–15
and NF 213–14
League of Iranian Socialists 204–5, 217,
218–19, 220–2, 229–33

McGhee, George 103, 108
McKay, Margaret 238–9
Mahamedi, Hamid 230, 237, 238
Majlis xv, xvi, xvii, xviii, 1–2, 11
and basts 162, 163–4
and eighteenth session 181
and fifteenth session 61, 64–5
and fourteenth session 37–8, 49
and oil 40, 41, 90–2
and referendum 164–6, 169
and repossession bill 96–7
and Reza Shah 29
and seventeenth session 112,
113–15
and seventh session 10
and twenty-first session 219–20
Makki, Hossein 65, 91–2, 164
Makkinezhad, Taqi 2
Malek, Hossein (half-brother) 2, 68, 100,
177, 206, 210
and Baqa'i 121
and Maleki 244, 246, 247
Maleki, Khalil xi, xii, xiv, 243–9, 251–4
and Amini 203–6
and Azerbaijan 43–4, 46, 50
and Baqa'i 120, 121, 122, 123–4, 125
and Berlin 5–8
and Britain 47–9
and communism 12, 13
and conspiracy theory 73–6
and Constitutional Revolution 1, 2